Truth, Denial and Transition

Truth, Denial and Transition: Northern Ireland and the Contested Past makes a unique and timely contribution to the transitional justice field. In contrast to the focus on truth and those societies where truth recovery has been central to dealing with the aftermath of human rights violations, comparatively little scholarly attention has been paid to those jurisdictions whose transition from violent conflict has been marked by the absence or rejection of a formal truth process. This book draws upon the case study of Northern Ireland, where, despite a lengthy debate, the question of establishing a formal truth recovery process remains hotly contested. The strongest and most vocal opposition has been from unionist political elites, loyalist ex-combatants and members of the security forces. Based on empirical research, their opposition is unpicked and interrogated at length throughout this book. Critically exploring notions of national imagination and blamelessness, the politics of victimhood and the tension between traditions of sacrifice and the fear of betrayal, this book is the first substantive effort to concentrate on the opponents of truth recovery rather than its advocates.

This book will interest those studying truth processes and transitional justice in the fields of Law, Politics and Criminology.

Cheryl Lawther is a Lecturer in Criminology in the School of Sociology, Social Policy and Social Work, Queen's University Belfast.

Professor Colin Harvey, Professor of Human Rights Law, School of Law, Queen's University Belfast:

"Dr Lawther's work is a timely and necessary intervention in discussions of the contested past in Northern Ireland. Her argument has considerable explanatory and normative power and assists greatly in understanding how unionism and loyalism grapples with the legacies of the conflict. This impressive volume is required reading for anyone seeking to understand transitional contexts where formal truth processes are not in place."

Professor John Brewer, Professor of Post Conflict Studies, Institute for the Study of Conflict Transformation and Social Justice, Queen's University Belfast:

"Great social science is mostly deeply embedded in personal experience and transitional justice studies is producing a new generation of young scholars struggling to understand the ambivalences of peace and the ambiguities of truth in the wake of some dramatic political transitions at the time of the new millennium. Cheryl Lawther is primary among them. She deals skilfully and intelligently with the problems Northern Ireland has in being reconciled to its past and has produced a first class book. Her work will be greatly admired by academics and lay readers alike."

Professor Richard English, Wardlaw Professor of Politics, School of International Relations, University of St Andrews:

"Thoughtful, serious-minded and well-researched, this study represents an important contribution to a vital and urgent debate."

Professor Kieran McEvoy, Professor of Law and Transitional Justice, School of Law, Queen's University Belfast:

"This is what top notch transitional justice scholarship looks like. It is a formidable achievement and a very welcome addition to the Routledge Transitional Justice Series."

Transitional Justice
Series Editor: Kieran McEvoy
Queen's University Belfast

The study of justice in transition has emerged as one of the most diverse and intellectually exciting developments in the social sciences. From its origins in human rights activism and comparative political science, the field is increasingly characterised by its geographic and disciplinary breadth. This series aims to publish the most innovative scholarship from a range of disciplines working on transitional justice related topics, including law, sociology, criminology, psychology, anthropology, political science, development studies and international relations.

Titles in the series:

Transitional Justice, Judicial Accountability and the Rule of Law
Hakeem O. Yusuf (2010)

The Era of Transitional Justice
The Aftermath of the Truth and Reconciliation Commission in South Africa and Beyond
Paul Gready (2010)

The Dynamics of Transitional Justice
Lia Kent (2012)

Gender Politics in Transitional Justice
Catherine O'Rourke (2013)

Identity, Reconciliation and Transitional Justice
Nevin T. Aiken (2013)

Corporate Accountability in the context of Transitional Justice
Sabine Michalowski (2013)

Families of the Missing
Simon Robins (2013)

Transitional Justice Theories
Edited by Susanne Buckley Zistel, Teresa Koloma Beck, Christian Braun and Friederike Mieth (2014)

Truth, Denial and Transition
Northern Ireland and the Contested Past
Cheryl Lawther (2014)

Forthcoming titles in the series:

The Concept of the Civilian
Claire Garbett

Transitional Justice and the Arab Spring
Edited by Kirsten Fisher and Robert Stewart

The Judiciary and the Politics of Transition
Saviours, Scoundrels, Scapegoats
Marny Requa

The Art of Post-Dictatorship
Ethics and Aesthetics in Transitional Argentina
Vikki Bell

International Trials and Reconciliation
Janine Clark

The Trouble with Truth
Dealing with the Past in Northern Ireland
Kieran McEvoy

Transitional Justice, Peace and Democracy
Conflict Resolution in Context
Elin Skaar, Camila Gianella and Trine Eide

Truth, Denial and Transition

Northern Ireland and the Contested Past

Cheryl Lawther

Routledge
Taylor & Francis Group
a GlassHouse Book

First published 2014
by Routledge
2 Park Square, Milton Park, Abingdon, Oxon, OX14 4RN

and by Routledge
711 Third Avenue, New York, NY 10017

a GlassHouse Book

Routledge is an imprint of the Taylor & Francis Group, an informa business

British Library Cataloguing in Publication Data
A catalogue record for this book is available from the British Library

Library of Congress Cataloging-in-Publication Data
Lawther, Cheryl, author.
Truth, denial and transition : the contested past in northern ireland / Cheryl Lawther.
p. cm.
ISBN 978-0-415-51014-1 (hardback) — ISBN 978-0-415-51015-8 (ebk)
1. Transitional justice—Northern Ireland. 2. Reparation (Criminal justice)—Northern Ireland. 3. Reconciliation—Political aspects—Northern Ireland. 4. Northern Ireland—Politics and government—1969–1994. I. Title.
KDE210.L39 2014
323.4'909416—dc23
2013035989

ISBN: 978-0-415-51014-1 (hbk)
ISBN: 978-1-315-79809-7 (ebk)

Typeset in Garamond
by FiSH Books Ltd, Enfield

MIX
Paper from responsible sources
FSC® C013604

Printed and bound by CPI Group (UK) Ltd, Croydon, CR0 4YY

Contents

Abbreviations

CAJ	Committee on the Administration of Justice
CCRC	Criminal Cases Review Commission
CEH	Historical Clarification Commission
CGP	Consultative Group on the Past
CJINI	Criminal Justice Inspection Northern Ireland
CLMC	Combined Loyalist Military Command
CVSNI	Commission for Victims and Survivors Northern Ireland
DUP	Democratic Unionist Party
EPIC	Ex-Prisoners Interpretive Centre
FAIR	Families Acting for Innocent Relatives
HET	Historical Enquiries Team
HMIC	Her Majesty's Inspectorate of Constabulary
HTR	Healing Through Remembering
ICLVR	International Commission on the Location of Victims' Remains
ICP	Independent Commission on Policing
ICTJ	International Centre for Transitional Justice
INLA	Irish National Liberation Army
IRA	Irish Republican Army
LVF	Loyalist Volunteer Force
MLA	Member of the Legislative Assembly
NIAC	Northern Ireland Affairs Committee
NIHRC	Northern Ireland Human Rights Commission
NIO	Northern Ireland Office
NIPB	Northern Ireland Policing Board
NIRPOA	Northern Ireland Retired Police Officers Association
OPONI	Office of the Police Ombudsman for Northern Ireland
PFNI	Police Federation for Northern Ireland
PIRA	Provisional Irish Republican Army
PSNI	Police Service of Northern Ireland
PUP	Progressive Unionist Party
RUC	Royal Ulster Constabulary

RUC GC F	Royal Ulster Constabulary George Cross Foundation
RUCR	Royal Ulster Constabulary Reserve
SATRC	South African Truth and Reconciliation Commission
SDLP	Social Democratic and Labour Party
SF	Sinn Fein
SLTRC	Sierra Leone Truth and Reconciliation Commission
TUV	Traditional Unionist Voice
UDA	Ulster Defence Association
UDP	Ulster Democratic Party
UDR	Ulster Defence Regiment
UFF	Ulster Freedom Fighters
UPRG	Ulster Political Research Group
UUP	Ulster Unionist Party
UVF	Ulster Volunteer Force

Acknowledgements

This book began life as a PhD thesis in the Institute of Criminology and Criminal Justice, School of Law, Queen's University Belfast. There, I was fortunate to be supervised by Professors Kieran McEvoy and Pete Shirlow. Both provided excellent support and guidance throughout the PhD process and beyond. Kieran, in particular, has been a constant source of encouragement, advice and friendship. During this time I was also fortunate to receive a Department of Education and Learning Northern Ireland studentship. Professors Brandon Hamber and Colin Harvey examined the thesis and provided valuable feedback and encouragement as regards publication.

In 2011, this book moved with me to the School of International Relations, University of St Andrews. While working there as a post-doctoral research fellow, Professor Richard English willingly gave up his time to provide invaluable career and publishing advice. His encouragement was, and is, much appreciated. The School of Sociology, Social Policy and Social Work, Queen's University Belfast provided a welcoming new environment in which to complete this manuscript.

This book would not, however, have been possible without the willing participation of interviewees. I would like to thank all of those individuals who generously took time out of their busy schedules to meet with me and to answer my questions. As this book will illustrate, the debate on truth recovery and dealing with the past in Northern Ireland is personal, political, emotional and hotly contested. Without their involvement, this book would not have been possible, or the process as enriching.

A number of parts of this book draw on my previously published research. I am grateful to Oxford University Press for permission to reproduce material from the following articles: Lawther, C. (2010) '"Securing" the Past: Policing and the Contest over Truth in Northern Ireland', *British Journal of Criminology*, 50, 3: 455–473 and Lawther, C. (2013) 'Denial, Silence and the Politics of the Past: Unpicking the Opposition to Truth Recovery in Northern Ireland', *International Journal of Transitional Justice*, 7, 1: 157–177. Taylor and Francis generously gave permission to reproduce material from Lawther, C. (2011) 'Unionism, Truth Recovery and the Fearful Past', *Irish Political Studies*, 26, 3: 361–382. Available at: www.tandfonline.com/doi/abs/10.1080/07907184.2011.593740. The cover image was sourced and supplied by the Press Association.

It was also a pleasure to work with Routledge throughout the publication process. From the outset, Commissioning Editor Colin Perrin showed considerable interest in, and enthusiasm for, this book. Rebekah Jenkins provided fantastic editorial support and readily answered my questions.

My final and most significant debt of gratitude goes towards my parents. 'Thank you' is not enough.

Cheryl Lawther
August 2013

Foreword

There are too many easy assumptions about truth recovery in transitional justice. Since the South African Truth and Reconciliation Commission (SATRC) completed its work, truth commissions have become a major part of the transitional justice toolkit. Some 40 official truth commissions, as well as a plethora of community-based initiatives, have been established in different countries in the past three decades. Notwithstanding their continued popularity, there has been a steady stream of critical research that questions some of the taken-for-granted axioms about the linkage between truth and reconciliation or the presumed healing benefits for victims of past violence. Less explored, and the gap that this book rather brilliantly fills, are the motives and understandings of those who are opposed to truth recovery. Broadly speaking, the assumption with such constituencies is that it is *only* the 'perpetrators' and their political apologists who advocate drawing a veil over the past. As Lawther well captures in terms of the Northern Ireland case study, sometimes it is also those who see themselves as 'victims' who appear least enthusiastic about organised truth-telling.

The bold 'facts' about the Northern Ireland conflict underline some of this complexity. Over 3,500 people were killed during the Northern Ireland conflict and it is estimated that over 100,000 were injured. Leaving aside for the moment the matter of state collusion – it is now clear that the security forces and intelligence services had infiltrated both Republican and Loyalist paramilitary organisations and were complicit in multiple murders – Republican organisations were responsible for over 2,000 deaths (approximately 60%), Loyalists over 1,000 (approximately 30%) and the state security forces for directly killing 363 people (approximately 10%). In a context where the IRA's political wing Sinn Fein is now sharing power with Unionists in Northern Ireland, and where many of its most prominent members are acknowledged former IRA members, one might be forgiven for assuming that Republicans would have the most to fear from organised truth-telling about the past. Loyalist paramilitaries no longer have any political representation at Stormont. While one might expect some embarrassing tales to be forthcoming about linkages between the Loyalist paramilitaries and Unionist politicians during the conflict, compared with a re-examination of some of the IRA's worst atrocities, the political discomfiture scales should be tilted firmly in favour of Unionism. However, to date at least, Unionists have largely set their face against truth recovery while Republicans continue to call for the establishment of an international truth commission. This is the paradox that Lawther tackles with some aplomb.

Clearly influenced by a couple of seminal texts – in particular Stan Cohen's work on denial and Benedict Anderson's reflections on nationalism – Lawther deftly identifies and explores the main factors that shape Unionist attitudes to truth. The centrality of victimhood to the Unionist understanding of the past permeates the whole text. Unionists appeared by and large to view the conflict through a prism where *their* state and *their* British identity was being attacked by Republican terrorists and where state and Loyalist violence was principally a reaction to that threat. From such a vantage point, Unionism and Unionists were *victims* of that terrorist campaign. For many of the Unionists interviewed herein, victims of terrorism and crime are deemed to expect justice (i.e. retribution) and therefore any discussions of methods of dealing with the past through fashionable techniques of transitional justice (such as truth recovery) appear highly suspicious. Of course, the legal reality is that few historical prosecutions will ever succeed, and that anyone convicted of a conflict-related offence that occurred before 1998 will only serve two years under the terms of the Good Friday Agreement. Regardless, as Lawther explores, a default recourse to the traditional criminal justice way of dealing with terrorism has provided a reassuring terra firma for many Unionists on which to stand one's ground against the competing versions of the past represented by organised truth-telling. The Unionist attachment to victimhood that Lawther identifies is also suffused with other complex themes – blamelessness and denial; a deep mistrust of both Republicans and the British state; factors related to political self-confidence; and long-celebrated traditions of loyalty and self-sacrifice that cannot be betrayed. Once one begins to consider these themes individually and cumulatively one begins to better understand how truth recovery can appear quite a threatening spectacle to Unionists in Northern Ireland.

This books draws variously from sociology, politics, law and anthropology to tell what is a complex tale. That tale is well told. It is also underpinned by some excellent fieldwork. The access to many of the major players is well used and gives the text significant richness and authenticity. It is a subtle, sympathetic and theoretically sophisticated discussion of the obstacles to truth recovery in one particular jurisdiction. However, its relevance and importance go well beyond Northern Ireland. The themes identified by Lawther need to be addressed and provide a template for those advocating truth recovery in any transitional context. A critical interrogation of the utility of truth recovery requires precisely such a nuanced grasp of the challenges articulated by those who are sceptical of its putative benefits.

As Lawther argues, conflicts such as Northern Ireland were sustained by competing versions of history. Unless we develop tools that can both take seriously those contested versions of history but also, where necessary, respectfully critique and interrogate some of the assumptions inherent within them, transitional justice will only ever preach to the converted.

This is what top-notch transitional justice scholarship looks like. It is a formidable achievement and a very welcome addition to the Routledge Transitional Justice Series.

Kieran McEvoy, Series Editor

Chapter 1

Introduction

The twenty-first century has been characterised by an 'urge' or 'rush' to truth in the aftermath of violent conflict. Declarations of 'Nunca Mas' and truth commissions in Latin America, the opening of Stasi police files in Eastern Europe and the establishment of the SATRC, among others, have all been influential. For advocates of truth recovery, the purported benefits of recovering truth about past human rights violations have been well rehearsed. They include reaffirming the rule of law; responding to victims' needs; fostering reconciliation; making known the range of forensic, personal and social 'truths' about past conflict; promoting accountability and broadening social and political ownership of the structural causes of violence and conflict transformation (Tutu 2000; Boraine 2000; Smyth 2007; Wiebelhaus-Brahm 2010). The extensive literature on the transitional justice 'success stories' – those societies that have successfully, at least, attempted to engage in a macro level process of dealing with past human rights violations and the speed at which discussions on the merits of truth commissions have developed in response to regime changes associated with the Arab Spring, for example, indicates how truth recovery is now considered an axiomatic element of post-conflict reconstruction (see, for example: International Centre for Transitional Justice [ICTJ] 2011; Michael 2011). That notions of 'truth', 'reconciliation' and 'forgiveness' permeate contemporary debates concerning, for example, the involvement of Ireland's Catholic Church in institutional child abuse and the forced assimilation and abuse of indigenous children at Canadian Indian Residential Schools – two 'settled' democracies – provides further evidence of the intellectual and practical mainstreaming of this discourse (McEvoy 2007; McAlinden 2013; James 2012).

This book seeks to broaden the transitional justice gaze. In contrast to the dominant focus on truth and those societies where truth recovery has been central to the transition, comparatively little scholarly attention has been paid to those jurisdictions whose transition from violent conflict has been marked by the rejection or absence of a formal truth process. In all transitional contexts, the dialectic between truth and denial – defined by Cohen (2001: 25) as 'the need to be innocent of a troubling recognition' –

is a key contest. This book engages with this debate to critically interrogate how post-conflict truth recovery is challenged and contested. It draws upon the case study of Northern Ireland, where, despite a protracted debate and significant energy around the question of establishing a formal truth process, at the time of writing, there has been little progress and the topic remains hotly contested. The strongest and most vocal opposition has been from unionist political elites, loyalist ex-combatants and members of the security forces. Based on empirical research, their opposition is unpicked and interrogated at length throughout this book. Critically exploring notions of national imagination and blamelessness, the politics of victimhood and the tension between traditions of sacrifice and the fear of betrayal among others, this book is the first substantive effort to concentrate on the opponents of truth recovery rather than its advocates.

Denial, silence and challenging the past: The international context

There are a number of jurisdictions, such as Spain, Mozambique and France, whose transition from a period of political violence and human rights abuses has been characterised by the absence of a formal truth process. In these sites and others, several powerful critiques of the perceived 'need' to recover truth about the past have been made (see also: Daly 2008). Couched within the euphemisms of 'getting peace' or promoting 'reconciliation', for example, some of the most slippery and strongly stated oppositional discourses to truth have been framed within a context of denial and silence (Payne 2008; Misztal 2003; Cohen 2001; Ben-Ze'ev *et al.* 2010). As Cohen (2001: 3) argues, 'Statements of denial are assertions that something did not happen, does not exist, is not true or is not known about' and are a common response to information that is too threatening or disturbing to be publicly acknowledged. Denial, then, includes cognition (not acknowledging the facts); emotion (not feeling); morality (not recognising wrongdoing or responsibility); and action (not taking active steps in response to knowledge) (Cohen 2001). Silence, the 'socially constructed space in which and about which subjects and words normally used in everyday life are not spoken' is also an active and deliberate response to past trauma (Ben-Ze'ev *et al.* 2010: 4). In contrast to denial, whereby the uncomfortable aspects of the past may be reframed or deflected, silence constitutes that which is 'generally known but cannot be spoken' (Zerubavel 2010: 32). Before exploring the Northern Ireland case in detail and broadening out the sociological, political and ideological objections to truth there, the five major models of opposition to truth recovery found in the international literature and borne out in practice are outlined below. As can be seen, these perspectives are often overlapping and the themes of denial and silence are often present.

Truth and pragmatic peacemaking

From a practical peacemaking perspective, it is often asserted that the demand for political stability and nascent democratisation is not well served by 'raking over' the past (Kovras 2013). Major arguments include that examining the past could derail or prevent fragile peace initiatives and/or provide an opportunity for the past to be re-interpreted and manipulated as a weapon for further conflict (see for example: Forsberg and Teivainen 2004; Aguilar 2001; Graybill and Lanegran 2004). The example of Spain is, ostensibly at least, a textbook illustration of a transition from violence in which the demands of peacemaking appeared to have taken precedence over the need to address the abuses of the past.[1] Approximately 500,000 citizens were killed either during the Spanish civil war of 1936–39 or under the dictatorial rule of General Francisco Franco until his death in 1975 (Preston 2012). For Spanish political elites, fears of a right-wing coup or return to civil war dominated the transitional period and led to the prioritisation of peace, order and democratic consolidation over an examination of the past (Aguilar 2001). The 'Pacto del Olvido' – the pact of forgetting was therefore founded on a pragmatic need for silence and was supported by the amnesty law of 1977 (Davies 2005; Blakely 2005; Ferran 2007). The amnesty law presents the civil war as a period of 'collective madness' where both sides committed heinous crimes and does not attribute responsibility to any party (Kovras 2013). According to Davies (2005), the law was intended to 'close' and 'forget' the past, heralding the beginning of a new democratic era in Spanish political life.

Truth, silence and 'moving on'

Work from the field of memory studies has shown that a common feature of post-conflict societies is the conscious decision to forget certain aspects of the past (Brewer 2010; Connerton 2008). In such contexts, silence may be a pragmatic choice in the quest to embed social stability and protect against retraumatisation (Winter 2010). Hayner (2011: 207) cautions that 'Remembrance must be balanced with forgetting so that … memories of the past don't overwhelm the present and the future'. In the Spanish case, the political dimension of the Pacto del Olvido was matched by a social consensus on the need for silence (Encarnacion 2001). For those communities most affected by violence and disappearances, 'the traumatic memory of a fratricidal conflict' and a fear of a return to totalitarianism offset many victims' demands for truth and the return of the bodies of the disappeared (Aguilar 2001: 97; Davies 2005; Farran and Amago 2010). Similar themes can be identified in the Republic of Ireland following the Civil War (June 1922–May 1923), which was fought between two opposing groups of the Irish Republican Army (IRA) and followed the War of

Independence (January 1919–July 1921). Neither were accompanied by any efforts to address the violence of the previous years. The intimacy of the Civil War, described as a 'war of the brothers', a desire to ensure that its bitterness was not transmitted to younger generations and a sense of shame about what had happened acted as codes for silence (Coogan 1998; Dolan 2003; Pine 2011). Not examining the past may therefore be linked to a particular understanding of reconciliation that suggests a need to silence the past in the name of the future. Raul Domingos, a former senior leader of the Mozambican guerrilla force Renamo, explicitly made this case in respect to the determination not to revisit the past in Mozambique following 16 years of war – 'The word "reconciliation" is a word used to mean forget the past and be tolerant. We killed each other, but we forget this because we are sons, brothers and we have to live together' (cited in Hayner 2011: 201; Cobban 2006).

Truth and trials as dominant scripts

In other cases, a formal overarching truth recovery process has been eschewed in favour of local, national, international or hybrid tribunals, designed to foster accountability, recover truth and provide restitution for victims. As Garland (1990) points out, criminal trials contribute to the construction of 'imagined communities' and generate meanings not only about crime and punishment, but are also about power, legitimacy and memory (Anderson 2006; Osiel 2000). For still powerful political actors, criminal tribunals can be a tool for perpetuating denial and silence and creating favourable narratives on the past (Wilson 2011; Scott 1992). The Extraordinary Chamber of the Criminal Courts of Cambodia, a hybrid court of international and local jurists, established in 2003 to try high-ranking members of the Khmer Rouge regime illustrates this case. Described as working to a 'politically pre-arranged script', the Chamber only has jurisdiction over five senior leaders of the Khmer Rouge and has not inspired confidence among the Cambodian people (Muddell 2003: np; Glaspy 2008). Trials have also been used in France to gloss over the extent and depth of the Vichy government's collaboration with the Nazi regime and, latterly, the use of torture by the French military during the Algerian War of Independence (1954–62) (Rousso 1991; Branche and House 2010; MacMaster 2002). As Loytomaki (2013) points out, the virtues of democracy, equality and human rights have been central to the traditional republican national identity. Not only has Vichy been presented as an authoritarian interlude in republican legality, but the French state has used criminal trials to claim that torture and other human rights abuses committed during the Algerian war were the acts of isolated individuals, helping to bolster a narrative that is supportive of French colonial history (Loytomaki 2013).

Truth, power and politics

Often related to the strategic use of criminal trials or a 'pragmatic' decision not to re-examine the past are the interests of political elites who remain in positions of power (Cohen 2001; Hayner 2011; Huyse 2013). A refusal to undertake a comprehensive truth recovery process has arguably been politically self-serving in a number of the jurisdictions already discussed. In Spain, for example, MacDonald and Bernardo (2006) have argued that silence has spared the main political parties – the Partido Popular and the Partido Socialista Obrero Espanol – discomfort and embarrassment. Likewise, Marks (1994) and Klosterman (1998) suggest that in Cambodia, one of the main reasons for the reluctance to fully examine the past is that few members of the Cambodian government have clean hands. Alternatively, in Turkey, successive governments have consistently engaged in a policy of 'literal denial' regarding responsibility for the 1915–17 Armenian genocide, during which approximately 1.25 million Armenians were massacred by the Turkish army or died during forced deportations (Cohen 2001; Dixon 2010; Hovannisian 1999). Power and political interest, particularly where the transition from political violence does not involve a complete break from members of the previous regime, may therefore contribute to a policy of denial and silence on the past (Huyse 2013). Kovras (2013) argues that in such contexts, as time passes, selective silence can become a well-entrenched and hegemonic feature of the political discourse and democratic institutions, narrowing the variety of alternative policies and sidelining dissenting voices.

Truth and cultural relativism

Finally, a preference for indigenous methods of conflict transformation, designed to symbolically deal with the past, has been expressed in societies such as Sierra Leone, Mozambique and Uganda (Shaw 2005; Honwana 1998, 1999; Baines 2007). In Mozambique, for example, ritual purification ceremonies are used to 'cleanse' and 'restore' victims and ex-combatants of their past experiences and are designed to symbolically 'lock' the past away (Nordstrom 2005). There, it is believed that to recall the past would open the space for malevolent forces to intervene and violence to return (Green and Honwana 1999). In Uganda, the most commonly known Acholi justice process – mato oput – has been used to deal with the legacy of the civil war between the Ugandan government and the rebel Lord's Resistance Army. Following a period of diplomacy and discussion aimed at reaching consensus on what happened and the amount of compensation to be paid, the mato oput ceremony is a means of promoting reconciliation between the clans of the victim and the perpetrator (Baines 2007). The height of the ceremony is the act of drinking the oput root, symbolising that both clans are willing and able to swallow any bitterness between them (Baines 2007). Many Acholi believe that the mato oput process can bring true healing in a way that the formal justice system cannot and scope has been provided for such community reconciliation processes in the Amnesty Act of 2000 (Jeffrey 2011).

Truth, transition and commissioning the past: Northern Ireland

The Northern Ireland conflict began in 1969 and lasted over 30 years. During this period, approximately 3,739 individuals died and over 40,000 were injured (McKittrick and McVea 2012). Following the signing of the Belfast Agreement in 1998, Northern Ireland has been an active site of transitional justice, with the reform of the criminal justice system and security forces, the release and reintegration of political prisoners, the decommissioning of paramilitary weapons and the development of the Northern Ireland Human Rights Commission (NIHRC) all forming part of the peace process (Northern Ireland Office [NIO] 1998; McEvoy 2001; Campbell and Ni Aolain 2003; Independent Commission on Policing [ICP] 1999; NIHRC 2003). The Belfast Agreement did not however make reference to the need to establish a formal truth recovery process and the absence of such a mechanism remains one of the outstanding factors of the peace process (NIO 1998). In this vacuum, an array of truth-finding efforts have emerged and a fierce contest over whether a formal truth recovery mechanism should be established has ensued. This book is structured against this backdrop. By way of introduction, the following discussion offers some preliminary comments on the development of the truth recovery debate in Northern Ireland. It draws attention to existing practices of truth recovery, outlines the arguments in support of a formal truth process and charts the major developments to date. It then goes on to consider the political contests that underpin much of the truth recovery debate and sets the aims and objectives of this book in that context.

At least four broad forms of truth recovery can be identified that make up Northern Ireland's 'piecemeal' approach to the past (Bell 2003: 1095). In brief, they are as follows.[2] At the legal end of the spectrum there have been a number of public inquiries, 'right to life cases' under Article 2 of the European Convention on Human Rights, civil actions and private prosecutions (Anthony and Mageean 2007; Bell and Keenan 2005). Public inquiries have a long legal pedigree in British political life and, designed to investigate events or actions by government agencies, have perhaps been the most visible form of truth recovery to date. As detailed throughout this book, public inquiries have been held into the events on Bloody Sunday, 30 January 1972, and into the deaths of Robert Hamill, Rosemary Nelson and Billy Wright, in which British security force collusion with loyalist, or in the case of Billy Wright, republican paramilitaries was alleged (Saville *et al.* 2010; Morland *et al.* 2011; MacLean *et al.* 2010). A documentary review has also been held into the case of Pat Finucane (de Silva 2012). Based in the Republic of Ireland, the Smithwick Tribunal is investigating the allegation that members of An Garda Siochana or other employees of the Irish State colluded in the fatal shootings of Royal Ulster Constabulary (RUC) Chief Superintendent Harry Breen and RUC Superintendent Robert Buchanan on 20 March 1989.[3] Smithwick's report is expected in late autumn 2013 (Stack 2013).

Police-led truth recovery has also featured prominently in Northern Ireland. Some of the earliest examples include the Stalker/Sampson investigations into the deaths of six men who were shot dead by the RUC in three separate incidents between November and December 1982, led by the Deputy Chief Constable of the Greater Manchester Police John Stalker and, latterly, following Stalker's removal from the inquiry, Colin Sampson from the West Yorkshire Police (Stalker 1988; Taylor 1987). Similarly, Sir John Stevens, the former head of the Metropolitan Police Service, conducted three investigations in 1990, 1993 and 2003 into suspected collusion between the Ulster Defence Association (UDA) and the security and intelligence forces in the murder of Pat Finucane and several others (Stevens 2003). Latterly, attention has focused on the work of the Office of the Police Ombudsman for Northern Ireland (OPONI) and the Historical Enquiries Team (HET). Established in 2000, alongside dealing with day-to-day complaints against the Police Service of Northern Ireland (PSNI), the OPONI has responsibility for investigating past actions and inactions associated with the RUC. The HET, established by the former Chief Constable of the PSNI, Sir Hugh Orde, is re-examining 3,286 deaths associated with the Northern Ireland conflict and aims to 'assist in bringing a measure of resolution to those families of victims affected by deaths attributable to the troubles in the years 1968 – 1998' (Northern Ireland Affairs Committee (NIAC) 2008: 10; HET undated). The contests concerning these forms of truth recovery are interrogated at length throughout this book.

Reflecting a grassroots approach to truth, there have been a number of community-lead truth recovery initiatives. This has included inquiries into specific events such as the New Lodge Six Community Inquiry held in 2003 into the deaths of six individuals shot dead by the British Army in 1973 in the New Lodge area of North Belfast and community-based truth recovery projects (Mullan 2003). The best known of these 'bottom-up' efforts at truth recovery is the Ardoyne Commemoration Project, a community-based truth-telling initiative designed to tell the stories of the 99 individuals who were victims of political violence in the nationalist Ardoyne community, and which resulted in the publication of 'Ardoyne: The Untold Truth', documenting those narratives (Ardoyne Commemoration Project 2002).

A number of victim-centred initiatives have also pertained to truth recovery. Examples include legislation to facilitate the recovery of the remains of individuals murdered and 'disappeared' by the IRA between 1972 and 1981 – the Northern Ireland (Location of Victims' Remains Act) 1999 and the Criminal Justice (Location of Victims' Remains Act) 1999 in the Republic of Ireland – and the documenting of who the victims are and the circumstances of their deaths (McKittrick *et al.* 2007). Other less-obvious forms of truth recovery include the issuing of apologies, the release of cabinet papers and other politically important material under the 'thirty-year' rule, journalistic research and books, autobiographies and memoirs written by former paramilitary activists, members of the security forces and intelligence services and former agents and informers (McEvoy 2006).

The debate on whether a formal truth recovery process should be established in Northern Ireland has been long and protracted (see for example: Hamber 1998, 2003; McEvoy 2006; Ni Aolain 2002; NIAC 2005a; Smyth 2007; Consultative Group on the Past [CGP] 2009; Commission for Victims and Survivors Northern Ireland [CVSNI] 2010a). Advocates of a formal truth process have made a number of compelling arguments. One of the best known of these is Christine Bell's (2003) assertion that in the absence of an official truth process, the past is continuing to haunt the present, destabilising the political institutions and impeding the peace process. In the 12 months prior to the publication of this book, there have been multiple instances where the past has dominated the present. They include the controversial Civil Service Special Advisors (Spad) Bill 2013, which prevents anyone with a serious conviction from being a special political advisor to ministers in the Northern Ireland Assembly; sharp political divisions concerning the transformation of the site of the former Maze/Long Kesh prison into a centre for peace building and conflict resolution; the dispute over the flying of the Union flag at Belfast City Hall; and the legal challenge over oral history tapes made by researchers at Boston College, which potentially contain information about the death and disappearance of one of the 'Disappeared' Jean McConville and are now held by the PSNI. 'Truths', which are often controversial and politically sensitive, are also continuing to emerge in a sporadic and unstructured manner (Watters 2003). Given the potential for social and political disruption and individual retraumatisation, it has been argued that a 'toxic bank' in which the unresolved questions of the past can be housed, handled and discharged is required (Clarke 2009).

A number of concerns have also been raised regarding the suitability and sustainability of the current approaches to dealing with the past. While the British government has ruled out further public inquiries, their selective nature and financial cost has been well documented (BBC News 2007; Belfast Telegraph 2007). Hegarty (2003, 2004) and Rolston and Scraton (2005) have further questioned their suitability on the grounds that government-appointed public inquiries can act as vehicles for the obfuscation of truth and minimisation of state culpability. In terms of the contribution to truth recovery from the policing family, it has been argued that the time- and resource-heavy nature of historical investigations are overshadowing the PSNI's ability to tackle present-day policing matters (Lawther 2010; NIAC 2008: ev.110, 86). The impartiality and operational independence of the HET and OPONI have also been the subject of some critique by academic Patricia Lundy (2009ab, 2012), the human rights non-governmental organisation (NGO) the Committee on the Administration of Justice (CAJ 2011a), the Criminal Justice Inspection Northern Ireland (CJINI 2011) and Her Majesty's Inspectorate of Constabulary (HMIC 2013). Perhaps most compelling of all is that in the absence of a formal truth process, there are victims whose stories and whose desire to know the truth about the past is falling through the gap (CVSNI 2010a, 2012). Many victims are ageing and with the passage of time and the absence of progress (for those who want truth), their chances of hearing or telling their truth is decreasing. The CVSNI (2010a, 2012) has actively called on the Government and political parties to agree structures, beyond the HET and OPONI, for dealing with the past. For these reasons and others, the concept of a formal truth process for Northern Ireland has been repeatedly placed on the public agenda.

The establishment of the CGP in June 2007 by the then Secretary of State Peter Hain is, at the time of writing, the most substantive development in Northern Ireland's truth recovery debate (NIO 2007). Co-chaired by Archbishop Robin Eames, the former Church of Ireland primate, and Denis Bradley, the former vice-chairman of the Northern Ireland Policing Board (NIPB), its official terms of reference were

> To consult across the community how Northern Ireland society can best approach the legacy of the events of the past 40 years; and to make recommendations, as appropriate, on any steps that might be taken to support Northern Ireland society in building a shared future that is not overshadowed by the events of the past.[4]

Following an extensive public consultation process, the Group published its report amid controversial scenes in January 2009, and detailed in full in Chapter 3.[5] Its main recommendations focused on six broad areas – 'The Legacy of the Past and Reconciliation', 'Victims and Survivors', 'The Legacy Commission', 'Society Issues', 'Processes of Justice and Information Recovery' and 'Remembering' (CGP 2009). In terms of truth recovery, the recommendation for a Legacy Commission – a bespoke truth commission-type body – is highly significant. The CGP envisaged four strands of work for the Legacy Commission. In the first strand, the Commission was designed to identify and engage with community concerns that have arisen as a result of the conflict and administer appropriate funds in the aim of helping build a shared and reconciled society (CGP 2009). The second strand, 'Review and Investigation' would review and investigate historical cases that resulted in death and establish whether there was a realistic chance of prosecution (CGP 2009). It would create a new independent unit, building on the existing work of the HET and OPONI (CGP 2009). The third strand of 'Information Recovery' would use both formal and informal means to establish answers to unresolved questions of importance to victims' families, in the aim of bringing a measure of resolution (CGP 2009). The fourth strand of 'Thematic Examination' would explore themes emerging from historical cases and the conflict as a whole (CGP 2009).

These proposals were immediately overshadowed by the recommendation that, based on the inclusive Victims and Survivors (Northern Ireland) Order 2006, a 'Recognition Payment' of £12,000 would be paid to *all* victims of the conflict – victim and ex-combatant alike. The intricacies of this debate are discussed in full in Chapter 3. While the Secretary of State withdrew this recommendation, the ensuing controversy instigated a period of lengthy debate and stalemate. This included a public consultation process on the Report of the CGP in mid-2009 and talks between the main political parties and the Secretary of State in early 2012 (NIO 2009, 2010). During this period, progress was not forthcoming and the then Conservative/Liberal Democrat Secretary of State Owen Paterson appeared to rule out a formal truth recovery body and asserted that there was no need for a 'shiny, glossy new organisation' (Paterson 2010; Belfast Telegraph 2011a). The former US envoy to Northern Ireland, Richard Haass, has recently been appointed to chair an all-party group being set up to deal with matters related to flags, emblems, parades and the past (NIO 2013). With Haass's report and recommendations due by the end of 2013, it is likely that this debate will continue for some time.

The politics of the past

Progress on dealing with the past has been curtailed by a lack of consensus among Northern Ireland's main political parties. In broad terms, the main nationalist and republican political parties, the Social Democratic and Labour Party (SDLP) and Sinn Fein (SF) have been supportive of a formal truth process. The SDLP is firmly committed to the principle that victims have a right to know the truth and to record the truth as it happens to them and has been largely supportive of the proposals put forward by the CGP (SDLP 2010, 2012a). The party has also advocated an 'ethical' approach to the past and the necessity of a 'robust truth process' (SDLP 2012b). SF has consistently called for the establishment of an independent international truth commission, overseen by the United Nations, and to which all parties to the conflict – unionists/loyalists, nationalists/republicans and the British state –

would be accountable (SF 2003, 2008, 2011, 2013). A major feature of the republican analysis concerning truth recovery is a focus on the activities of the British state and its security forces during the conflict, particularly regarding allegations of security force collusion with loyalist paramilitaries. A number of the party's discussion documents have emphasised the importance of reciprocity and inclusivity and have called on republicans to 'participate and play a full role' in any such body (Eolas 2003; An Phoblact 2009; SF 2012).

By contrast, unionist political elites, principally the Democratic Unionist Party (DUP), Ulster Unionist Party (UUP) and the Traditional Unionist Voice (TUV), loyalist ex-combatants, led by organisations such as the Ex-Prisoners Interpretive Centre (EPIC) and representatives of the security forces, including the Northern Ireland Retired Police Officers Association (NIRPOA) and the Police Federation for Northern Ireland (PFNI) have expressed consistent opposition to, and reluctance to engage with, the truth recovery debate and the concept of a formal truth process.[6] On one level, and echoing other international sites of transitional justice and truth recovery, unionists have articulated a number of practical objections to dealing with the past.[7] During interview, one of the most common arguments made to the author was that uncovering the 'dirty details' of the past would poison and polarise political relationships and the question of whether the devolved institutions would be able to withstand an investigation of the past was frequently raised (NIRPOA 2008, 2009; PFNI 2008a).[8] These arguments speak to the perception that a truth process would become another site of conflict, or, as expressed by one interviewee, that the process or final report would 'become a running sore' (Lundy and McGovern 2008a; McEvoy 2006).[9] Likewise, interviewees expressed concern that a truth process could heighten community tensions and lead to retaliatory violence.[10] The concern that young people would join paramilitary organisations to 'avenge' past wrongs added considerable weight to this point.[11] A number of loyalist ex-combatants argued that participating in a truth process could negatively affect the family and social relationships they have built up post-conflict.[12] Third, and in keeping with any attempt to deal with the legacy of a traumatic past, fears were raised as to the potential retraumatisation of participants (see for example: Hamber 2009; NIRPOA 2008; PFNI 2008a). Finally, others objected to the sequencing and financing of a truth process, arguing that the time is not 'right' for truth recovery – with one interviewee at least suggesting that the legacy of the conflict should be left for younger generations to examine and others raising objections on the grounds of financial cost (Fletcher *et al.* 2009; Olsen *et al.* 2010; Patterson 2008).[13]

As detailed above, many of these oppositional discourses have been echoed in other transitional societies and, in a number of cases, cited as the main reason for the rejection of a formal truth process. Given the legacy of violent conflict in Northern Ireland and the long transition to peace, these arguments are neither unreasonable nor unexpected. Indeed, and following international best practice, if a truth process was to be established in Northern Ireland, detailed consideration would be required on how best to alleviate these potentially negative effects (ICTJ 2013ab). However, what is particularly significant and interesting about unionists' opposition goes beyond practical objections to dealing with the past. Rather, and as is the focus of this book, their sociological, ideological and political objections are compelling. Typically found in press releases or other organisational documentation, unionists and loyalists have, for example, argued that a truth process would become a 'Brit-bashing session' and provide an opportunity for republican politicians and ex-combatants to 're-write' the past; distort 'innocence' and 'guilt', creating 'moral equivalence' between victims and perpetrators; that it would betray narratives of sacrifice and legacies of loss; and that it would perpetuate the 'illusion of collusion' and 'blame' the security forces and British state for the conflict (see for example: DUP 2003, 2009a; UUP 2009a, 2011a; EPIC 2004; NIRPOA 2009; PFNI 2008ab). Speaking to processes of denial and silence and the tension between how remembering and forgetting are constructed and maintained regarding past violence, this book engages with these themes (Cohen 2001; Ben-Ze'ev *et al.* 2010; Ricoeur 2004; Misztal 2003).

In doing so, the Northern Ireland case study provides an ideal prism through which to critically interrogate how opposition to truth recovery is manifested. Focusing on a society where truth recovery is piecemeal, heavily contested and, as yet, characterised by the absence of a formal truth process, this book has relevance and appeal beyond the Northern Ireland setting. Moreover, it stretches the boundaries of the Northern Ireland truth debate. To date, much of the literature on truth recovery in Northern Ireland has focused on existing truth recovery mechanisms, other feasible approaches or the views of civilians and community leaders (see for example: Hamber 1998; Bell 2003; McEvoy 2006; Campbell and Turner 2008; Duffy 2010; Lundy and McGovern 2005, 2007, 2008a; Lundy 2009ab, 2010; Simpson 2008, 2009). There has been no sustained attempt to explore the views of unionist and loyalist political elites or representatives of the security forces, a curious oversight given their centrality, and opposition to, this debate. Based on a critical theoretical and empirical examination of their views, this book contributes to filling that gap.

A caveat

One caveat is worth making at this juncture. As Cohen (2001) demonstrates, denial is neither a fixed psychological mechanism nor a universal social process. Neither is it likely to be one-dimensional or isolated, particularly in conflict-related situations (Cohen 2001). Instead, denial is likely to be widespread and multifaceted and, in the context of truth recovery, may translate into opposition or reluctance to reengage with the past, manifested, for example, through literal, implicatory or interpretive denial, or through silence (Cohen 2001; Winter 2010).

As argued throughout this book, in Northern Ireland, unionists and representatives of the security forces have articulated the strongest opposition to a formal truth recovery process. In 2009 at least, the NIAC (2009) cited unionist's hostility as the principle reason for the British government's delay in responding to the proposals of the CGP. However, a reluctance to engage with uncomfortable truths is not the sole preserve of unionists. As regards SF, there has been continued scepticism over the party's real commitment to truth-telling. For example, within the party in general, there has been little public acknowledgement that the IRA was responsible for the greatest loss of life during the conflict or any significant moves to investigate the deaths of ordinary Catholic civilians. In other cases, some of which are explored throughout this book, SF too have chosen silence rather than an active re-examination of their past. This includes the SF President Gerry Adams' refusal to admit that he was a member of the IRA and the Deputy First Minister Martin McGuinness' use of an IRA 'code of honour' when pressed on his knowledge of the past at the Saville Inquiry (see Chapter 4). The IRA also refused to meet the CGP on the basis that it was a British state body and more recently, former members of the organisation refused to give evidence in person to the Smithwick Tribunal, despite the promise of extensive safeguards to protect individual's identity and security (Patterson 2008; News Letter 2008a; Sheahan 2013). Judge Smithwick reported that he was 'very disappointed' that oral evidence would not be given (BBC News 2013a). A number of commentators have also suggested that SF's demand for an independent international truth commission is an act of obfuscation in itself. As Campbell and Connolly (2012) note, advocating for a 'high bar' may (deliberately) prevent the establishment of a truth commission, while simultaneously keeping the focus on state agencies and giving scope to SF's claim that the British state is intent on covering up the past (Rowan 2008, 2011).[14]

The British state is also arguably less than enamoured with the prospect of a full examination of its role during the conflict. As explored in Chapter 4, in 2005 the British government passed the Inquiries Act (2005) that provides for significant ministerial control over the operation of public inquiries and limits the potential for truth-telling (Requa 2007). There is some speculation that this Act was passed in direct response to Justice Cory's finding that members of the security forces colluded with loyalist paramilitaries in the death of Catholic solicitor Pat Finucane and subsequent recommendation for a public inquiry (Requa 2007). The British government later reneged on its commitment to a full public inquiry into this case, offering a documentary review instead (Paterson 2011). There has also been persistent scepticism concerning whether British intelligence agencies such as MI5 and MI6 would play a full role in a truth process (Rolston and Scraton 2005; Rowan 2011).[15]

Denial and silence are therefore not unique to unionists, loyalists and the security forces and I am conscious that this book presents a limited gaze on the protagonists. A fuller perspective would require a substantive analysis of the position of unionists and loyalists, nationalists and republicans and the British and Irish states. While not understating the importance of unionists' opposition, either for the Northern Ireland context or the transitional justice field more broadly, this book only speaks to one aspect of that triangle.

The politics of definitions

For readers who are less familiar with the Northern Ireland context, it is helpful at this juncture to define what is meant by unionism, the security forces and loyalism.

Unionism

As a political ideology, unionism seeks to preserve the union between Northern Ireland and Great Britain and is based on a sense of loyalty to, and sacrifice on behalf of, the British state (McAuley 2010). However, unionism is not homogenous and its political constituents are drawn from a wide range of groupings and from a variety of social backgrounds and cultural perspectives (McAuley 2010; Coulter 1994). To try to capture this diversity, a number of scholarly definitions of unionism have been made. Aughey (1989) for example has suggested that the concept of unionism, essentially concerned with the role of the state and its citizenship, is predicated on the notion that membership of the UK represents a clear, unequivocal and durable definition of British political status (Loughlin 1995). For some, unionism is the consequence of neo-colonial relationships in Ireland. McGarry and O'Leary (1995: 354), for example, argue that unionists constitute a residual social and political category, the legacy of relationships between settlers and natives on the island that has created an 'ethno-national' conflict between two groupings 'who want their state to be ruled by their nation, or who want what they perceive as "their" state to protect their nation'. Alternatively, unionism has been presented as an expression of supremacist politics (McVeigh and Rolston 2007); a direct reflection of Protestant ethnic identity (Bruce 1986, 2007); or the political expression of a distinct religious grouping (Hickey 1984). Others argue that unionism is based on an understanding of Irish nationalism as the 'dangerous other' (McAuley 2010: 17). Bowyer Bell (1996: 115, cited in Spencer 2008: 23) argues that 'if they do not know exactly who they are, they know all too well what they do not want to be'. Identity is thus predicated on an imagined community and constructed in relation to the exclusion of the 'other' (Anderson 2006). For Mitchell (2003), this process of negative identity formation is self-perpetuating, maintaining an insecure identity that requires enemies, fears and conspiracies to sustain its dynamism and entrenches the tendency to evaluate political conflict through a lens of good versus evil.

The two main unionist political parties are the UUP and the DUP. The UUP is the older of the two parties, and following the partition of Ireland in 1920 and establishment of the Stormont Parliament, enjoyed approximately 50 years as Northern Ireland's largest political party, until the instigation of direct rule by the British government in 1972, due to worsening political and social tensions at that time (Walker 2004). McAuley (2010) argues that much of the focus of these years was in response to the sense of physical threat that many unionists believed themselves – and the Northern Ireland state – to be under. Three measures became central to the creation of a political culture that cast members of the Catholic community as 'disloyal' (Buckland 1979). First, in 1922, the new administration introduced the Civil Authorities (Special Powers) Act and transferred law and order powers from the judiciary to the Executive (Boyle, Hadden and Hillyard 1980). This legislation provided the legal basis for many of the counter-insurgency activities of the 1970s and 1980s and was disproportionately used against members of the Catholic nationalist community (Cochrane 2013). Second, the Northern Ireland government took direct control of the new police force, the almost wholly Protestant RUC (Ellison and Smyth 2000). Third, under the Local Government Act (Northern Ireland) of September 1922, local political representation was reorganised, abolishing the existing system of proportional representation and implementing structures under which unionist control and gerrymandering (the manipulation of electoral boundaries) was made possible (McAuley 2010). Unionists thus dominated the state apparatus and the structure of policy and politics (McAuley 2010).

Throughout its history, the UUP has maintained its commitment to principles such as to, 'Promote, strengthen and maintain the Union of Great Britain and Northern Ireland under the Crown and uphold all democratic institutions in Northern Ireland'; 'Safeguard the British Citizenship of the people of Northern Ireland where the rights of all individuals as equal citizens within the Union are fully recognized'; and to 'Support the maintenance of the rule of law'.[16] The UUP was an active participant in the peace process and has, despite concerns over factors such as the decommissioning of paramilitary weapons and reform of the RUC, largely remained committed to the Belfast Agreement (Walker 2004). Following the signing of the peace accord, the party was returned to office as Northern Ireland's largest political party. Electoral fortunes have, however, declined in recent years. Currently led by Mike Nesbitt, the party has slipped to the fourth largest party, with 13 Members of the Legislative Assembly (MLAs), behind the DUP, SF and the SDLP.[17] An electoral alliance with David Cameron's Conservative Party failed to win any seats in the 2010 British parliamentary general election.

The DUP, founded in 1971 by the Reverend Ian Paisley and now led by Peter Robinson, is the largest party in Northern Ireland, with 38 seats in the Northern Ireland Assembly.[18] Historically, the party has been regarded as an advocate of a more hard-line unionism and has been associated with religious fundamentalism (Bruce 1986, 2007). The party has also traditionally been opposed to power sharing in Northern Ireland and did not participate in the negotiation of the Belfast Agreement, raising political and moral objections to many of its major components, including the early release of paramilitary prisoners, the reform of the RUC and the presence of SF in government (Tonge 2002). Following the signing of the St Andrews Agreement in October 2006, which restored the devolved institutions, the DUP has claimed to have 're-negotiated' the Belfast Agreement and sits in the Northern Ireland Assembly, with party leader Peter Robinson as First Minister alongside the Deputy First Minister, SF MLA Martin McGuinness.

Security forces

Throughout this book, the term 'security forces' refers to the RUC and its role during the conflict. Established in the wake of partition, the RUC was formed in March 1922 and was, historically, overwhelmingly Protestant in composition. Over the course of the conflict, 305 police officers were killed and over 9,000 seriously injured. The relationship between the police and state was deeply entwined. In part, this was due to two generic points about the nature of policing in deeply divided societies – first, that the relationship between police and state tends to be more deeply institutionalised in socially divided contexts and, second, the police in such societies are invariably recruited from the dominant social group and so reflect their culture and worldview (Weitzer 1995; Brogden and Shearing 1993). From the outset, the RUC's duties involved not only combating crime, but also maintaining the state and its unionist character, and, for this reason, their political and social views have been largely interchangeable (Brewer *et al.*, 1988; Weitzer 1995). Reflecting Anderson's (2006) work on imagined communities, the RUC acted as an embodiment of the unionist state and provoking a deep visceral attachment among those unionists who regarded it as vital to the protection of their interests, became a key site through which recognition was claimed, accorded or denied (Loader and Mulcahy 2003).

As explored later in this book, while official discourse on the RUC privileges the themes of legitimacy, acceptability and police professionalism, supported by emergency legislation, the RUC became a crucial part of the Unionist regime of hegemonic control and represented the 'coercive arm' of the state (O'Leary and McGarry 1996: 51).[19] Given that nationalists and republicans represented the most visible threat to the state, the RUC concentrated its resources on policing those communities (Mulcahy 2006). The 'sharp end' of policing included an aggressive paramilitary policing of dissent, through to allegations of 'shoot-to-kill' policies and collusion with loyalist paramilitaries. Lacking legitimacy and viewed with considerable mistrust and suspicion by a significant part of the community in Northern Ireland, policing was perhaps the most emotive, divisive and controversial aspect of the conflict (Mulcahy 2006). Reform of the RUC was therefore central to the peace process and, chaired by Chris Patten, the ICP was tasked with developing a model of policing that could attract widespread community support. Its report, 'A New Beginning', emphasised the importance of policing that is accountable to the law and community and is free from partisan control (ICP 1999). In light of these recommendations, significant changes were made to the RUC and the new police service, the PSNI, was established in 2001. Where appropriate, detailed distinctions are made throughout the text to the PSNI and other post-Patten policing bodies.

Loyalism

This book adopts the definition that 'Loyalists are understood as those who have been involved in paramilitarism and/or loyalist-inspired political and community-centred activity' (Shirlow 2012: 8). The two main loyalist paramilitary organisations active during the Northern Ireland conflict were the Ulster Volunteer Force (UVF) and the UDA.[20] Their political manifestations are the Progressive Unionist Party (PUP), associated with the UVF and the Ulster Political Research Group (UPRG), linked with the UDA.

Attachment to the British Crown and flag and a feeling of belonging to the 6 counties of Northern Ireland has been a defining feature of loyalism (McAuley 2004). Although the histories, tactics and leadership values of the UVF and UDA differed, both were concerned that Northern Ireland's constitutional position was under direct threat from militant republicanism and were willing to counter this threat with violence against Republican targets (when available) and more often, the Catholic civilian population (McAuley 2010). Neither felt that the state was effectively dealing with the challenge to its existence (Taylor 1999). Their 'crimes' were therefore those of 'loyalty' (Wood 2006). In total, loyalists were responsible for 996 deaths – including 54 nationalist or republican activists and 712 Catholic civilians (Shirlow 2012). In October 1994, under the auspices of Combined Loyalist Military Command (CLMC), the UVF and UDA publicly announced their cessation from violence and offered 'to the loved ones of all innocent victims...abject and true remorse' (CLMC 1994). Despite sporadic violence and intra-loyalist feuding, the ceasefire has continued to hold and, in both personal and structural terms, there is evidence of former combatants working to decrease political and social tensions in their respective communities (Shirlow *et al.* 2010).

The UVF and UDA are represented politically by the PUP and UPRG. At the time of writing, neither is represented in the Northern Ireland Assembly. Informed by their proximity to the conflict and socio-economic location, common themes include a sense of powerlessness, inequality, structural injustice and, at times, social dislocation (Farrington 2008; Wood 2006; Gallaher 2007). Steeped in the prison experience of founding members such as the late David Ervine, Billy Hutchinson and Gusty Spence, the PUP has historically presented a strand of political thought which is socialist in orientation and particularly receptive to the conditions of loyalist prisoners (McAuley 2004). Critical of the intransigence within mainstream unionism, the party has emphasised a need for all communities to accept their social responsibilities and an attempt has been made to establish class as a reference point (Spencer 2008; McAuley 2005). In recent years, the party leadership has demonstrated a willingness to enter into political debate with representatives of Irish republicanism (McAuley 2005). At the time of writing, the party is led by Billy Hutchinson, a former member of the UVF. The UPRG is the successor of the Ulster Democratic Party (UDP), which emerged in the post-ceasefire period and promised 'effective leadership' and a different type of loyalism (McAuley 2005). After the UDP failed to win any Assembly seats, it was dissolved and replaced by the UPRG. The UPRG is not a registered political party and provides 'political analysis' to the UDA.[21] Like the PUP, the UPRG has argued that the UUP and DUP have abandoned the Protestant working class (Farrington 2008). The organisation has also played an influential role in moving the UDA away from violence and criminality and supported the decommissioning of loyalist weaponry (Shirlow 2012).

Research design and methodology

The research for this book is based on over 40 'elite' interviews. Participants stemmed from three main cohorts. Over 27 interviews took place with representatives of the main unionist and loyalist political parties and associations – the UUP, DUP, TUV, PUP, UPRG and The Union Group. Policing representatives included a number of senior members of the PSNI, OPONI, HET, PFNI, the NIRPOA and the RUC George Cross Foundation (RUC GC F). Third, a number of academics and members of civil society with an interest and expertise in this area were interviewed. This included the co-chairs of the CGP. A form of purposeful sampling was used whereby potential interviewees were approached on the basis of their relevancy to the research questions (Bryman 2004; Goldstein 2002). In this case this meant those individuals who were, for example, professionally placed to represent the views of their organisation or who were publicly engaged in the debate on dealing with the past. These actors' expertise and experience in their respective areas meant they were ideally situated to offer valuable contributions to this work. The overwhelming majority of interviewees were male and participants stemmed from a range of socio-economic backgrounds and geographical locations throughout Northern Ireland.

This approach did however mean that a number of groups and patterns of investigation did not form part of this research. Specifically, this means that the findings of this book are not geographically representative of unionist or loyalist spokespersons across Northern Ireland and do not represent the views of ordinary rank and file unionist and loyalist civilians. Neither does it include the views of unionist victim and community groups. Given the legacy of the Northern Ireland conflict and its continuing impact on those on the receiving end of loss, violence and destruction, the concerns of victim and community groups are highly important. Significant points of common interest and divergence with political leaders and other opinion formers can often be identified. However, as detailed above, the views of unionist civilians and victim and community groups have been explored elsewhere and are the focus of ongoing research. By contrast, this was an elite focused study and to move beyond this objective could have compromised the clarity of the arguments expressed within. The choice of interviewees hence reflected this aim.

All interviews took place between March and October 2009, in light of the publication of the Report of the CGP in January 2009. This timely approach took advantage of the immediate political reaction to the Group's work and a time of greater reflection on the truth recovery debate. Access to interviewees was, in the main, more straightforward to facilitate than initially anticipated. In the first instance, I followed well-established guidelines for conducting successful elite interviews, sending a formal request to potential participants outlining the nature of the research project and why I wished to interview them (Lilleker 2003; Peabody *et al.* 1990). Latterly, a small number of interviewees acted as valuable 'gatekeepers' to facilitate access to harder to reach individuals (May 2001). While not all those approached agreed to be interviewed, citing understandable time constraints, the vast majority were extremely willing, including a number of high-profile political and professional actors. The highly topical nature of this debate was undoubtedly of benefit. Moreover, a number of former loyalist ex-combatants, who are now in positions of political and communal leadership in their local areas, expressed gratitude that their views and experiences were being taken into consideration.

All interviews were 'semi-structured' in nature and the rationale for this approach was threefold. First, the open-ended nature of semi-structured interviewing encourages participants to 'ramble' in their responses and offer feedback within their own frames of reference, combining structure with flexibility (Bryman 2004: 320; Bachman and Schutt 2001). Responses were therefore highly individual and the social and cultural backdrop to interviewee's responses was readily identifiable. This provided a detailed insight into how participants understanding of relevant social factors shaped and refined their perspectives and contributed to the quality and richness of the data collected (May 2001). In this respect, the use of semi-structured interviews had a distinct advantage over the use of focus groups in which the sensitive nature of this research could have led to the over domination of certain voices and the silencing of others. With focus groups there was also the potential that the discussion would have rapidly gone off topic and into a wider political debate.

Second, during the interviews, the use of a semi-structured approach allowed the author to 'listen, then prompt and encourage where appropriate' (Davies 2000, cited in Jupp, Davies and Francis 2000: 91). Having the flexibility to raise questions not previously formulated, I was able to enter into a process of dialogue and exchange with participants, facilitating clarification and elaboration of key topics (May 2001; Noaks and Wincup 2004). In many instances, this revealed detailed intricacies of participant's positions that were of major significance to this research, but which had not come to light through the literature review. I would argue this approach encouraged a refinement of the research topics and, ultimately, a greater depth of knowledge and insight.

Third, the possession of a clear interview guide provided a number of benefits, not least in terms of ensuring that the interview stayed with the boundaries of the research question. Deviation from the specific question and the subsequent generation of large amounts of irrelevant and unsuitable data were the disadvantages of focus groups and unstructured interviews that I was keen to avoid (Corbetta 2003). Concomitantly, a clear focus of investigation made it less easy for participants to evade more-challenging questions. Combined with the above argument, this meant I had the freedom to formulate new questions yet ensure all the relevant themes were dealt with and necessary information produced. Having a core interview guide also provided a concrete frame of reference that was invaluable when analysing the data and illuminating differences and similarities between participant's positions (May 2001; Marshall and Rossman 1999). Again, neither unstructured interviewing nor focus groups would have provided such a clear analytical framework.

This research was also conducted according to strict ethical guidelines and underwent a process of ethical review.[22] In addition to standard ethical principles, such as the importance of informed consent and the ability to withdraw from the research at any time, all interviewees were asked to sign a document stating whether they consented to their name being used in this research. The vast majority gave consent. Those who did not are referred to anonymously throughout the text. With the participant's permission, all interviews were recorded and transcribed. Participants were also offered the opportunity to receive a copy of the interview transcript and make any changes they saw fit. A number of interviewees requested to do so, and, in a small number of cases, some minor changes to the text were made.

There are a number of well-established critiques of focusing exclusively on elite actors. This research was conducted with these critiques in mind and a number of counter-arguments can be made. One obvious downfall is that the research may reify hegemonic understandings of a given social or political issue, while simultaneously silencing the voices 'from below'. As discussed above, one feature of the debate on truth recovery in Northern Ireland is that much of the most informed and nuanced discussions have come from beyond the political and policy elites. Using elite interviews, I was able to gain an in-depth insight into arguments that had previously only been accessible in the form of one-dimensional press releases and under-developed discussion documents and articles. Second, I was able to explore how participants' position on the truth recovery debate related to broader political, social and cultural forces. Lilleker (2003: 208) has argued that such interviews 'provide insights into ... the inner workings of the political process, the machinations between influential actors and how a sequence of events was viewed and responded to within the political machine'. The scope of the research sample also provided a greater breadth and depth of opinion than had previously been attained.

Dexter (2006) also suggests that elite interviewees may be particularly skilled at avoiding difficult or challenging questions. For a small jurisdiction, Northern Ireland has been extensively researched and among many political and community leaders, there is (understandably) a degree of 'research weariness' (Reed 2012). It is my view that the topical nature of this research project and the high media profile afforded to the truth recovery debate at the time of interview sparked participant's interest and willingness to be interviewed. I would also argue that the original nature of the research encouraged participants to directly answer my questions rather than diverge into well-rehearsed 'political monologues' often employed by political elites during interviews and particularly so in politically polarised societies such as Northern Ireland (Puwar 1997).

Third, I would argue that my identity as a young female academic whose name denotes a Protestant background influenced participant's responses and attitudes towards me during interview. This dynamic is of particular importance in a 'divided society' where

> the mutual impact of identity between researcher and respondent matters because the data may vary from an interview where the respondent assumes the researcher is on their 'side', to one where the researcher is assumed to be from the opposing ethnic group.
>
> (McEvoy, J. 2006)

During the course of interview, a number of interviewees asked subtle questions in regard to my background, including where I live and the school I attended. As discussed by Finlay (2001), in Northern Ireland, these factors are key features in the quest to ascertain one's identity. Given that the overwhelming majority of those interviewed were from a Protestant-unionist background, it is my view that many were comfortable and open in discussing their views with me because they assumed that I was from the same community. It is likely that this 'identity element' contributed to the richness of the data obtained. This did not, however, prevent at least one interviewee expressing 'surprise' that someone of my assumed background would have any desire to look at the sensitive or uncomfortable issue of dealing with the past and one participant appeared to be concerned that that I would be shocked or upset by the detail of their responses.[23] More encouragingly, and echoing the aims and objectives of this research, several interviewees emphasised the need for this research and showed great enthusiasm for this work.[24] Such interviews were a considerable source of motivation for this author.

Chapter structure

This book is structured as follows.

Chapter 2 begins the analysis by concentrating on the themes of denial, blame and blamelessness. After outlining unionists' preferred vision of the past and their sense of collective memory, this chapter explores how different techniques of denial are used to deny responsibility for their role in the causes and consequences of the Northern Ireland conflict and to deflect calls for truth recovery. Privileging a highly polarised conceptualisation of 'right' and 'wrong' and a singular interpretation of truth, this chapter argues that truth recovery challenges unionists' narratives of the past, the present and their imagined future (Leebaw 2011). It also demonstrates how truth recovery and dealing with the past can be readily equated with apportioning 'blame' and responsibility for the conflict.

Chapter 3 continues to develop these themes by examining the complexity and politicisation of how to define victims and perpetrators in the aftermath of violent conflict. It argues that this contest is related to competing interpretations of moral authority, legitimacy, innocence and guilt. This chapter illustrates that such contested understandings of victimhood can directly inform opposition to a formal truth process. In Northern Ireland, unionists and representatives of the security forces have argued that they are the *real* and *innocent* victims of the conflict. The allegation that a truth process would create 'moral equivalence' between victims and combatants, denying and exacerbating legacies of loss and that it would undermine hierarchal understandings of victimhood and a hierarchy of truth are key areas of investigation.

The intersection between trust and truth-telling is examined in Chapter 4. While truth processes are often presented as being able to 'narrow the range of permissible lies', or to challenge the capacity for historical revisionism, this chapter argues that in the absence of trust, the converse is equally true – that truth recovery may be used to 're-write' the past in a partial and selective manner or that not all parties to the conflict will openly participate (Ignatieff 1996: 113). Two areas that have a fundamental bearing on unionists' opposition to truth recovery in Northern Ireland are examined – the argument that truth recovery has, and will, overwhelmingly concentrate on the actions of the state during the conflict and that republican politicians and ex-combatants cannot be trusted to tell the truth about their involvement in the conflict.

Chapter 5 moves on from considering the lack of trust in the 'other' to how a lack of trust in the 'self' and how to present one's narratives of the conflict may shape opposition to truth recovery. Concentrating on the concept of loyalty, this chapter argues that unionists' and loyalists' status as pro-state actors has had a negative impact on their confidence to participate in a truth process. It will be suggested that loyalty has mediated unionists' and loyalists' willingness or capacity to speak out about problematic aspects of the state's conduct during the conflict, engendering silence rather than voice; that there is a lack of confidence in terms of how to 'sell' their story; and particularly, in terms of loyalists, a lack of resourcing to help build community confidence in truth recovery.

The flipside to loyalty is betrayal and as regards dealing with the past, the question of how examining past actions can be interpreted as betraying the sacrifices that have been made. Focusing largely on the security forces, Chapter 6 will highlight the importance of a narrative of sacrifice and of 'keeping faith with the dead' (Ignatieff 1998: 188). It will suggest that for former members of the RUC, current and prospective methods of truth recovery have been interpreted as betraying their sacrifice and have called into question the meaning of their death. By contrast, a significant difference of opinion on the need for a formal truth process can be found at the elite level of the post-Patten policing bodies. This chapter argues that these tensions are part of the debate over 'ownership' of the past.

Chapter 7 concludes the book. Drawing together the previous chapters, it offers some comments on the local and global significance of this work. It ends with a call to move beyond denial and silence in Northern Ireland to a broader notion of political responsibility for the past. In this chapter I argue that doing so is vital to taking ownership of the past *and* the future.

Notes

1 Since 2000, there has however been an increased momentum around remembering the past in Spain (Farran and Amago 2010). The Association for the Recovery of Historical Memory was established in 2000 and collects oral

and written testimonies about Franco's victims and attempts to excavate and identify bodies dumped in mass graves (Renshaw 2011). In October 2008, Spanish judge Baltasar Garzon, at the behest of victims' relatives, also attempted to open an inquiry into crimes committed during Franco's dictatorship. The investigation was short lived, and in 2010, the political right took legal action against Garzon, alleging that he had abused his powers vis-à-vis the 1977 amnesty law (The Economist 2010). In 2012, the Spanish Supreme Court acquitted Garzon but the terms of 1977 amnesty law were upheld (Tremlett 2012).

2 While many of these examples are discussed in greater depth throughout this book, for a comprehensive guide to truth recovery initiatives in Northern Ireland see: McEvoy (2006) and Healing Through Remembering (2013).

3 See: www.smithwicktribunal.ie/smithwick/HOMEPAGE.html (accessed on 10 July 2013).

4 See: www.cgpni.org (accessed 1 October 2007).

5 The group received 290 written submissions, 2,086 standardised letters and met privately with 141 individuals and groups.

6 As explored throughout this book, this does not mean that unionists are opposed to 'truth' per se.

7 These concerns are arguably of significance to all parties to the conflict. However, it is interesting to note that the preponderance of these arguments have been made by representatives of the pro-state community.

8 Interview, Richard Bullick, DUP, 25 March 2009; Interview, Trevor Ringland, One Small Step Campaign, 21 May 2009; Interview, Danny Kennedy, UUP, 5 May 2009; Interview, Sir Reg Empey, UUP, 17 April 2009; Interview, Dermott Nesbitt, former UUP representative, 23 March 2009.

9 Interview, Richard Bullick, DUP, 25 March 2009.

10 Interview, Jeffrey Donaldson, DUP, 11 May 2009; Interview, Frankie Gallagher, UPRG, 11 June 2009.

As The UUP's Sir Reg Empey stated, 'People are still subject to intimidation in this place not a hundred yards from where we are sitting, in all directions ... the organisations are still there and while they may not be rattling their sabres as overtly as they once were, on all sides they are still operating ... now if somebody comes up and says, even with protection of some sort, "I know it was Billy over there did it in 1978, I was with him", what is the reaction to that going to be? – "I'll kill him'". Interview, Sir Reg Empey, UUP, 17 April 2009.

11 Interview, Frankie Gallagher, UPRG, 11 June 2009; Interview, Trevor Ringland, One Small Step Campaign, 21 May 2009.

12 Interview, Billy McQuiston, UPRG, 18 June 2009; Interview, North Belfast community worker, 24 June 2009.

13 Interview, Tom Elliott, UUP, 20 April 2009.

On the financial cost of investigating the past, the DUP's Ian Paisley Junior argued, 'Getting justice is an incredibly expensive luxury and a high ticket item like that in the current economic climate is going nowhere. That is not the right reason as to why but I think it is an explanation'. Interview, Ian Paisley Junior, DUP, 12 September 2009.

14 As detailed in Chapter 4, the former PUP leader Dawn Purvis has also recognised this point.

15 It is interesting to note that during interview, Archbishop Robin Eames, co-chair of the Consultative Group on the Past, claimed that MI5, MI6, Special Branch and the Ministry of Defence were committed to participating in the Legacy Commission designed by the CGP. Interview, Archbishop Robin Eames, 23 October 2009.

16 Ulster Unionist Party Rules, 2007. Available at: www.uup.org/policy/the-objectives-of -the-party-shall-be-to-.php (accessed on 5 March 2008).

It should be noted that the argument that unionists supported the rule of law at all times is not entirely accurate. Having supported practices such as internment, the torture of terrorist suspects and the supergrass trials, their support for the rule of law was essentially politically contingent.

17 See: http://aims.niassembly.gov.uk/mlas/statistics.aspx (accessed on 25 June 2013).

18 See: http://aims.niassembly.gov.uk/mlas/statistics.aspx (accessed on 25 June 2013).

19 Brewer *et al.* (1988: 50) and Tomlinson (1980, cited in Ellison and Martin 2000: 694) have respectively described the RUC as the 'armed wing of unionism' and as the 'umbilical cord of unionism'.

20 While space prevents an exhaustive examination of each of the loyalist paramilitary organisations, the following descriptions provide a brief overview.

a. The modern UVF was formed in 1966 under the leadership of Gusty Spence. Its origins can be traced to the mass mobilisation of Protestants against the Irish Home Rule movement (Bruce 1992a). From the late 1960s onwards its main aim was to exert military force 'to destroy the forces and resources of the enemy by means of counter terrorism' (Taylor 1999; UVF 1974, cited in Spencer 2008: 62).

b. The UDA was officially formed in 1971, and like the UVF, emerged as a community-defence organisation. The UDA's cover organisation, the Ulster Freedom Fighters (UFF) engaged in campaigns of sectarian murder (Wood 2006). Such activity was often justified with the claim that the victim was a member of the IRA, yet people were frequently murdered simply because they were members of the Catholic community (Bruce 1992a). Throughout its history the UDA has been plagued by criminality, power struggles, feuding and allegations of collusion with the British intelligence services (Wood 2006).

c. The breakaway Loyalist Volunteer Force (LVF) formed in 1996 in opposition to loyalist paramilitary support for the peace process (Spencer 2008). Led by Billy 'King Rat' Wright (murdered by the Irish National Liberation Army [INLA] while in prison in 1997) and composed of disenchanted UVF and UDA elements, the LVF presented an Evangelical form of resistance to the peace process (Bruce 2004).

21 Interview, Frankie Gallagher, UPRG, 11 June 2009.

22 See: www.law.qub.ac.uk/schools/SchoolofLaw/Research/EthicsApproval/ (accessed on 1 February 2008).

23 As these remarks were made 'off the record', these sources will remain anonymous.

24 As above.

Chapter 2

Truth, denial and blamelessness

Introduction

Defined by Cohen (2001: 25) as 'the need to be innocent of a troubling recognition', the capacity of a truth process to challenge myths and falsehoods is one of the most compelling and challenging features of transitional justice (Leebaw 2008, 2011). In South Africa, for example, the manner in which the South African Truth and Reconciliation Commission (SATRC) held sectoral hearings into the role of the business, medical, legal, religious and prison communities during the apartheid era and, via the media, brought the horrors of apartheid into the living rooms of white South African's who could no longer say 'I didn't know' has been widely applauded (Dyzenhaus 1998; Boraine 1999, cited in Rolston 2002: 96). Similarly in Chile, Argentina and elsewhere, part of the argument for truth recovery has been to seek to encourage, if not compel, pro-state sectors to acknowledge not just the reality of past abuses but also their complicity (through actions or silence) in such acts (Payne 2008; Stanley 2005; Jamieson and McEvoy 2005).

These aspirations rest on a number of points. The first calls for a broader notion of accountability – the need to problematise and complicate simple, yet polarised histories, inculcating the idea that 'all sides in the struggle did bad things'. In terms of Christie's (1977) idea of 'conflicts as property', as is emphasised in the restorative justice literature, cultivating a more equal distribution of responsibility requires political generosity and the willingness of all parties to the conflict to take ownership of and acknowledge their role in the past (Braithwaite 2002; McEvoy and Eriksson 2006). Gibson's (2004: 204) description of the SATRC's 'multifaceted truth' as 'an amalgam of ideas about the past with which all South Africans must at least contend' is indicative of the plurality of truths, which will exist in any post-conflict jurisdiction. This does not mean an uncritical acceptance of all narratives of the past – while there are some facts that are fundamental enough that broad acceptance of their truth is necessary, challenging myths and falsehoods also requires acknowledging that some versions of the past are simply wrong

(Minow 1998; Hayner 2011). Gready (2011: 73) argues that 'Truth, in this process, must take sides and make enemies'. Rather, as Ignatieff (1996: 113) and Jelin (2007: 140) respectively state, the objective is to 'narrow the range of permissible lies', because 'it is unthinkable to find one memory, a single version and interpretation of the past shared by a whole society whatever its scope and size'. For Arendt (1968: 20), the challenge 'is to see precisely what it [the past] was, and to endure this knowledge'.

While victims of past human rights violations often welcome official acknowledgement of their experiences, for once and still powerful actors keen to conceal their past actions and inactions, denying and silencing the past may be part of an attempt to protect oneself or one's community from the unpalatable realities of a violent past (Stanley 2005; Ben-Ze'ev *et al.* 2010). Rejecting a broader notion of ownership and responsibility for conflict, doing so speaks to a reluctance to move away from polarised conceptions of 'innocence' and 'guilt' or 'good' and 'evil' (Rousso 1991; Misztal 2003; Payne 2008; Bouris 2007). This chapter will argue that for those unionists, loyalists and representatives of the security forces who are opposed to the establishment of a formal truth process in Northern Ireland, the dynamics of denial and silence have been instrumental in shaping their concerns. It will do so through five overlapping sections. By way of background, the first section explores unionist representations of the history and context of the Northern Ireland conflict. Focusing on the concept of denial, the second section addresses how unionist political elite's reluctance to countenance the idea that their actions or inactions played a role in the causes and consequences of the conflict has structured their opposition to a truth process. The third part of this chapter will argue that Northern Ireland's status as part of a liberal democracy with a stated commitment to the rule of law has led to particular difficulties as regards 'seeing' past human rights violations. That a truth process would challenge these claims and the blameless identity they represent closely links to the fourth argument explored in this chapter – the perception that a truth process would be used to *blame* unionists and members of the security forces for the conflict. This is also coupled with the argument, made by a number of interviewees, that a truth process should seek to place all responsibility for the conflict with republican paramilitaries and that their 'repentance' should be sought. Past efforts at truth recovery and a number of the recommendations of the CGP have been framed in such a way as to support this oppositional stance. Finally, and against this backdrop, it will be suggested that while loyalist ex-combatants and their political representatives are often more willing to acknowledge their role in the past, the concern that they could be exploited by members of the unionist political elite, determined to avoid implication in the events of the conflict, has contributed to their reluctance to participate in a formal truth process. Bound up with notions of blamelessness, denial and apportioning 'right' and 'wrong', this chapter will argue that a version of the 'past perfect' is often preferred to a more open acknowledgment of past actions and inactions.

Unionism, identity and imagining the past

Defined by Misztal (2003: 103) as 'the creative imagining of the past in the service of the present and an imagined future', collective memory is not merely historical knowledge shared by a group (Novick 1999). Rather, according to Halbwachs (1950, cited in Novick 1999), collective memory is understood to express some eternal or essential truth about the group: it has to resonate with how we understand ourselves, how we see our present circumstances and how we think about our future. By way of background, the following discussion will outline the dominant unionist view of the history and context of the Northern Ireland conflict. It will argue that for many of those representatives of the UUP, DUP and security forces interviewed for the purposes of this book, a specific understanding of the causes of the conflict in Northern Ireland was articulated – one in which they, and by extension, the British state, bore little to no responsibility for its events (Lawther 2010, 2011, 2013). The assertion by the TUV MLA Jim Allister that 'nationalists and republicans set up a terror campaign to butcher you, so anyone in their right mind can see where right and where wrong is' is a particularly stark representation of this narrative.[1] Major aspects of this discourse include an emphasis on the state's legitimacy, the importance of upholding the rule of law and the role of the security forces in securing peace and stability, often by way of death and sacrifice. As I will argue below, seeking to create a 'new' imagined political community, a truth process would challenge the validity and legitimacy of this collective memory (Teitel 2000; Leebaw 2011; Anderson 2006).

At least three main points can be deduced from the field of memory studies which are relevant to this analysis. First, is the circularity between memory and a group or an individual's sense of identity and legitimacy. Novick (1999: 7), for example, comments that 'we choose to center certain memories because they seem to express to us what is central to our collective identity. Those memories, once brought to the fore, reinforce that form of identity'. Forming coherent narratives of the past and the 'continuity of conscience' that links past, present and future, collective memory helps structure the imagined political community (Oakeshott 1983: 15). As Anderson (2006: 6) has argued, the imagined political community is both limited and sovereign, yet different from an actual community because it is not a community based on the everyday face-to-face interactions of members – '…it is imagined because members of even the smallest nation will never know most of their fellow members…yet in the minds of each lives the image of their communion'. Those outside this imagined community are deemed a threat to its values and experiences (Anderson

2006). Shaping this imagined political community may necessarily involve silencing, denying or forgetting certain aspects of the past (Connerton 2008; Ricoeur 2004; Brewer 2010).

While an exhaustive overview of the history of the Northern Ireland state is beyond the scope of this book, some brief comments on unionist narratives are useful for illustrative purposes. As detailed in the introduction, following the Government of Ireland Act in 1920 and until the instigation of Direct Rule in 1972, the Northern Ireland state was unionist dominated (Farrington 2006). For successive governments, the state was a legitimate political entity that properly expressed the political outlook of the majority of the local population (Bourke 2003). In this version of the past, discrimination against the one-third nationalist population – found for example in the manipulation of local government electoral boundaries to help establish unionist control in areas where nationalists where the majority community or the existence of partial policing practices is absent (Cochrane 2013). Rather, much of contemporary unionist discourse appears to privilege a version of history in which the period of unionist rule from 1921 onwards was characterised by good community relations and in which the place and treatment of the nationalist minority did not validate the rise in communal and political agitation (Bourke 2003). The liberal–democratic nature of the Northern Ireland state is often emphasised and linked to the suggestion that the seeds of violence lay in republican irredentism rather than discrimination or maltreatment of the minority population:

> Northern Ireland remained a parliamentary democracy, in which government was conducted on the same lines as in the rest of the UK. It was never a police state, because the police, like every other branch of the executive was subject to the scrutiny of parliament. There was no question which could not be aired in parliament. The press was not censored. With one important exception, there were no official curbs on free speech or the free expression of political opinion...Moreover, the period of unionist rule was, with the exception of some ugly riots in the early 1930s, almost free of sectarian violence.
>
> (Stewart 1986: 177, cited in McGarry and O'Leary 1995: 133–34; Cochrane 1999)

Paralleling unionists' narratives, much of the organisational memory of the RUC draws attention to officers' belief in a period of trouble-free and consensual policing prior to the onset of the conflict (Boyce 1979). Narratives of public acceptability, political neutrality, impartiality and a primary concern with enforcing ordinary criminal law rather than exceptional security measures formed the basis of the RUC's legitimation discourse (Brogden and Shearing 1993; Ellison and Smyth 2000; Pockrass 1986; Ryder 2000; Mulcahy

2006). As illustrated by the former Chief Constable Sir Ronnie Flanagan's statement – 'we are no more, we are no less, than public servants delivering a public good – that of the policing service', this discourse presented the image of a police force upholding the 'service ideal' of British policing standards and corresponding to Loader and Walker's (2001) conceptualisation of 'policing as a public good' (Mulcahy 2006: 151; Mulcahy and Ellison 2001). Building upon their self-professed status as a 'law-bound, disciplined, visible public service, in order to protect life and property' and conveying the ideologically satisfying view of police officers as neutral umpires, accountable to the law, rather than political actors advancing a political agenda, dealing with 'unnecessary' and 'unjustified' terrorist activity was presented as a 'regrettable necessity' (NIRPOA 2009: 19; Ellison and Smyth 2000). The following statement by an RUC Chief Inspector well captures these sentiments:

> The RUC are what I like to call the 'thin green line' – it's a phrase I have used many times – and it sums up quite well what I perceive the role of the RUC to be in this community. Basically, we try and maintain some semblance of order and stability until the politicians can agree on a solution. The force has no interest in the politics of the situation – we are just the umpire holding the ring.
>
> (cited in Mulcahy and Ellison 2001: 398)

Pointing to the 'living' quality of memory and therefore the difference between memory and history – as Novick (1999) argues, while history focuses on the historicity of past events, memory, by contrast, is seen as not having a sense of the passage of time, it denies the 'pastness' of objects and insists on their continuing presence – such images have a continuing salience.[2] For many unionist political elites and representatives of the security forces, their sense of identity and collective memory is founded on the notion of the 'past perfect', whereby the criminal origins of the IRA's campaign and the legitimacy of the state and its security forces actions are heavily emphasised (Booth 2001: 786; Halbwachs 1992; Misztal 2003; Cochrane 1997; Ryder 2000). The unionist 'usable past' is therefore one where the 'myth of blamelessness' has been articulated and reproduced to deny responsibility for the conditions which gave rise to or emerged during the conflict (Booth 2001; Lawther 2013). This perspective was clearly articulated by one representative of the DUP and his remarks are worth repeating at some length:

> I think that unionists come to the troubles with a view that they are completely guiltless in all of this and that they were victims of a revolutionary organisation who wanted to overthrow their state and all they wanted to do was to see their state functioning normally. I

> actually have a great deal of sympathy for that point of view because I am in that situation. I grew up in a country that was undergoing a revolutionary war and thanks be to God the only thing that didn't happen was a civil war in response and I think many many times when I read about the history of other countries that God was extremely merciful to this country that the unionist community did not revolt in anger as to what happened. I see a community that suffered and suffered terribly and could have involved themselves in a civil war and didn't because they decided to throw their lot in with a State and a State that has quite frankly let them down. To me that is an amazing story of passiveness in the face of human suffering.[3]

Instead, responsibility for the conflict is laid at the door of the Republican movement: 'let me make it clear and beyond doubt…the Provisional IRA [PIRA], its leadership and members, were co-conspirators in a criminal insurrection designed to overthrow the lawful order in Northern Ireland' (DUP 2009a: 6). A defence of the RUC often runs in tandem with this view:

> People have to know who were responsible for the atrocities. It wasn't the security forces. The security forces, on the whole, held the line, in fact I would say the police service, the RUC, and history I think will be favorable on this, many many times held this province from going into anarchy.[4]

Yet, as Teitel (2000) and Leebaw (2011) have argued, transitional justice institutions cannot simply rely on a set of commonly accepted norms for guidance; instead, they seek to naturalise the compromises, distortions and irregularities that frame their investigations, creating a 'new' imagined political community (Anderson 2006; Wilson 2001). Such efforts are inevitably contested and problematic and, in a transitional environment, the myriad of often competing identities has influenced the shape of truth recovery mechanisms and responses to them (Arthur 2011). As illustrated in South Africa and Guatemala, for example, the often privileged position of the security forces, who acted as embodiments of the state and the challenge the respective truth processes posed to this (imagined) identity, was often central to the narratives of those who opposed the SATRC and Guatemalan Commission for Historical Clarification (Gready 2011). For unionists this is the problem. According to their narratives of the past, there was little wrong with the unionist state and hence little need for reform or the critical interrogation of that past that a truth process would entail. Unionists' opposition to truth recovery is therefore resistance to the challenge a truth process would pose to the construction of their identity, specifically that of the 'imagined' blameless political community (Anderson 2006). This tension was well captured by a former political advisor to the UUP:

> When political traditions are dealing with their past they are dealing with something precious to the adherents of that tradition and I think we face some of those complications too. I think our past creates our identity, I think that is true across the board. It should be a creative dialogue with your past, a creative tension, not a bland acceptance and I guess that is where we are not at.[5]

Truth, denial and blamelessness

As detailed above, one of the most lauded values of recovering truth about past human rights violations is the purported capacity of a truth process 'to establish an accurate record of a country's past, clarify uncertain events and lift the lid of silence and denial from a contentious and painful period of history' (Hayner 2011: 20). Yet, for unionists, the very existence of a truth process and its capacity to reveal uncomfortable truths challenges the 'myth of blamelessness' and undermines the argument that republican culpability is at the root of all that has troubled Northern Ireland (Hamber 1998; Smyth 2007; Ignatieff 1996; Hayner 2011). According to Cohen (2001), information, which is too threatening or disturbing to be publicly acknowledged, is often reframed, justified and reappropriated through sophisticated techniques of denial. Cohen (2001) suggests a standard rhetoric of response, comprising three sequential, or more often, simultaneous elements: 'literal' or outright denial; 'interpretive' denial; and 'implicatory' denial. Unionists have, to varying degrees, used all three elements of this architecture of denial to deflect their share of ownership and responsibility for the conflict and, by extension, calls for truth recovery.[6] Drawing on a selection of examples, the following discussion sets out this case.

Literal denial

The most overt form of denial is literal denial – the assertion that something did not happen or is not true (Cohen 2001). Challenging the fact or knowledge of the fact, this form of denial is typified by statements such as 'nothing happened here', 'there was no massacre', 'we don't believe you' (Cohen 2001: 7). In Northern Ireland, elements of literal denial were levied against the CGP's attempt to encourage unionists to begin to accommodate the idea that all parties to the conflict committed wrongs (Cohen 2001). The CGP made several such attempts. For example, an early speech by the Group's co-chairs Archbishop Eames and Denis Bradley noted that while it is difficult, unionist's need to countenance their own 'ugly truths', including the fact that the State at times acted outside the law (Eames and Bradley 2008). As Archbishop Eames argued, 'This is one of the crucial issues facing us as a Group, difficult as it may be for some in our society to hear that elements of the State, on occasions, acted outside the law' (Eames and Bradley 2008). Likewise, the Report of the CGP expressed sentiments such as 'versions of the past differ not so much in the facts of what happened but more in the moral assessment of the rightness and wrongness of what was done by opposing sides' and suggests that 'just as rights were present on both sides, wrongs were also committed by both' (CGP 2009: 53, 55).

Such efforts were not well received. In large part, they were interpreted as betraying unionist's self-identity as upholders of the rule of law and as part of the attempt to blame the RUC for much of the responsibility for the conflict. For example, the former leader of the UUP Tom Elliott argued that the Report was 'promoting the view that it is the fault of Unionism from 1921', while a former party advisor has noted there is an 'implicit acceptance of one theory of the origins of the Troubles' and an assumption of 'too much guilt' (Birnie 2009; UUP 2009a). DUP leader Peter Robinson was no less unequivocal, arguing, 'I think most people in Northern Ireland will readily grasp who might gain from a focus on "*conflicting moral judgements*" rather than "*just the facts*" (DUP 2009a: 7). Robinson's formal response to the Report of the CGP also appears to suggest that it is Archbishop Eames and Denis Bradley who are in denial about the causes of the conflict – 'in offering an a la carte choice of interpretations and justifications about the 'cause of the conflict', the authors ask the rest of us to deny what we know and hold to be true' (DUP 2009a: 4). As explored below, these arguments are not inseparable from Northern Ireland's place in the UK – a liberal democracy with a stated commitment to the rule of law (Ni Aolain and Campbell 2005).

Interpretive denial

The second substantive form of denial identified by Cohen (2001: 7) is interpretive denial – the idea that 'what happened is not what you think it is, not what it looks like, not what you call it'. In this case, the raw facts (that something happened) are not denied, but are given a different meaning from what seems apparent to others. The reaction of a number of prominent unionist politicians to the Saville Inquiry into the events on Bloody Sunday illustrates this technique. On 30 January 1972, 13 civilians who were attending a civil rights march in Londonderry were killed when soldiers from the 1st Parachute Regiment of the British Army opened fire, claiming that protestors had fired shots. The British government established the Widgery Tribunal to investigate the chain of events in full and the tribunal reported 11 weeks later, in April 1972. Widgery (1972) largely exonerated the British soldiers, reporting that soldiers from the parachute regiment had been fired on first and that some victims had handled weapons, despite witness evidence stating that the victims were unarmed civilians. Widgery (1972: np) concluded that there would have been no deaths if there had not been an illegal march and one that created 'a highly dangerous situation'.[7] The victims' families and their supporters denounced the report as a whitewash and following a long campaign for truth and justice, in 1998, the then Prime Minister Tony Blair established the Saville Inquiry to investigate as 'a definite matter of urgent public importance' the events of that day.[8] Published on 15 June 2010, the long-awaited Saville Report overturned Widgery's (1972) conclusions, finding the 13 victims to be innocent, 'none of whom was posing a threat of causing death or injury' (Saville *et al.* 2010: 58). Saville further concluded that 'We found no instances where it appeared to us that soldiers either were or might have been justified in firing'; that army paratroopers fired the first shot and that a number of soldiers knowingly gave false evidence to the inquiry (Saville *et al.* 2010: 45).

Since the establishment of the inquiry in 1998, there has been a persistent cynicism from unionists, particularly in regard to its financial cost, what they perceive to be a hierarchy of victims and the challenge it poses to the memory and legitimacy of the state forces (DUP 2009b, 2010a; UUP 2007a). The following comments made by the DUP's Gregory Campbell on a BBC Northern Ireland 'Spotlight' programme, aired on the night of the report's publication, demonstrate Cohen's (2001) argument that in cases of interpretive denial, by changing words or using euphemisms, the cognitive meaning of events are reinterpreted and re-allocated to another class of event. Responding to the question of whether it was difficult to hear 'a British Prime Minister – a Conservative–Unionist Prime Minister saying that Saville's conclusions were absolutely clear and unambiguous', Campbell sought to reinterpret the Report's findings.[9] Instead, Campbell laid emphasis on the importance of looking at the events of Bloody Sunday in their wider socio-political context, and, in particular, the murder of two police officers in Londonderry two days previously (Campbell, G 2010; DUP 2010b). In doing so, Campbell attempted to deflect attention from the actions of the paratroopers, provide 'justification' for their mind-set and place responsibility with the IRA:

> It wasn't difficult at all when you know David Cameron as we have begun to know him over recent months; it is just a pity that either he or Lord Saville weren't prepared to face up to the truth and the reality and all the revisionism that we have heard over the last 15 or 20 minutes on your programme and I have heard it all day, will not change the truth, it will not change the truth. What is the truth? Whether Lord Saville wants to write about it or ignore it, whether

> David Cameron wants to try and ignore it or not – the truth is this – why were the soldiers of the parachute regiment deployed into the Bogside initially, why were they there anyway? ... The reason they were deployed was because there was murder, terror, there was shooting, there was bombing ... however much people in politics or in the media don't like this, this is the reality.[10]

An emphasis on other injustices, particularly those perpetrated by the IRA, ran in tandem with this view:

> I am not out of step with the reality of the picture and the reality is that there have been 30 years, 10,000 bloody days were innocent people have been murdered, mostly by an organisation set up with government assistance in the Irish Republic. That was state aided murder for 30 years ... there was no investigation into that, there was no £200 million spent on that.[11]

Corresponding to Cohen's (2001) concept of the denial of the victim, DUP minister Jeffrey Donaldson displayed a similar reluctance to recognise the importance of Saville's outcome for the families of those bereaved on Bloody Sunday. Responding to the question of 'is this not a time in history to have the maturity to rejoice that justice has been done?', made by a member of the audience at the 17 June 2010 BBC 'Question Time' broadcast, Donaldson remarked that 'Justice cannot be a partial thing' and claimed 'I will rejoice when there is justice for the people that I represent as well. Justice for all who lost a loved one – that is what justice is about'.[12]

Implicatory denial

In other instances, unionist reluctance to engage with the truth recovery debate can be likened to a form of implicatory denial, whereby there is no attempt to deny the facts or their conventional meaning, but an effort to deny or minimise the psychological, political or moral implications that often follow (Cohen 2001). In part, this may be traced to a historical tendency towards passivity in unionist political culture that, linked by Cohen (2001: 140) to implicatory denial, is the 'absence of reaction' by 'those who have seen, known or heard about the situation – yet have still not reacted'. The following comments illustrate this case:

> We believed in the justness of our case, we believed that the public, when the public at large saw people being slain on their farms, slaughtered in the streets, blown to pieces, that every right thinking person across the world would say that is wrong, that is horrendous.[13]

> Because of that story telling became less relevant because for unionists it is obvious – you shouldn't have to go on a six-week course to describe all of this. It was very clear, people started protesting and marching and murdering and shooting and you can't reconcile yourself to that. Eventually after a period of time they had to stop. What is there to tell a story about?[14]

At one level, silence in the aftermath of violent conflict is not unexpected or unanticipated. Winter (2010), for example, suggests that touching on the themes of loss, mourning, sacrifice and redemption, silence is always a part of the framing of public understandings of war and violence. The above quotations however suggest that among unionist political elites there was a perception that the causes and consequences of the conflict were so 'obvious' that there was no need to articulate the trauma they were experiencing or to make their case.[15] Moreover, as Zerubavel (2010) suggests, the intensity of silence is self-reinforcing, whereby the longer people remain silent, the harder it is to find things to say and where the longer things go undiscussed, the harder it becomes to talk about them. When faced with the prospect of a truth process and the inevitable challenge to their preferred vision of the past, this legacy of silence is problematic:

> There is also the fact built into the DNA of our party, as a party of government for 50 years in the state of Northern Ireland, of basically not having to answer questions. It was almost as if the unionist party only spoke to unionist voters and therefore it was closed, hermeneutic almost, there was no need to go outside and try to explain ourselves and we got intellectually lazy. When you get intellectually lazy and then you face a crisis and a conflict and you have to articulate yourself in front of people who may not be sympathetic to you, then you hit a brick wall.[16]

Constituting what Aughey (1989) and Graham (1998) have respectively termed an 'inheritance of political inarticulateness, an inheritance which almost constitutes a form of a-politicism' and a 'masterly inactivity' in terms of developing a well-defined sense of place and past, this backdrop has negatively affected unionists' attitudes to truth recovery.

Equally problematic is Winter's (2010: 28–29) argument that the more insidious side to this form of silence arises when the 'morally ambiguous chapters of a country's history cannot be faced easily', when 'talking about the past presents the danger of a breakdown of the legitimacy or authority of a regime…silence then is the insurance policy people take to protect this given order, even at the cost of the truth'. As detailed above, much of contemporary unionist discourse privileges a narrative of blamelessness in which the security forces, British state and wider unionist community are absolved from any responsibility for the conflict in Northern Ireland. Maintaining a silence on the past is therefore a form of resistance *and* a type of communication. On one level and speaking to the above discussion on the intersection of memory and identity, resisting truth through silence is a form of loyalty to the memory of the past. As Ricoeur (2004: 21) states, 'to memory is tied an ambition, a claim – that of being faithful to the past'. It may also be a form of protection against the uncomfortable idea that not only do the state and its agents need to be investigated, but, having expressed unswerving loyalty to that state, of the implications for their identity. Misztal's (2003) use of trauma theory substantiates this argument. As Frijda (1997) and Paez *et al.* (1997) point out, forgetting and silence are frequent reactions to a traumatic past as a way to protect and defend the value and image of specific social groups. The trauma associated with the 'growing realization that not everything that was done by the security forces during the conflict adhered to the rule of law'[17] has consequently engendered a silence that is both strategic and grounded in fear. However, silence is also a form of communication – as Blanchot (1986, cited in Winter 2010: 3) notes, 'To be silent is still to speak'. Silence may therefore be a rational choice for unionists. Given the state's rule of law status, as Campbell and Connolly (2012) argue, collusion and other such practices had to be well concealed. Thus, by maintaining a silence on the past, it may be possible to limit the provable truths and assist in turning the state and unionist community's role in the past into a non-event. In such contexts, 'Silence, then, is not the opposite of speech but, indeed, its very condition of possibility, the precondition of knowing and of meaning' (Eng 2002: 86).

For those who have been more willing to countenance the idea that not all was perfect in the past, doing so has been extremely difficult. According to Cohen (2001), this tension concerns bridging the moral and psychic gap between what you know and what you do, between your sense of who you are and how your action (or inaction) looks. It also concerns doing the 'right' thing with this knowledge (Cohen 2001). The following comments illustrate this case:

> For me the most difficult thing I have had to do in the party in recent years was sit down with a friend of mine from a republican background saying about how she was harassed by police officers going to Mass when she was growing up in County Down. I was thinking, 'I know a lot of police officers but not a single one who would have done that. I *know* she is not lying to me, I *know* it happened.'[18]

For Ignatieff (1996: 118), when caught between the tension of an idealised vision of the RUC and more unpalatable realities, 'denial is actually a defense of everything one holds dear'. The obvious difficulty this interviewee had when attempting to articulate the silent struggles he has personally grappled with reflects Cohen's (2001: 131) argument that 'The problem is not remembering the story…but you have to locate and make sense of memories which you yourself cannot fully believe. The impossibility lies not in seeing the past reality, but in perceiving it *as* reality'. Against a history of denial, the question of how to deal with these concerns and the implications for unionist's sense of identity and legitimacy has engendered an uncertainty and nervousness amongst such voices.[19] Denial has therefore been maintained through silence, which, as Wittgenstein suggests, is an act of language in itself (Morris 2008). In this form of ideological denial, silence is 'choosing, ostrich-like not to know' (Makiya 1993: 325, cited in Cohen 2001: 116). It is also underpinned by profoundly political considerations (Sider and Smith 1997; Trouillot 1995).

Denial, silence and the liberal democratic state

Northern Ireland's status as a part of the UK, a jurisdiction with an impressive democratic pedigree and ideological commitment to the rule of law may also influence unionists and the British state's willingness or ability to 'see' past violations (Ni Aolain and Campbell 2005). In the Western liberal transition, the identification as a rule of law state presupposes the existence of a legal system in which laws are equal in their application, clear in meaning and publicly accessible; that the legal system is based on the presumption of innocence and its central institutions – courts, prosecutors, the police and judiciary are fair, competent and independent; and in which the idea of government by law, rather than by people is supreme (Carothers 1998; Minow 1998). Forming a social contract between the citizen and state and in which no one is above or outside the law creates a community in which each member is *protected* and *prohibited* by the law and its institutions (Geertz 1983). As explored throughout this book, for unionists and the security forces, the conviction that they, and the British state, at all times upheld the rule of law has been unbending and a major legitimation device. The declaration contained in the UUP Party Rules that members will 'Support the maintenance of the rule of law' and the former Chairman of the PFNI Les Rodgers assertion that 'We have stood firm in an unenviable and isolated position doing our best to keep communities from each others throats. At all times we have worked to bring communities together in support of the rule of law' typify this mind-set (Rodgers 1997, cited in Ryder 2000: 484-485). As Geertz (1983: 234) has argued, law represents a way of conceptualising and articulating an ideal vision of the social world and enables people 'to imagine principled lives they can practically lead'. For supporters of the state, privileging this status has been central to imagining their identity and 'principled' lives.

Yet, the British state and its agents played an active role in the conflict, raising the problem that state-led human rights abuses can and do occur in Western liberal democracies, ostensibly at least, founded on their commitment to the rule of law (Bell *et al.* 2004). A number of distinct manifestations can be identified. As has been well documented, in Northern Ireland, the law both operated to manage and ameliorate the state's involvement in the conflict (Boyle *et al.* 1980; Walsh 1983; Ni Aolain 2000). The architecture of emergency legislation under the Civil Authorities (Special Powers) Act of 1922, latterly the Emergency Provisions Act 1973, is indicative of this paradox, permitting, for example, the internment of suspected members of paramilitary organisations without trial, many of whom were subject to torture and degrading treatment and Diplock courts (juryless trials in cases of suspected paramilitary activity) while simultaneously, as an Act of a sovereign parliament, conferring legality and rule of law compliance (Boyle *et al.* 1980). Described as 'legislation in respect of the defence of the realm' and as straying 'perilously close to the point of merely rewriting laws to cover any required action', in Northern Ireland, law became partly constituent of the conflict (Campbell, C 1994; Townshend 1986, cited in Hogan and Walker 1989: 171; Campbell and Ni Aolain 2003). Likewise, as critiqued in detail in later chapters, despite professing a commitment to the rule of law and impartial policing, evidence of collusion between members of loyalist paramilitary organisations and state forces, and other partial policing practices has been found. With the 'sharp end' of state legislation and the use of force largely falling on nationalist and republican communities, such practices undoubtedly inflamed communal tensions and played a direct role in the conflict.

That a truth process would investigate human rights violations the state's legal architecture should have rendered impossible is therefore paradoxical and uncomfortable for the British state and its unionist supporters (Jamieson and McEvoy 2005; Campbell and Connolly 2012). As Campbell and Connolly (2012) argue, that such violations conflict with the state's preferred self-image has arguably made them difficult to 'see' (Cohen 2001; Stanley 2005). In O'Rawe's (2003) opinion, the state's reluctance to identify with unresolved questions concerning its conduct during the conflict is typified by the British government's handling of contentious matters thrown up for review by the Belfast Agreement. Drawing on the examples of reform of policing, emergency legislation and the criminal justice system, O'Rawe (2003) argues that the manner in which the three separate review bodies had clearly demarcated areas of responsibility ensured they worked in isolation and prevented a more collaborative approach. Likewise, discussion on a truth commission or other form of truth recovery body was entirely absent (NIO 1998). Instead, the preference has been for an atomised or piecemeal approach to the past (Campbell and Connolly 2012; Bell 2003). That the 'need' to change and question many of the main institutions of the state goes to the heart of the political order and the

British state's narrative of the conflict may, therefore, have been decisive in the decision to engineer a process of disaggregated and incremental change, which effectively silenced comprehensive discussion on the state's role during the conflict. In O'Rawe's (2003: 1025) opinion, this deliberate compartmentalisation of issues contributed to a climate of false change in which the British government could avoid the 'deconstruction of dearly held truths and assumptions'. A second and related difficulty is that achieving legal accountability for covert violations has been particularly challenging, because, given the challenge to the state's self-image, historically, such acts were organised well below legal radars (Campbell and Connolly 2012). Third, and finally, given the state's self-image as a rule of law state, it has difficulty 'seeing' that it committed any serious and systemic violations (Campbell, C. 2010). From this perspective, as a 'fully functioning' 'liberal democracy', the employment of transitional justice mechanisms, such as a truth process, traditionally associated with dealing with the legacy of authoritarian regimes, is both deeply unsettling and perceived to produce little benefit, other than a unnecessary and harmful attack on the legitimacy and identity of the state, its institutions and supporters. Unionist's relationship of loyalty for and sacrifice on behalf of the British state may therefore have contributed to the creation of selective 'blind spots' regarding the state's conduct.

Truth and playing the blame game

Tied into this polarised reading of the causes and context of the Northern Ireland conflict is a particular understanding of the relationship between truth recovery and the notion of blame. For Ignatieff (1998), the very point of a truth recovery exercise is to leave no one untarnished – the contribution of such a venture is to expose the myth of blamelessness. Rejecting the need to broaden ownership and responsibility for the conflict, two distinct arguments have been made by unionists, which further their opposition to, and distance from, the truth recovery debate. On one hand, and informed by what many believe to be a structural bias at the heart of the peace process, is the argument that a truth process would be used to 'blame' unionists and members of the security forces for the conflict. Conversely, there is a strong element within the DUP in particular who believe that a truth process should be used to place all responsibility for the conflict with republican paramilitaries. This is closely linked to a privileging of forensic truth and criminal trials, and the argument that republican's 'repentance' should be sought. Both factors are explored in turn below.

The perception that a truth process would be used to 'blame' unionists and members of the security forces is grounded in a wider interpretation of the peace process and associated conflict transformation initiatives. As Bell *et al.* (2004: 315) and Mulcahy (2006: 199) suggest, carrying an 'implicit narrative of institutional failure', the Belfast Agreement created 'massive ideological dissonance' for many unionists, challenging their narratives of the state, its history and the conflict. That the police and other aspects of the Northern Ireland state needed to be reformed is undeniable. However, as Memmi (1990) suggests, the conflict over the past reflects broader conflicts over the need to legitimise power relations. Having characterised the conflict as a battle between 'good' and 'evil' – the state and republicanism, the need for reform and the implication of previous failings was subsequently interpreted as a direct attempt to saddle the pro-state community with a disproportionate amount of blame and responsibility for the conflict. The following statement on the proposed changes to policing is illustrative of these concerns and is useful by way of context at this juncture:

> Over the years the RUC has held this community together when at times it would almost have disintegrated under the pressures of civil disorder. We have stood firm in an unenviable and isolated position doing our best to keep communities from each other's throats. At all times we have worked to bring communities together in support of the rule of law. We are now being portrayed by our enemies as part of the problem of Northern Ireland rather than its essential protective binding.
>
> (Rodgers 1997, cited in Ryder 2000: 484–5)

Against this backdrop, efforts at truth recovery have been viewed in a similar vein and interpreted as another mechanism through which unionists and the security forces (and the British state) would continue to be 'blamed' for the conflict. The fact, as explored in full in Chapter 4, that the most visible efforts at truth recovery have, to date, been largely 'state centric', and often involve allegations of collusion between loyalist paramilitaries and the security forces has reinforced this perception. It is also the case that such efforts correspond to republicans' demands for truth and their insistence on investigating the British state, with a lack of visible *quid pro quo* in terms of investigations into matters of significance for the unionist/loyalist community (see for example: SF 2013). That collusion was mentioned in the Report of the CGP as a potential area of 'Thematic Investigation' has hence been singled out by its critics as evidence of its 'intent' (or that of an alternative truth mechanism), the NIRPOA (2009: 20–21) concluding 'It is clear that members of the CGP have listened well to propagandists whose efforts over the last 20 years have been rewarded with a number of mud-slinging opportunities at vast public expense'. While the topic of collusion has not been singled out as an area of thematic investigation – in the report it is preceded by suggestions of cases linked by circumstances, death, the identity of the culprits or specific areas of paramilitary activity – the perception that the Legacy Commission, or an alternative truth body, would focus on the activities of the state and security forces has continued to structure unionists' opposition (CGP 2009).

This perception has a number of consequences. For example, during interview, an attempt was made to counter the argument that a truth process would be a one-sided venture, the question often being put to interviewees as to what areas they would like a potential truth process to investigate. While a number of respondents raised the issue of the experiences of Protestants who lived in the border counties during the conflict, in the main, other proactive suggestions were not forthcoming.[20] Instead, most opted to critique the idea of a formal truth process. Likewise, unionists' assumption that they would be 'blamed' for the conflict obscures the fact that the objective of a truth process is to move beyond polarised conceptions of 'right' and 'wrong', to a thicker, more complex truth about the past (SATRC 1998). Justice Albie Sachs, the former South African Constitutional Court Judge and anti-apartheid activist, has well captured this objective with regard to the work of the SATRC:

> I think the TRC Report is a brilliant document. I loved it because it was so uneven, it was rough, it had its seams, you could see the stitching, and it was authentic, it was real. It was not one of these boring, homogenised commissioned reports that are read only by a few experts. It contained the passion, the variety, and even the contradictions of the process itself...The TRC was a site of struggle, an ideological, conceptual, political, emotional, personal struggle'.
>
> (NIAC 2005a: ev.262)

The creation of a formal record of the past also narrows the capacity of politicians, ex-combatants, victims or other actors to assert partial or untrue versions of history (McEvoy 2006; Leebaw 2011). However, adhering to a binary interpretation of the conflict, for unionists, there can only be one outcome from a truth process – the apportioning of guilt and innocence and the assumption that such a body could only be to their detriment.[21]

That said, it is also significant to note that alongside the fear that they would be 'blamed' for much of the responsibility for the conflict, there is a profound desire among many unionists to use a truth process to place all responsibility for the conflict with paramilitary organisations. Such arguments are not unusual elsewhere and, given the emotion, pain and loss suffered by opposing sides during conflict, are not unexpected. Daly (2008) for example has commented that for the most part, people expect a commission not to tell *the* truth, but to tell *their* truth. Mendeloff (2004) suggests that it is in this light that Croatians supported the International Criminal Tribunal for the former Yugoslavia because they believed it would demonstrate that Serbs committed more crimes against Croatians than Croatians did against Serbs. As regards the Northern Ireland context, the DUP's Maurice Morrow made this case in the immediate wake of the publication of the Report of the CGP:

> ...the Consultative Group on the Past has missed an opportunity to address the legacy of the past properly. The manner in which it referred to the 'blame game' trivialises the fundamentals of right and wrong, truth and justice. The Consultative Group had a moral duty to place the blame where it lay – with those who took up arms. However, instead, it has blatantly dodged the issue...It is time that the tables were turned; the Consultative Group on the Past should have grasped that nettle.[22]

The DUP's Gregory Campbell advocated the idea that a truth process should, in fact, be predicated on this basis:

> That is why a unionist analysis of the truth recovery process has to start from that perspective, that the campaign to dismantle and destroy the state was wrong and then all the other things were reactions to that, whether it was military checkpoints, whether it was excesses on the part of one or two police officers, all of that existed and happened because there was a republican campaign to try and destroy Northern Ireland. So, if anyone looking at this starts from that base, square one, then they will better understand the unionist approach to truth recovery, start from another perspective, they will end up with the wrong conclusion.[23]

I would argue that for unionists, this linear focus on accountability and apportioning right and wrong is evidenced by their unswerving belief in the judicial process and their continued emphasis on the relationship between victims' needs, dealing with the past and criminal prosecutions, regardless of the practicalities of this argument. Alluding to this point, the TUV's Jim Allister has argued that 'My own view is that the proper forum for truth recovery is the criminal court and that there all men are equal and that there should be a product which is punishment for the guilty and some satisfaction for the victim'.[24] Writing in response to the Report of the CGP, DUP leader Peter Robinson echoed this line, noting that 'Any proposal which suggests moving towards a system which removes the possibility of justice or removes the right to have access to justice by the victim and their families must be rejected. ...The right to justice for all must be maintained' (DUP 2009a: 9).

On one level, these sentiments reflect some victims' wishes and desires (CVSNI 2012). However, they also point to what Bronwyn Leebaw (2012) has critiqued as the tendency to see justice as a synonym for prosecution or what McEvoy (2007) has characterised as the seductive qualities of legalism and the recourse to law as a form of symbolic censure. As McEvoy (2007) argues, in periods of political transition, law can become an important practical and symbolic break with the past, a part of the effort to publicly demonstrate the new-found legitimacy and accountability of the new regime (Osiel 2000). For those who remain attached to the past, the opposite is equally true – as a long-standing form of collective memory making, law, exercised through criminal trials and the determination of judicial punishment can become part of the 'battle for the past' – that by apportioning innocence and guilt in individual cases, the collective markers of right and wrong are re-emphasised and the meaning of power, authority and legitimacy re-inscribed (Teitel 2000; Osiel 2000; Garland 1990; Bell 2009). While not denying victims' right to justice, focusing on the individualisation of guilt and responsibility, unionists' continuing emphasis on the need for criminal trials and judicial punishment may be part of the effort to use the law as a form of symbolic censure.

Equally, as a matter of practicality – namely the availability of forensic evidence and time constraints, the criminal justice system will only ever be able to look at a limited number of cases (Boyd and Doran 2006). The implications are twofold. First, as pointed out by Chief Prosecutor Robert Jackson in his opening statement at the Nuremberg Trials, there is a danger that trials 'may be protracted by the details of particular wrongs and that we may become lost in a "wilderness of single instances" ' (Leebaw 2008: 104). Second, the 'law "sees" only a limited range of wrongs' (Campbell and Turner 2008: 376). Given the institutional nature and framework of the judicial process, the narrative that emerges is a narrow or 'forensic' construction of truth (McAlinden 2013). By definition, criminal trials or public inquiries cannot engage in a broader examination of the causes, context or consequences of a period of political violence, or produce a 'social' or 'restorative' truth (Posel 1999). Their findings may therefore obscure the broader context of patterns of abuse and systemic wrongdoing over time (Campbell and Turner 2008). Indeed, Rolston and Scraton (2005) have argued that public inquiries can become legalistic vehicles for the obfuscation of truth and minimisation of state culpability. For those unionists who seek to minimise their own role in the conflict, calling for criminal prosecutions may therefore be part of the effort to deny or minimise their own role in the conflict and to reinforce the distance between their 'imagined selves' and the reality of a complex past (McAlinden 2013; Cohen 2001; Anderson 2006).

Allied to these arguments is the claim that a truth process should be used to secure 'repentance' from republican ex-combatants. In the international literature on transitional justice, the notion of 'repentance' is commonly linked with apology and forgiveness (Bouris 2007; Borneman 2005). Often focusing on the building or restoring of social relationships, apology is the verbal acknowledgement of responsibility for wrongdoing (Minow 1998). Its characteristics include authenticity in the intent of the wrongdoer, the wrongdoer voluntarily lowering their own status as a person and the vindication of the victim and rehabilitation of the wrongdoer (Brooks 1999; Borneman 2005). In part and within the DUP in particular, it is undoubted that Biblical associations of forgiveness and repentance affect their attitudes towards republican participation in a truth process. The remarks of the DUP's Nelson McCausland are indicative:

> There is a sense within the Protestant mind-set that if I do wrong, I really should admit that I have done wrong and say I am sorry for what I have done wrong; there should be honesty about it, there should be some form of, in theological terms, repentance or remorse for it...With the whole thing around truth recovery and the Protestant mind-set, I think that's the biggest issue. People want to hear others saying, standing up and admitting that 'I did wrong'.[25]

The demand that 'There has to be repentance' has also been made at various junctures and the former DUP leader Ian Paisley's 2004 declaration that republicans need to wear the 'sack cloth and ashes' of repentance is similarly infamous (interview, 1998, cited in Southern 2005: 131; Rowan 2005).[26] As these sentiments suggest, the equation of notions of apology and repentance with a truth process speaks to a continuing battle over power relations and presents a truth process as a potential theatre in which this struggle would continue to be contested. The danger then is that apology is not about establishing a 'morally appropriate relationship' but constitutes a political instrument that is linked to questions of blame and responsibility (Harvey 1995: 62, cited in Moon 2007: 321). These points again illustrate the importance that is attached to ascribing right and wrong and so fighting for supremacy of the moral and political high ground.

Blame, 'Othering' and loyalists

Efforts to deny and allocate blame and responsibility for the conflict have also structured one of loyalist ex-combatants most significant objections to a truth process. As detailed above, arguably one of the greatest strengths of a truth recovery process is to flatten the hierarchy of blame and responsibility for conflict-related events. For ex-combatants who are seeking to re-integrate into their former communities, participation in a truth process may be particularly beneficial, providing participants with an opportunity to contextualise and complicate their own involvement in conflict (Duthie 2005; Waldorf 2010). However, in many transitional societies, a substantial body of opposition to the establishment of a formal truth process has been from ex-combatants. Of particular interest to this analysis is the argument that ex-combatants may be scapegoated and blamed for much responsibility for the conflict (Pride 2002; Penal Reform International 2004; Shaw 2005). In South Africa, for example, Gear (2002) notes that while a number of former members of the South African National Defence Force felt engaging with the SATRC was beneficial, it was generally 'a fundamental factor in the stigmatisation of ex-combatants who were part of the apartheid security forces' (Gear 2002: 7). Cock (1998: 126, cited in Gear 2002: 8), describes such practices as part of a 'transition anxiety' that seeks readily available 'scapegoats' however complex the reality of the conflict may be.

In contrast to mainstream unionism, loyalist ex-combatants have, in the main, been much more willing to acknowledge their role in the conflict and support the notion that every community has to share responsibility for the past (CLMC 1994; Spencer 2008; Shirlow 2012; Shirlow and McEvoy 2008).[27] The former PUP leader Dawn Purvis has, for example, publicly stated that 'There is no question that people on all sides committed acts of violence. However, we all need to take responsibility for our actions or inactions during the conflict and everyone should ask themselves the question: What should I have done differently?'[28] However, one of loyalists most commonly expressed grievances is that while some unionist politicians provided the leadership for and context in which violence could flourish, they have 'used and abused' loyalist activists by privately encouraging and publicly denouncing their actions.[29] This point was clearly made during interview:

> There are many members of the mainstream unionist fraternity that have marched along the streets and quietly applauded loyalism as it took up arms. In actual fact they directed loyalists to take up arms and kept their powder dry in the past.[30]

A substantial body of anecdotal and documentary material supports this assertion (O'Callaghan and O'Donnell 2006). The DUP, notably Ian Paisley and Peter Robinson, have been singled out for particular attention. Both men, for example, played a leadership role in the Ulster Resistance, an armed paramilitary movement established in opposition to the Anglo-Irish Agreement (Bruce 1992a).[31] Several inflammatory speeches designed to lure and raise loyalists into action were made by Paisley, including his declaration at a recruitment rally for the Ulster Resistance that 'There are many like myself who'd like to see the agreement brought down by democratic means, but wouldn't we all be fools if we weren't prepared' (Paisley 1985, cited in Bruce 1994: 33). Based on original documentation held by the Northern Ireland Public Records Office, O'Callaghan and O'Donnell (2006) have also shown that, in the late-1960s at least, both the Prime Minister Terrence O'Neill and senior figures in the RUC believed there to be an extremely close connection between Paisley and the UVF (News Letter 2012a).

However, many unionist politicians have continued to deny any association with loyalist paramilitary organisations during the conflict (Shirlow 2012).[32] In the opinion of Rankin and Ganiel (2008), this is part of the DUP's efforts to present itself as a party with 'clean hands', democratic and morally fit to exercise power, in contrast to the 'immorality' of republican terrorists and deviant loyalist criminals. In part, loyalists' experiences can also be traced to the nature of pro-state terrorism (Bruce 1992b; EPIC 2004). As outlined by Bruce (1992b: 71), the nature and 'awkwardness' of pro-state terrorist groups means that they are in competition with and vulnerable to criminalisation and disassociation from the state and its forces that they purport to defend. In Northern Ireland, given unionists' emphasis on law and order and loyalty to the crown forces, joining the RUC, Ulster Defence Regiment (UDR) or B-Specials was the 'correct' and 'legitimate' response to terrorism (Shirlow *et al.* 2005). By contrast, within republicanism, given the nature of the conflict, there was a more positive attitude towards imprisonment and a stronger sense of support from relatives and community members (Shirlow and McEvoy 2008). This distinction is also part of the competing interpretation of the conflict as criminal versus political for unionists and nationalists, respectively (McEvoy 2001). According to this interpretation, unionist politicians claimed terrorism was driven by a small number of 'men of violence' with criminal and psychopathic tendencies, rather than in response to any wider structural or ideological context. Loyalist combatants in Northern Ireland were consequently deemed 'beyond the pale' and regarded as much less socially acceptable than 'political prisoners' among republicans (Mitchell 2008).[33] Leaving many loyalists feeling they were a 'sabre' to be rattled and as 'cannon fodder', the resulting perception is 'the pro-state or the pro-status quo combatants feel they are the ones who are hung out to dry if you like, the whipping boys for the conflict' (McAuley 2004; Spencer 2008).[34]

This attempt to maintain a distance from loyalist paramilitaries has continued into the post-conflict period. It is well established that loyalist ex-combatants have displayed political, military and communal leadership, which has helped challenge local cultures of violence (McEvoy and Shirlow 2009). Such work has included leading restorative justice projects, dealing with interface tensions and promoting cross-community projects (Shirlow *et al.* 2010). However, for many of those ex-combatants now involved in community work and conflict transformation projects, residual criminalisation, dismissal and intolerance has characterised much of their interaction with unionist political elites (Shirlow *et al.* 2005; Shirlow and McEvoy 2008; Shirlow 2012). As Gormally (2001: 16, cited in Mitchell 2008: 10) has opined, 'The issue [for the state] is whether to support clearly peaceful activities or to assume that paramilitary leopards will never change their spots and oppose any extension of their influence'. Paralleling narratives of betrayal and hypocrisy discussed above, Mitchell (2008) and Cassidy (2008) have noted that there are various examples of mainstream unionist politicians privately using former combatants to diffuse violent situations on the ground, while simultaneously denouncing them in the media. As one focus group participant argued, 'Unionist politicians will talk to paramilitaries and communities quietly to sort things out, but they will not do it publicly' (Mitchell 2008: 15). There is consequently an abiding sense that loyalists are working on behalf of 'a community within a community…an underclass (marginalised) by middle unionists, the media…middle unionism doesn't like [conflict transformation] because they don't want a working class movement…' (Shirlow and McEvoy 2008: 138–9). 'There is also a feeling of being abandoned by unionists who were, in the words of one former combatant, "quite happy when I was dirtying my hands" ' (Mitchell 2008: 15). Senior figures within the PUP and UPRG substantiated these points during interview.[35]

Against this backdrop, and despite the above arguments on contributing to a thicker notion of ownership and responsibility, many loyalists feel that participating in a truth process would further their criminalisation and stigmatisation (EPIC 2004).[36] The potential benefits for loyalists were only recognised by two interviewees, one of whom argued that loyalists would welcome the opportunity to publicly make their case and one of whom felt that a truth process would help ex-combatants more critically engage with their own sense of identity and belonging.[37] These views were, however, at the margins of debate. Instead, it was felt that a truth process would be used to allocate 'blame' and 'credit' and so draw a line between 'worthy and 'unworthy' citizens or create what Tonry (2004: 24) has described as a few 'viscerally plausible scapegoats' (Tilly 2008). Reflecting Said's (2003) work on 'othering', the UPRG's Billy McQuiston well captured these sentiments.

> At the end of every conflict there has to be someone that people can lay the blame on and it suits unionists to point at loyalists to keep unionists clean…They have to bear the blame for it but they never will. I think it is going to perpetuate the thing…where blame is laid and it is going to allow unionists to say 'it was them bad boys, it wasn't us', but the fact remains that the loyalist paramilitaries could not have survived unless they had that sea to swim in and unionists created that sea for them to swim in. There is culpability all the way round here.[38]

That these remarks are not mere speculation is borne out, at least on the part of some, by the DUP member Gregory Campbell's reaction to the suggestion that one of loyalists major objections to a formal truth process is it would be used to criminalise their activities during the conflict. Firmly locating their actions within a framework of gangsterism and illegal activity, he replied, 'they would be quite right that that's what would happen but it would be quite correct and proper that it would happen'.[39] On one level such constructions of former members of paramilitary organisations as ruthless and criminal is understandable given the emotional terrain of loss (McAuley *et al.* 2009). It does however obscure the socio-political and cultural causes that led to many ex-combatants involvement in conflict. That loyalist ex-combatants could be used as scapegoats by unionist politicians eager to maintain their image of blamelessness may be well founded and has been instrumental in shaping their reluctance to participate in a formal truth process.

Conclusion

Charles Villa-Vicencio (2003: 240), the former director of the research department of the SATRC, which was responsible for producing the TRC's final report has argued that in South Africa, the commissioners aspired to 'a shared and ceaselessly debated memory' of the past, 'a complex, perhaps contradictory, set of narratives about the past'. This ethos has informed much of the subsequent 'truth cascade' and corresponds to Hayner's (2011) argument that there is never just one truth – we each carry our own distinct memories and sometimes, they contradict each other (Sikkink 2011). For Ricoeur (1999: 12–16), showing respect for the 'Other' means accepting this 'difference of memory'.

These sentiments sit at odds with unionist perspectives on the truth recovery debate in Northern Ireland. This chapter has argued that many unionist political elites and representatives of the security forces have expressed opposition to a formal truth recovery mechanism because of the challenge it poses to their narratives of the past, the present and *their* imagined future (Leebaw 2011). These narratives coalesce around a singular version of 'truth' and the argument that the actions of unionist political elites or the security forces did not contribute to or perpetuate the conflict in Northern Ireland. That a formal truth process would seek to broaden ownership and responsibility for the past across all parties to the conflict has grated against this backdrop and an architecture of denial has been constructed in response. Alongside aspects of literal, interpretive and implicatory denial, this reluctance to engage in a broader examination of the causes, consequences and context of the conflict has extended to a difficulty 'seeing' past human rights violations on the part of the state. It has also lead to an equation between dealing with the past and apportioning 'blame' and responsibility for the conflict, a factor of particular concern for loyalist ex-combatants. Reflecting starkly polarised conceptions of 'innocence' and 'guilt' and 'right' and 'wrong', as explored in Chapter 3, this backdrop has informed unionists' perspectives on victimhood and has further strengthened their opposition to a formal truth process.

Notes

1 Interview, Jim Allister, TUV, 20 March 2009. See also: NIRPOA (2009: 20) for a discussion on the 'substantive conflict' – that between good and evil – rather than that between Republicanism and the State.
2 See Nora (1996: 3) on the living quality of memory – 'Memory is life, always embodied in living societies and as such in permanent evolution, subject to the dialectic of remembering and forgetting, unconscious of the distortions to which it is subject, vulnerable in various ways to appropriation and manipulation, and capable of lying dormant for long periods only to be suddenly reawakened. History, on the other hand, is the reconstruction, always problematic and incomplete, of what is no longer'.
3 Interview, Ian Paisley Junior, DUP, 12 September 2009.
4 Interview, Jimmy Spratt, DUP, 20 May 2009.
5 Interview, name withheld, UUP, 23 June 2009. On this point, the same interviewee acknowledged that part of the problem is that unionists do not realise Northern Ireland is a contested political landscape.
6 Interview, Lesley Carroll, 10 June 2009; Interview, Archbishop Robin Eames, 23 October 2009; Interview, Denis Bradley, 8 October 2009.
7 Following the reintroduction of internment in August 1971 by the then Northern Ireland Prime Minister Brian Faulkner, and in response to escalating violence, all processions and parades in Northern Ireland were banned (Blom-Cooper 2006).
8 See: www.bloody-sunday-inquiry.org.uk (accessed on 26 March 2013).
9 'Bloody Sunday Report', Spotlight, BBC1, 15 June 2010. Author's recording.
10 'Bloody Sunday Report', Spotlight, BBC1, 15 June 2010. Author's recording.
11 'Bloody Sunday Report', Spotlight, BBC1, 15 June 2010. Author's recording.
12 'Question Time', BBC1, 17 June 2010. Author's recording.
13 Interview, Maurice Morrow, DUP, 20 April 2009.
14 Interview, Gregory Campbell, DUP, 12 May 2009.
15 There were of course times when many unionists felt they simply could not speak out. Donnan and Simpson's (2007) work on Protestants living in the border counties of Northern Ireland well illustrates this case.
16 Interview, name withheld, UUP, 23 June 2009.
17 Interview, name withheld, UUP, 23 June 2009.
18 Interview, name withheld, UUP, 23 June 2009. Author's emphasis.
19 Interview, name withheld, UUP, 23 June 2009; Interview, Esmond Birnie, UUP, 19 May 2009; Interview, Lesley Carroll, 10 June 2009.
20 Interview, Maurice Morrow, DUP, 20 April 2009; Interview, Professor Henry Patterson, 22 April 2009.
21 I would argue that many of the misconceptions associated with the mechanics of a truth process, such as the tenuous parallels drawn between Northern Ireland and South Africa and the concern that perpetrators would be named publicly, are informed by this reading. These points and others are explored in full in Chapter 5.
22 Consultative Group on the Past. Private Members' Business, Northern Ireland Assembly debates, 2 February 2009.
23 Interview, Gregory Campbell, DUP, 12 May 2009.
24 Interview, Jim Allister, TUV, 20 March 2009.
25 Interview, Nelson McCausland, DUP, 3 April 2009.

26 Extracts from speech by Ian Paisley, leader of the DUP, at the North Antrim DUP Association annual dinner, Saturday 27 November 2004. Online. Available at: http://cain.ulst.ac.uk/issues/politics/docs/dup/dup/ip271104.htm (accessed on 27 January 2008).

For Arthur Aughey, the unionist 'mythology of righteousness' alluded to above and its theological implications allows the DUP to portray itself as the 'justified sinner' because 'they have got God on their side'. Interview, Arthur Aughey, 1 June 2009.

27 Interview, Dawn Purvis, 6 April 2009.

28 Eames/Bradley Consultative Group on the Past. Private Members' Business, Northern Ireland Assembly debates, 10 March 2008.

29 Interview, Martin Snodden, 3 April 2009; Interview, Tom Roberts, EPIC, 28 April 2009.

30 Interview, Martin Snodden, 3 April 2009. This is not to argue that such loyalists were without agency. McAuley *et al.* (2009) make the point that many who heard rousing and potentially inflammatory political statements did not join paramilitary organisations.

31 The Ulster Resistance, a loyalist paramilitary-style organisation – was formed on 10 November 1986 by Ian Paisley, Peter Robinson and Ivan Foster, a Fermanagh Free Presbyterian cleric (Bruce 1994). The movement comprised nine battalions and organised a series of recruitment rallies across Northern Ireland. In July 1987, the Ulster Resistance collaborated with the UVF and UDA in a bank robbery in Portadown that funded a large purchase of arms from South Africa (Bruce 2003). A cache of weapons was found in County Armagh in November 1988, alongside a number of Ulster Resistance berets, and a DUP member was arrested in connection with the find (Southern 2005). The DUP subsequently began to distance itself from the Ulster Resistance. After 1989 and the arrest of three members in Paris in connection with arms trafficking offences, the organisation itself began to fade out of existence (Bruce 2003).

32 Interview, Gregory Campbell, DUP, 12 May 2009; Interview, Jimmy Spratt, DUP, 20 May 2009.

33 Interview, Billy McQuiston, UPRG, 18 June 2009.

34 Interview, Tom Roberts, EPIC, 28 April 2009.

35 Interview, Dawn Purvis, 6 April 2009; Interview, Frankie Gallagher, UPRG, 11 June 2009.

36 Interview, Martin Snodden, 3 April 2009; Interview, Frankie Gallagher, UPRG, 11 June 2009; Interview, Billy McQuiston, UPRG, 18 June 2009; Interview, Eric McKee, UPRG, 18 June 2009; Interview, Tom Roberts, EPIC, 28 April 2009; Interview, Dawn Purvis, 6 April 2009.

37 Interview, Martin Snodden, 3 April 2009; Interview, Dawn Purvis, 6 April 2009.

38 Interview, Billy McQuiston, UPRG, 18 June 2009.

39 Interview, Gregory Campbell, DUP, 12 May 2009.

Chapter 3

Truth, politics and victimhood

Introduction

In Northern Ireland, the notion of blamelessness has been closely associated with the argument that unionists and the security forces are the *real* and *innocent* victims of the conflict. Imported from long-standing criminal justice and victimology debates, this contest is integrally related to political claims making and the continuation of the meta-conflict (McEvoy and McConnachie 2012). Before exploring this dynamic further, the following discussion will critically unpack the complexity of defining 'victims' or 'perpetrators' in international criminal justice debates. The 'allure of victimhood' and the ready politicisation of these terms will be highlighted (Gready 2011: 169). This discussion will then be brought to bear on Northern Ireland where the statutory definition of a victim is inclusive of all victims and survivors of the conflict – civilians, members of the security forces and former members of paramilitary organisations and has been a considerable source of angst for many unionists. As explored below, unionists' memories and narratives of the conflict privilege a hierarchal conception of victimhood and a sharp demarcation between victims and combatants. To blur these categories challenges their sense of identity and is perceived to afford legitimacy to the actions of republican paramilitaries and elide Protestant narratives of loss. The second half of this chapter will argue that this backdrop has caused two broad sources of tension in terms of a truth process. The first focuses on the notion of the 'myth of equivalence' and the argument that a truth process would seek to create moral equivalence between 'innocent' victims, particularly members of the security forces, and 'guilty' combatants. The second maps hierarchal constructions of victimhood onto a hierarchal understanding of truth and critiques the tendency to use the truth recovery debate as a forum for 'whataboutery'. Exploring these areas in turn, this chapter will argue that the relationship between innocence, legitimacy and hierarchies of victimhood is integral to unionist's sense of identity and collective memory.

Constructing the complex political victim

Defining who is a 'victim' or 'combatant' in the aftermath of violent conflict is neither neat nor easy (Bouris 2007; Borer 2003). As Govier and Verwoerd (2004) point out, such definitions are embedded in the broader socio-political context of post-conflict societies and the recognition that individuals within each subset are not homogenous. Based on a critical analysis of the final Report of the SATRC, Borer (2003) has created a taxonomy of victims and perpetrators in response to what she argues are several incorrect assumptions in human rights scholarship. They include:

1 The separation of victims and perpetrators into two distinct groups.
2 The assumption that both groups are homogenous – 'The victims', 'The perpetrators'.
3 That the two are diametrically opposed – in the worst case victims versus perpetrators (Borer 2003).

Instead, Borer (2003: 1115) has presented a nuanced and complex challenge to the assumption of homogeneity, arguing that 'not all victims are the same, nor are all perpetrators the same, and some victims are also perpetrators'. The following analysis traces this complexity and points to the inherently competitive and politicised nature of these debates.

Turning to the question of victim identity first, the most commonly recognised phrase is that of the 'innocent victim', often used to describe the non-combatant status of the victim as defined in international law and the Geneva Conventions (Bouris 2007). Typically, the victim is not only innocent in terms of not functioning as a combatant, but also in the sense that they had not done anything to invite or 'deserve' their victimisation (Bouris 2007). Yet, victimhood is also a matter of self-identity, and the reasons for describing oneself as a victim can be multiple and competing. They range, for example, from the desire for acknowledgement, to a label against which the degeneracy of the other side can be highlighted, to the construction of a narrative of moral legitimacy (Borer 2003; Smyth 2007; Dillenburger *et al.* 2005).[1] In a number of instances, a preference for the term 'survivor' has been expressed (Du Toit 1997, cited in Minow 1998). By contrast, others have displayed a reluctance to identify with the word 'victim' due to its connotations of passivity and helplessness. In the words of Rama Mani, a scholar who has worked in several African countries, 'The term victim defines individuals in terms of their past; makes them appear ill and in need of treatment; impotent and in need of help' (cited in Huyse 2003: 60). For others, 'victim' is eschewed in favour of that of soldier, hero, freedom fighter or martyr (Gear 2002). In other cases, there are those whose victim status has been repressed or denied (Brewer and Hayes 2011; Butalia 2000; Cohen 2001). Such repressed or unrecognised victimhood is often the product of social, political and legal practices that result in cultures of silence and denial in the public sphere.

Yet, victims can be perpetrators themselves. The following example provides a way into this complexity: 'A student watches his parents being harassed by secret police; the student joins protest or freedom-fighting groups and then is arrested; the student emerges willing to use terrorist tactics against the secret police, and sets off bombs that kill civilians' (Minow 1998: 63). In this example, the student has been a victim, combatant and bystander. However, as Smyth (1998: 40) argues, 'If victims harm others it is supposedly understandable in the light of their suffering and above all, those who claim victimhood are not to be blamed'. Thus, in cases such as those of Winnie Mandela, who, while involved in abduction and torture, was the target of state harassment and abuse for years, the definition of 'victim' or 'combatant' can be personal, political and inherently subjective (Borer 2003). Further complicating these boundaries is the nuanced and self-reflective argument provided by Primo Levi whose discussion on his and others' 'inadequate' efforts at resistance during their time in German concentration camps hints at a belief that through their 'failure' to 'resist', he and fellow prisoners were also complicit in the atrocities that took place (Levi 1989). In doing so, Levi (1989: 56–57) implicates all humans in the acts of others, encompassing not only deeds of depravity, but also the failure to act to prevent such deeds –

> What guilt? When all was over, the awareness emerged that we had not done anything or not enough, against the system into which we had been absorbed...on a rational plane, there should not have been much to be ashamed of, but shame persisted nonetheless, especially for the few, bright examples of those who had the strength and possibility to resist.

Unpacking the term 'ex-combatant' is similarly complex. The SATRC (1998) for example acknowledged that the word 'perpetrator' made no distinction between the kinds of acts committed, the reasons why they were committed, their consequences or their context, nor did it distinguish between individuals who committed just one act and those whose entire operation and purpose was the commission of such acts. The first argument to be made is that while victims can be perpetrators, perpetrators can also be victims. While this may seem to dishonour those who have suffered, Boraine (2000: 128) argues that

> To think of the perpetrators as victims is not to condone their actions or their deeds, nor is it to turn away from the many victims whose lives they destroyed by their activities. It is simply to try to understand something of the ambiguity, the contradictions, of war, of conflict, of prejudice.

The most obvious example of perpetrators who can also be thought of as victims are child soldiers (Happold 2008; Zack-Williams 2001; Druba 2002; Honwana 2006; Rosen 2005; Wessells 2006). Similarly, in South Africa it is arguable that young Afrikaner soldiers and policemen can be viewed as victims of an authoritarian, masculinised militarised society, in which they were forced to go through a cadet system at school, were conscripted into the army and were subjected to daily state propaganda (Borer 2003). Arguably those who fall within this rubric can be viewed as victims of larger societal factors and the question of perpetrator agency must be raised (Pride 2002). In other instances, many ex-combatants continue to suffer as a result of their militarised histories and involvement in violent conflict (Gear 2002). Sources of trauma among former combatants in South Africa include the brutalisation of South African Defence Force (SADF) conscripts in training; the conditions under which Umkhonto we Sizwe (MK) members lived in exile; the resulting paranoia that comes from a culture of infiltration; government security-force harassment of liberation fighters families and the consequences of witnessing and participating in violent acts (Gear 2002). Post-traumatic stress disorder (PTSD), anxiety, depression, substance dependence and increased rates of divorce and suicide have, for example, been associated with Vietnam veterans.[2] For these reasons and others, Kingma (2001) argues that one argument for the emphasis on post-conflict Disarmament Demobilisation and Reintegration (DDR) schemes is humanitarianism – that ex-combatants can also be victims of the conflict in which they were participants.

More broadly, distinctions between direct and indirect perpetrators have been made and are another useful example of these complexities. The Report of the SATRC (1998) for example notes that alongside direct perpetrators – those who came forward, applied for and were granted amnesty, there was also a 'Chain of Command' phenomenon, providing cover for those in senior positions who were the architects of atrocities, filtering down from senior members of government, to elite level security and police officers, and then to their subordinates, entrusted with carrying out criminal acts (Dyzenhaus 1998; Payne 2008; Borer 2003). Institutions can also bear some responsibility for past actions and inactions. As outlined by Dyzenhaus (1998), in South Africa this included structural agents of civil society such as churches, the media and legal profession. Explicitly acknowledging the problem of wider complicity, the TRC drew a distinction between acts of commission and omission, stating, 'It would...be misleading and wrong to assign blame for the gross violation of human rights only to those who confronted each other on the political and military battlefields, engaged in acts of commission' (SATRC 1998: 211). Termed 'silent beneficiaries' and 'onlookers' by Huyse (2003), indirect offenders may also belong to the international community.

As this discussion suggests, the terms victim and combatant are neither static nor mono-causal. Echoing Boraine (2000), Bouris (2007) advocates embracing the complexities and contradictions of the victim identity in order to better recognise and respond to their needs and to help contribute to peace. Yet, as Bouris (2007) also points out, images of the victim are powerful, gripping and integral to helping us make sense of conflict, particularly in making moral calculations, and determining who is 'good' and who is 'evil'. One inevitable consequence is that the identity of victim or combatant contains a valuable political currency and, in the aftermath of violent conflict, may be appropriated or rejected by competing parties to the conflict. In particular, articulating a narrative of victimhood has been interpreted as a way of garnering support and sympathy and, based on the argument that 'in as far as they are victims, they are devoid of volition or intent', can be used to claim legitimacy and justification for past actions (Gilligan 2003: 30; Ignatieff 1994; Lu 2002; Cohen 2001; Smyth 2003). As Smyth (2003: 126–127) argues, for those who participated in the violence of the past, without the status of victimhood, 'their violence becomes too naked, politically inexplicable, and morally indefensible'. By implication, to be outside this categorisation of victimhood is to be aligned with notions of guilt, illegitimacy and complicity. It may also involve a reluctance to countenance the victimhood of the 'other', which as Nadler and Schnabel (2008, cited in Aiken 2010: 181) warn, is a common danger in post-conflict societies where a sense of 'double victimhood' prevails and in which each identity group perceives itself to be the sole legitimate victim of past violence and expects its enemies to accept responsibility for past wrongdoing (Brewer 2006, 2010). Multiple victimhood may further increase the temptation to deny the culpability of one's own group and to impose a hierarchy of victimhood in which some deaths are held to be more important and so merit more recognition than others (Brewer 2010). In this context, defining who is a 'victim' or 'combatant' can become one of the sharpest post-conflict debates.

Unionism, innocence and the politics of victimhood

The politicisation of victimhood has been a prominent feature of the 'post-conflict' landscape in Northern Ireland where the so called 'victims debate' is closely related to competing interpretations of the causes and context of the conflict and has been contested through notions of 'guilt' and 'innocence' and discussions over a 'hierarchy of victimhood' (Bell 2003; Ignatieff 1994; Cohen 2001). Value judgements of blame and responsibility and polarised conceptions of the 'other' are key elements of this debate and recognition of one groups suffering by state and/or international actors is frequently interpreted as a slight against or a silencing of the moral integrity and 'innocence' of the 'other' community (Hamber *et al.* 2001, cited in

Stevenson *et al.* 2007; Little 2012). However, as Ferguson *et al.* (2010) point out, such competition is also a natural extension of the persistence of fear, anger, hurt and loss that is attached to memories of the past. While manifested at various junctures throughout the peace process and period of conflict transformation, the ongoing debate over who can be considered a victim or survivor of the Northern Ireland conflict provides a useful prism through which to explore this contest. As explored below, unionists have privileged a hierarchal conception of victimhood and the identity of the 'real' and 'innocent' victims of the conflict. To complicate these starkly polarised definitions of 'innocent victims' and 'guilty combatants' erodes their sense of self-identity and is perceived as offering justification and legitimacy to the actions of paramilitary organisations.[3] Challenging their narratives of the conflict, as explored throughout this chapter, for many unionist political elites, the need to preserve their status as the 'real' and 'innocent' victims of the conflict has directly informed their opposition to much of the debate on dealing with the past.

The Victims and Survivors (Northern Ireland) Order 2006 provides the statutory definition of a victim or survivor of the Northern Ireland conflict. According to Article 3, Paragraph 1 of the Order this is,

> (a) someone who is or has been physically or psychologically injured as a result of or in consequence of a conflict-related incident;
> (b) someone who provides a substantial amount of care on a regular basis for an individual mentioned in paragraph (a); or
> (c) someone who has been bereaved as a result of or in consequence of a conflict-related event.[4]

As an inclusive definition of victimhood, the Order includes *all* those affected by the conflict – civilians, members of the security forces, former members of paramilitary organisations and their families. It does not imply that all members of society experienced victimhood equally, nor does it suggest that all parties to the conflict, or all members of society, are equally to blame. Nor does it obfuscate individual or collective responsibility. Rather, it is need focused and takes the individual experience of suffering as its starting point – 'we are talking about victims and a victim is someone who has been bereaved' (NIAC 2009: ev.4). In doing so, it does not condone violence in any way, but does correspond to Bouris' (2007: 10) argument that in aftermath of political violence, the political victim is complex and messy – 'a victim who is no longer chained to characteristics of complete innocence and purity, but remains a victim nonetheless'.

For the main nationalist and republican political parties, the SDLP and SF, the definition of a victim contained in the Victims and Survivors (Northern Ireland) Order 2006 is broadly agreeable. Both have advocated an inclusive definition of victimhood and rejected the suggestion that a distinction between 'deserving' and 'non-deserving' victims can be made (Lundy and McGovern 2005; McEvoy 2014). The SDLP has proposed a wide-ranging definition of victimhood that focuses on those 'whose life has altered its course as a result of the bitterness and division in our society and who believes that the alteration was negative' and 'includes individuals who might be perceived by some to have brought suffering upon themselves' (SDLP 1999, cited in McDowell 2007: np). Rejecting the criminalisation of their dead and the idea of a hierarchy of victimhood, SF has also proposed a definition of victimhood that 'includes all of the victims of the conflict, combatants and non-combatants' (cited in Smyth 2009: 37). In the attempt to legitimise the actions of armed republicans and delegitimise those of the British state, this definition of victimhood speaks to the argument that the conflict was political in nature, and reflects the long-held view that the British government and its security forces, at times in collusion with loyalist paramilitaries, were a source of victimisation for the nationalist and republican community (Brewer and Hayes 2011). The remarks of SF member Pat Sheehan are illustrative:

> The current definition of victims and survivors is fair because it enshrines in legislation the equality of victims and is totally inclusive of all victims. The members on the other side of the House should, at some stage, remove the scales from their eyes and recognise that there was a conflict here, which was a political conflict, and that, as a result, terrible things happened and people became victims...The British or unionist victims of the conflict should not be given a position over and above victims from the republican or nationalist community, and, likewise, republican and nationalist victims should not be given a place over and above victims from the British or unionist community. All victims should be equal.[5]

The statutory definition of a victim or survivor has, however, been a considerable source of angst for many unionists and members of the security forces. In contrast to the inclusive approach to victimhood advocated above, many unionist political elites have called for an exclusive definition of victimhood that is structured by rigid definitions of the terms 'victim' and 'perpetrator' and their connotations of 'innocence' and 'guilt' and 'legitimate' and 'illegitimate' victims (DUP 2007, 2011; UUP 2011a). Claiming ownership of the 'real' and 'innocent' victims of the conflict – 'our innocent victims' – the unionist politics of victimhood is centred on the memory of suffering inflicted on the Protestant community by republican paramilitaries, the 'disproportionate' nature of the same and the illegitimate and unjustified nature of the IRA's campaign (Ganiel 2007; Dawson 2007; Simpson 2009). Within this conceptualisation of victimhood, only 'innocent' victims or 'undeserving' victims are considered 'true' victims of the conflict (Brewer and Hayes 2011; Smyth 2003). The following statement by the DUP MLA Jonathan Bell illustrates this case – 'an innocent victim is an innocent victim. It means exactly what it says on the tin, they are innocent victims'.[6] For many unionists, and conforming to Christie's (1986) concept of the 'ideal victim' – the innocent victim, engaged in respectable behaviour when victimised, topping this hierarchal construction of victimhood are members of the security forces. Ian Paisley Junior's remarks on this point are worth repeating at some length:

> I understand the view that all tears are equal...I think that if the call by our Lord and Saviour is to love thy neighbour, then you have got to understand that that loss for the individual is equal. That doesn't mean to say that you empathise or agree with the circumstances behind what led up to it. I do however take the view that security service personnel who were murdered for doing their duty, for simply putting on their uniform, do have a higher standing, or should have a higher standing when it comes to any recognition of victimhood in Northern Ireland. Why? Take the impartial view – a police officer in New York who is gunned down in the line of duty dies a hero. Why? Because he is, because he put on a uniform and was killed solely because he was a police officer. A police officer in Northern Ireland should be afforded no less and I take the view that that needs to be established in the minds of people, that if you are doing your job, which happens to be protecting the citizens of a nation, no matter what those citizens background might be, no matter what their religion might be, you are protecting them, serving them and if you are killed for simply doing that job, you deserve a heck of a lot more standing as a victim than this notion of someone who has died as a result of the troubles and who was a participant in those troubles...The short answer is, is there a hierarchy of victims? I actually think there is.[7]

In many cases, unionist's claim to innocent victimhood is empirically correct, both as detailed earlier, in respect to the victim's non-combatant status and where individuals and communities had violence visited upon them without any morally or politically justifiable reason (Bouris 2007). The wrongness of such actions and the absolute entitlement of those wronged to identify themselves as victims or survivors (if they so wish) is a given (McEvoy and McConnachie 2012). The emphasis on innocence is also a natural and expected reaction to traumatic loss – as Enns (2012: 98) argues, 'we seem devoted to upholding the absolute innocence of victims' and the defence of victims' stories and images is often a duty of memory (Sivan 2000, cited in Enns 2012; Brown 2011). For unionists, an essential part of the 'duty of memory' is to challenge 'the lie of anything but innocence and guilt'.[8] As James Booth (2001: 779) argues, these sentiments relate to the 'great fear' for memory-justice – that victims will be remembered, but also, that the wrongness of the crime and the effect of the perpetrators actions will not be forgotten. That the Victims and Survivors (Northern Ireland) Order 2006 provides an inclusive definition of victimhood has been perceived to blur these boundaries and create 'moral equivalence' between the 'innocent victim' and the 'guilty perpetrator', 'spreading culpability among all the parties' (Williams and Scharf 2002: 27). In the opinion of the DUP's Nelson McCausland, the implication of parity between victims and combatants contravenes the Protestant mind-set of right and wrong and therefore where blame and responsibility for the conflict lie.[9] Thus, as argued by the former UUP leader Tom Elliott,

> ...we do not believe that the person who was killed by the bomb, the innocent victim, and that guy who set out to do it are equal. We would suggest anyway that there has been a determination from government to actually bring that about, this equality and that has meant that what we would call the real and innocent victimhood has been eclipsed.[10]

Conversely, from a unionist perspective, those at the bottom of this hierarchy of victimhood are members of paramilitary organisations – particularly IRA members – killed in active service (either by the British security forces, other paramilitaries or by their own actions) and who are considered deserving of their fate (Duffy 2010). As Brown (2011: 75) notes with reference to the relatives of the eight IRA men and one civilian who were killed by the Special Air Service (SAS) in Loughgall, Co. Armagh, in 1987, family members of paramilitary activists also sit outside this hierarchy of victimhood – 'we were also constantly presented in the media as 'IRA Relatives' it was like using a dirty word to describe us. They wouldn't see us simply as bereaved relatives – that didn't suit many people, we had to be presented as something more than that, something evil'. Representatives of nationalist victims groups have also argued that victims of state violence are often marginalised and presented as in some way contributing to their own deaths or that their community is responsible for creating the conditions under which their deaths occurred (Dawson 2007; Lundy and McGovern 2006; Smyth 2003).[11]

As Moeller (1999) argues and as illustrated by the above examples, innocence not only signals that the victim has done nothing wrong, but also that the perpetrator has done something wrong and is evil in character. Innocence and guilt are therefore mutually dependent – in the process of political claims making, the positioning of the guilty perpetrator is required to satisfy and exemplify the innocence of the victim. For Gready (2011: 168), such hierarchies are founded on the politics of recognition and legitimisation: 'We suffer[ed] therefore we are' (Duffy 2010; Smyth 1998, 2003; Bar-Tal 2003). Innocence therefore not only denotes suffering, but only relates to 'our' community, not 'theirs' and can provide a means of blaming past violence on the 'other' and escaping one's own share of blame and responsibility (McEvoy and McConnachie 2012; Brewer and Hayes 2011). As explored in Chapter 2, privileging a narrative of blamelessness, from a unionist perspective, this hierarchal and tightly delineated definition of victimhood is essential to delegitimising and criminalising the republican campaign of armed violence and reinforcing their own self-identity and understanding of the conflict. I would argue that the election of the security forces to the top of the hierarchy of victimhood is part of this effort, reflecting both the long-standing narrative in which members of the RUC have been presented as willing to pay the ultimate sacrifice – death – in the name of peace and stability and Ignatieff's (1994: 6) argument that 'myths of innocence and victimhood' can be used to provide protection against one's own side's complicity in acts of violence – the denial of their role during the conflict (Ryder 2000; Ellison and Smyth 2000).

Some difference of opinion can however be found amongst representatives of the PUP and loyalist ex-combatants. The former PUP leader Dawn Purvis has, for example, argued against distinctions between victims, on the basis that 'hurt and pain is the same for every individual'.[12] Purvis was also quick to point out that the notion of a hierarchy of victims is part of the competing interpretation of the causes of the conflict (see also: PUP 2013).[13] In many cases, and reflecting broader international trends, a rejection of static and mono-cultural readings of victimhood was provided by loyalist interviewees (Waldorf 2010; Sriram *et al.* 2012; Shirlow 2012). One former loyalist combatant for example argued that while he was able to acknowledge and take responsibility for his role in the past, he also believed himself to be a victim of societal factors that lead to his involvement with paramilitarism.[14] Conversely, Eric McKee, a former member of the UDA, made a clear distinction between his own experience and that of someone who has been bereaved:

> I am a loyalist prisoner. In trying to equate me with a victim, even in my terms it just doesn't work, not for a minute. I might be a victim of the troubles and the conflict we have been brought up in, but certainly not in the same light as someone who has lost a loved one. I could never see that.[15]

While these differing perspectives highlight the complexity of the victim–combatant axis, many unionists have failed to recognise this diversity of views or acknowledged the perspective of those such as McKee. Instead, politicians and commentators have been keen to emphasise the criminality and moral degeneracy of loyalist and republican ex-combatants alike (Kane 2009). Maintaining such a stance has contributed to the criminalisation and stigmatisation of former loyalist combatants.

The battle for 'public victimhood' – the contest over the 'right' to the status of 'victim' has therefore become an arena in which contested notions of past violence and suffering have been constructed and reproduced (Brewer 2010: 164; McEvoy and McConnachie 2012). As Marie Breen Smyth (2007: 78) argues, it has also become central in 'determining which side in a conflict is deserving of sympathy, which is most profligate in inflicting harm; which has violated the rules of war; which is guilty of human rights violations'. That the statutory definition of a victim has complicated and challenged rigid hierarchies of victimhood has caused outrage among unionist politicians and representatives of the RUC (DUP 2009a; UUP 2009b). To do so challenges their claim to innocence and has been interpreted as implying 'moral equivalence' between the actions of victims, the security forces and paramilitaries. This backdrop has been highly influential in regards to their opposition to the truth recovery debate.

Truth, victimhood and the myth of equivalence

In this context of hierarchies and polarised definitions of victims and combatants, the perception that a formal truth process would seek to create or imply 'moral equivalence' between the actions of victims and combatants – particularly between members of the security forces and paramilitary organisations – has been a major element of unionists' opposition (Williams and Scharf 2002). Following the resumption of talks in early 2012 on how to deal with the past, DUP leader Peter Robinson explicitly made this point: 'The DUP will not allow any talks to become a rewriting of history. We will not support any perversion of the definition of a victim or dilute the hurt and suffering caused' (McAdam 2012). Similar critiques have been made in other transitional jurisdictions, notably South Africa. For example, while the Report of the SATRC begins with an exposition of the role of the state, it is immediately juxtaposed to a discussion on the 'liberation movements' and their role in abuses (Teitel 2000). According to Sarkin (2004: 111), the Commission's subsequent findings on the culpability of the African National Congress (ANC) for human rights violations caused protest from the ANC as the 'liberation movement objected to the label "perpetrators" ' and argued that 'fighting for and against apartheid' were not equivalent. More controversial is that in the spirit of 'national reconciliation', frequent analogies were drawn between victims and combatants (Wilson 2001; Moon 2009). Explaining this point, Tutu (1996: 43, cited in Moon 2009: 103) claimed:

> There is no distinction between someone who is a victim of human rights violations, perpetrated by, say, the liberation movements, or

> one who is a victim of violations perpetrated by the apartheid dispensation…In the matter of amnesty, no moral distinction is going to be made between acts perpetrated by the liberation movements and acts perpetrated by the apartheid dispensation.

The objective of recognising both victims and combatants experiences is not to suspend moral judgement or to deny combatants agency and responsibility – Tutu, in his foreword to the Report of the SATRC, for example, stressed the importance of moral difference – 'I cannot, however, be asked to be neutral about apartheid. It is an intrinsically evil system' (Asmal 2000, cited in Leebaw 2011; TRC 1998 vol. 1: 12, 13, cited in Gready 2011: 41). Rather, as Villa-Vicencio (2003) points out, it is to acknowledge the complexity of conflict and the experience of loss. Yet, alluding to the delicacy of this argument, as Teitel (2000) argues, when two sets of previously diametrically opposed narratives are conjoined in one forum and document, the implication is one of relativisation and, therefore, moral equivalence.[16]

In Northern Ireland, the concern that a formal truth process would be an exercise that could be 'used in the service of equivalence' has been expressed by several unionists and members of the security forces.[17] A number of manifestations of this critique can be identified and are illustrative of the competing narratives that attempt to explain the causes of the conflict. For many unionists, their views have been largely conditioned by two proposals associated with the CGP. The first of these is the CGP's (2009: 91) proposal that a £12,000 'Recognition Payment' would be paid 'to all those who have lost loved ones because of the conflict'.[18] This decision was based on the definition of a victim contained in the Victims and Survivors (Northern Ireland) Order 2006 and reflects the Group's belief that the 'true nature of the hierarchy of victims lies in the level of loss and suffering experienced during the conflict' (CGP 2009: 68). On one level, the CGP's (2009) recommendation echoed international norms whereby making reparations in the aftermath of violent conflict is regarded as one of the most tangible manifestations of a state's efforts to acknowledge and remedy harms (De Greiff 2006; Laplante and Theidon 2007; Minow 1998).[19] Given that the Northern Ireland conflict had a financial impact for many victims and survivors, the proposed Recognition Payment also had the potential to alleviate practical concerns and go some way to countering the historically low rates of compensation associated with the conflict (MacBride 2011).

Its symbolic dimension was, however, problematic. Payable to all victims of the conflict, the proposal immediately became part of the debate on who is a victim of the conflict. Variously described as 'immoral', 'repugnant', 'disgusting' and a betrayal of innocent victims, the lead up to, launch (attended by the author) and immediate aftermath of the Report's publication was marked by angry scenes and fierce debates in the media and Northern Ireland Assembly (see for example: DUP 2009cd; UUP 2009c; TUV 2009; Smyth and Rowan 2009; News Letter 2009).[20] The British government subsequently rejected the proposal (Belfast Telegraph 2009a). Conforming to Gregory Campbell's assertion that the distinction between 'innocent' and 'guilty' is *black and white*, a particularly popular parallel was drawn between the status of the innocent victims of the Shankill bomb and that of the bomber Thomas Begley and his accomplice Sean Kelly.[21] Writing in respect to Argentina's Madres de la Plaza de Mayo, Claire Moon has also used Simmel's (2004) equivalence of exchange theory to explain opposition to (financial) reparations on the grounds that applying the core idea behind reparations – a compensatory theory of justice – to the loss of human life and injury, involves crossing different lexicons of value (Moon 2012; Minow 1998).[22] Moreover, the attempt to 'value' the loss of life has been described as staining 'the moral imagination' (Minow 1998: 104). This thesis is also directly applicable to unionists' opposition to the Recognition Payment and the implication of equivalence between 'the service and sacrifice of members of the security forces' and those 'who were setting out to plan murder'.[23]

Equally controversial was speculation during the CGP's public consultation phase on whether the group would recommend an amnesty to aid the truth finding process and its later recommendation for a limited immunity from prosecution (CGP 2009). By extinguishing criminal and/or civil liability, conditional amnesties have accompanied truth recovery processes in a number of transitional environments (Mallinder 2008). One of the main purposes of an amnesty in such contexts is to encourage combatants to reveal information and potentially provide a greater degree of truth recovery than may have been possible under formal criminal proceedings (Mallinder 2008). Doing so can help provide answers for victims and their families. Application for and acceptance of the terms of an amnesty law can also act as a form of accountability in itself (Mallinder and McEvoy 2011; Slye 2000). For these reasons and others, amnesty's or other processes to shield individuals from prosecution are not without precedent in Northern Ireland. During the earliest stages of the conflict, an amnesty covering 'events associated with, or arising out of, political protests, utterances, marches, meetings and demonstrations occurring between 5 October 1968 and 6 May 1969' was passed by the Stormont government in an effort to de-escalate the conflict, or, in the words of the then Prime Minister Chichester-Clarke, to 'wipe the slate clean and look to the future' (Bell 2003: 1101). Its beneficiaries included members of the RUC and the former DUP First Minister Ian Paisley. Limited immunity from prosecution was also offered by the Independent Commission for the Location of Victims' Remains (ICLVR)[24] and formed a main element of the architecture of the Saville and Nelson inquiries into the events on Bloody Sunday 30 January 1972 and the death of solicitor Rosemary Nelson, who was murdered by loyalist paramilitaries in March 1999 (Morgan 2002; Hegarty 2003; Duffy 2010). In these cases, the offer of limited immunity was a pragmatic tool to incentivise truth recovery.

In my view, the CGP appeared to recognise that an amnesty or measure of limited immunity was essential to encourage the full and frank disclosure an effective truth process requires. Given that with the passage of time, among other variables, the likelihood of large numbers of criminal prosecutions is ever decreasing, it is also difficult to envisage how any truth process could operate without a guarantee of immunity from prosecution (Boyd and Doran 2006; McEvoy and Mallinder 2008). Early revelations in the media in January 2008 that an amnesty may be offered were arguably part of a deliberate attempt to begin to 'acclimatise' politicians and civil society towards this idea (Bradfield 2008). However, the suggestion of amnesty was not well received by many unionists and members of the security forces who regarded it as affording legitimacy and justification to the actions of republican paramilitaries (see for example: DUP 2008; UUP 2008; News Letter 2008b; Henry 2008).[25] Discussions on amnesty thus blur the line between *innocence* and *intent* that has been crucial in their self-legitimising narratives (Beetham 1991).[26] The NIRPOA's (2008: 15) submission to the CGP clearly makes this point: 'The undeniable truth remains that no police officer ever set out from his/her home with the intent of causing the death of any citizen'. These oppositional narratives carried over to the CGP's (2009) recommendation for the use of 'Protected Statements' – a form of limited immunity whereby information contained in statements made to the Information Recovery unit would not be admissible in criminal or civil proceedings. Despite the fact that the Group's co-chairs Archbishop Eames and Denis Bradley were at pains to emphasise that the Report did not recommend an amnesty, their arguments had little impact on critic's belief that the Report contained an amnesty 'in all but name' or in the erroneous equation of the limited immunity recommendation with a general amnesty.[27] The resulting perception is that

> The UK Government treated the paramilitaries as criminals; an amnesty removes this designation. Such a move may please the paramilitary principals but it immediately invites the legitimate state forces to review their own status during the conflict.
>
> (PFNI 2008a: 3)

These themes were repeated in early 2012. At this time, there was a renewed emphasis on dealing with the past following talks between the main political parties and the then Secretary of State Owen Paterson and the controversy surrounding the operational independence of the OPONI. Speaking on the difficulties faced by the OPONI, the former Ombudsman Al Hutchinson publicly stated that conditional amnesties, depending on the wishes of individual victims and their families, should be part of any process for dealing with the past. In response to these developments, the DUP's Arlene Foster argued that 'Any process dealing with the past must not include any amnesty or proposal which could allow some individuals to escape justice for their actions...It is important no one in Northern Ireland believes they can walk away from crimes they committed in the past and have a veil drawn over the campaign of terrorism waged here' (DUP 2012; UUP 2012a; BBC News 2012a; McAdam 2012). As Osiel (2000) argues, in this context, for unionists, amnesty exploits the binary logic of criminal liability.[28]

It is however interesting to note that while these views have been loudly and publicly expressed, in private, a number of important figures within unionism and the security forces have been more open to the idea of an amnesty or limited immunity.[29] For example, during interview, Ian Paisley Junior conceded in a pragmatic and victim-centred argument that:

> I do think that some victims are entitled to be asked that question...If I had lost a brother, or a wife or a father, I think I would be entitled to answer that question for myself, to say that if it means that I now know exactly who, what, why, whatever and I will get the truth and nothing but the truth and that person will get some form of a limited immunity, I think I am entitled to make that judgement call...I think that sometimes the right people to ask that question of are never asked and never get a chance to give their answer.[30]

Members of the CGP supported this point during interview, claiming that during the Group's consultation phase, there was a strong demand for an amnesty from representatives of the security forces.[31] Co-chair Denis Bradley has since publicly stated that 'the people who want an amnesty in all of this and I'm going to say it for them, are the security forces'.[32] These perspectives speak to the use of amnesties as both a pragmatic tool to encourage truth recovery and, for those involved in violent conflict, to draw a line under the past and remove the threat of prosecution (Mallinder 2008). However, as can be seen, there is a considerable distinction between some unionist's public and private views. Seeking to maintain a highly stratified distinction between victims and combatants, for many unionists, an amnesty, even if it could benefit members of their community, simply cannot be countenanced.

For others, and largely conditioned by this backdrop, the idea of establishing a truth process and the objective of truth telling was closely associated with the idea of creating moral equivalence. One of the strongest of these critiques was expressed by a member of the TUV who argued that the entire purpose of the Legacy Commission proposed by the CGP would be to create moral equivalence:

> [It] is based upon this distorting fallacy of equating victims with perpetrators, on the spread of this gospel of equivalence that we are all victims and that really there is no real difference to make the innocent feel as guilty as the perpetrator. That is an obnoxious concept to me and since the whole thing is based on that conception, the whole thing is flawed.[33]

A more subtle version of this concern is related to the idea that there should be a hierarchy of narratives on the past. One interviewee for example suggested that unionists self-constructed boundaries of right and wrong will neither welcome the story's of the 'other' being told in anything other than local level initiatives nor will they be willing to listen to them.[34] Another lamented statements such as 'This listening must then lead to honest assessment of what the other is saying and to recognition of the truth within their story' on the grounds that the view that 'the Northern Ireland conflict has a number of "sides" and they all deserve to be heard' is implying moral equivalence (Birnie 2009; CGP 2009: 53). In a similar vein, Professor Henry Patterson has argued that the Legacy Commission proposed by the CGP would provide a 'poor man's post-modernism of 'story-telling' where the 'police story' or the 'army story' has the same truth value and moral content as the 'former combatants' story' (Patterson 2009: np).

As explored in detail below, such remarks illustrate the hierarchal construction of victimhood in unionist discourse (Dawson 2007). They also speak to Sivan's (2002, cited in Enns 2012) observation that while we defend the emphasis on victims' stories and images as a duty of memory, to bring former perpetrators into this analysis is more risky. As Sivan (2002, cited in Enns 2012: 113) suggests, it is at this point that the charge of moral equivalence can be made – 'It is true that to focus on the perpetrator is to risk making us identify with him; as he explains and justifies himself, tells us about his work, his joys, his sorrows, he looks like anyone else and we grant him our understanding'. For unionists, this is the danger. Relatives of republican paramilitaries killed in Gibraltar and at Loughgall have, for example, called for a truth process to 'level the political playing pitch' and to question 'What is it that turns a world upside down and makes ordinary people, coming from ordinary homes, do extraordinary things? That's the story that needs to be told and accepted' (cited in Brown 2011: 75–76). Seeking to challenge their criminalisation, some loyalist ex-combatants have made similar claims (Shirlow 2012; Shirlow *et al.* 2010). For those unionists and representatives of the security forces who have prided themselves on the fiction of blamelessness, the prospect that a truth process would examine all aspects of the past has (incorrectly) been interpreted as implying parity between victims and members of paramilitary organisations and negating true levels of loss and responsibility.[35] Given that a major function of any truth process is to provide a space in which all accounts of the past can be rehearsed and examined, these concerns present a significant hurdle to the establishment of such a process (Hayner 2011).

Victimhood, hierarchies and truth as 'whataboutery'

While Gready (2011: 166) argues that in 'the cast of the past...the victim question is important, but does not warrant a monopoly on the past', as illustrated above, the pull of victimhood can readily translate into claims of moral authority and superiority. Truth processes are, ostensibly at least, designed to level such hierarchies, constructing a more plural, 'democratising truth', and helping to diffuse contests over the past (Smyth 2007; Teitel 2000). Inevitably, some voices may be prioritised. In South Africa, for example, despite its laudable aims, the SATRC has been criticised for elevating the voice of the 'forgiving victim' who directly contributed to the project of national reconciliation (Wilson 2001; Moon 2008; McEvoy and McConnachie 2013). In other cases and where truth recovery becomes part of the continuation of the conflict, memories and voices may be selected for partial ends. Hierarchies of victimhood may therefore translate into hierarchies of truth.

As detailed above, a hierarchal construction of victimhood can be found in unionist discourse. I would argue that this has led to a complex picture as regards dealing with the past. First, and as explored in detail in Chapters 4 and 6, within unionism and loyalism, there is a clear rejection of the selective nature of public inquiries and investigations in the coroners' courts on the grounds that they create a 'hierarchy of victims', privileging certain deaths at the expense of the vast majority of those affected by the conflict. The Saville Inquiry and its financial cost of £195million has been a particular source of critique (DUP 2010c).[36] The UUP's Tom Elliott later re-emphasised this point in light of the announcement that the PSNI are to carry out a murder inquiry into the events of Bloody Sunday:

> Here we see the hierarchy of victims. Those who received a fully funded public inquiry have the Director of Public Prosecutions as part of setting up a murder investigation. Those who's loved ones died at the hands of terrorists and who have been denied such an Inquiry are not being afforded equality.
>
> (UUP 2012b)

As Dawson (2007) points out, this critique is, in principle, egalitarian and fair. Indeed, in early 2013, Tom Elliott argued that there is a need to develop an agreed method of ensuring that all victims can pursue the truth (UUP 2013). The insistence that the process of establishing truth and justice in terms of conflict-related deaths needs to be extended beyond a few high-profile and largely 'state-centric' cases is also important and one of the central arguments for establishing a formal overarching truth process (Bell 2003; CGP 2009; Lundy 2010).

However, a closer reading of unionist discourse reveals that competitive notions continue to influence their attitudes towards calls for, or the recovery of, truth. (This competition is not, of course, unique to unionists, though they are the focus of investigation here). As Dawson (2007: 287) notes, it is found in:

> the perception that the extent of the *other* side's gain is the extent of *our* side's loss, and its corollary: that the necessary response to the telling of *their* story is not to listen, understand and acknowledge it, but to deny, and then to set the record straight by telling *our* side of the story [emphasis in original].

Among certain unionist political elites, one manifestation of this dynamic is the tendency to downplay or have difficulty accepting evidence of well-documented atrocities against members of the nationalist or republican community (Lawther 2013). This links to the perception that unionist memories of loss and their claim to innocent victimhood are being exacerbated, if not marginalised (Brewer 2006; Ganiel 2007; Mulcahy 2000; Hayward and Mitchell 2003). According to Dawson (2007), it is further associated with the assumption that among nationalists, only the 'deserving' – terrorists and their accomplices – have been harmed by the state security forces and a dismissal of campaigns for truth about state violence as republican propaganda. It also displays little understanding of either the role of the State in hindering, rather than advancing a human rights agenda of this kind, or of the immense effort that relatives and supporters have put in over many years to build and sustain justice campaigns such as that relating to Bloody Sunday (Dawson 2007). The DUP MLA Paul Girvan's remarks in the Northern Ireland Assembly following the British government's decision to hold a documentary review rather than a public inquiry into the case of Belfast solicitor Pat Finucane, murdered by loyalist paramilitaries in collusion with British state forces, well illustrates this dynamic:

> Pat Finucane was killed in 1989. He along with more than 3,000 other people, suffered as a consequence of the terrorist campaign that took place during that terrible 30 year period. Members on this side of the House find it difficult to understand why Pat Finucane should be elevated above all other victims of the Troubles. What is so special about Pat Finucane that he and that family need to have that public inquiry?[37]

The competitive nature of truth recovery in Northern Ireland is also apparent in the fact that when calls for truth into matters of significance for the nationalist or republican community are made, or when evidence is produced to support long-standing claims of misconduct by the police or British state, they are often immediately countered by calls for truth into matters of significance for the unionist community. Such calls for truth are natural and expected and, I would strongly argue, should be encouraged. Indeed, their sequencing may relate to international transitional justice norms. In any transitional jurisdiction, the timing of a truth process requires careful consideration (Theissen 2004; Dimitrijevic 2006). Levels of political momentum, popular mobilisation and the balance of peace are all influential (Fletcher *et al.* 2009; Olsen *et al.* 2010; Sikkink 2011). That unionist politicians have often voiced their calls for truth on the back of other successful campaigns may be part of an attempt to take advantage of a favourable political climate – Kofi Annan (2004: 1), the former Secretary-General of the United Nations, for example, has argued that 'justice, peace and democracy are not mutually exclusive objectives, but rather mutually reinforcing imperatives. Advancing all three in fragile post-conflict settings requires strategic planning, careful integration and sensible sequencing of activities' and is likely to be closely tied to their determination to ensure unionist narratives of loss are not lost from public accountings of the past (Simpson 2009). However, there is also, at times, a reactionary quality to their calls for truth, suggesting, in part, a 'truth as trumps' dynamic in which one call for truth or the production of truth is countered by that of a more 'significant' or more 'important' truth. This can, for example, be seen in respect to the actions of DUP member William McCrea, who, following the publication of the Saville Report and the naming of the Bloody Sunday victims in Parliament, named more than 100 victims of IRA atrocities during a parliamentary debate on terrorism to give them the same 'privilege' and to 'put them formally on record' (Lister 2010). As McCrea argued, the families of those individuals have many unanswered questions and the importance of achieving truth (if so desired) and some measure of resolution cannot be understated (Lister 2010). However, this dynamic does, at times, point to an attempt to secure political points, rather than respond to victims' needs.

I would argue that this constant trading and jostling for truth or the 'best' truth has led to a situation, applicable to the two main ethno-national blocs in Northern Ireland, where calls for truth and the recovery of truth have become a form of 'whataboutery'. This phrase, originally associated with Cardinal Cahal Daly, refers to the long-standing tradition in Northern Ireland of using past sins visited by either community (or the British or Irish state) upon each other to avoid uncomfortable questions about one's own past or contemporary responsibilities for making peace (Fealty 2005; McEvoy 2006).[38] As Brewer (2010) argues, people often have predetermined preferences in the way they intend to use so-called 'truths', which limit their capacity to genuinely receive the results of a truth process. In terms of dealing with the past, whataboutery is premised on the denial of the truths of the 'other' as a way to highlight the innocence and moral integrity of one's own experiences. Previous commentaries on prospects for truth recovery in Northern Ireland have noted the concern that a formal truth process could become a forum for the institutionalisation of whataboutery (McEvoy 2006).[39] In the battle over remembering and forgetting, unionists have privileged a hierarchy of victimhood and a hierarchy of truth (Ricoeur 2004). In doing so, they too have used truth recovery to fight 'the war' by other means (Barton 2000, cited in Dawson 2003).

Conclusion

While the past is a collection of narratives about human tragedy, the construction of 'victims' and the attribution of 'victimhood' are not innocent acts – they require what Elias (1986) calls 'victimhood work' and result in a 'politics of victimhood'. This process of claims making is dichotomous, creating 'us' and 'them' and collectivities of victimhood (Rosland 2009). As this chapter has argued, claiming victimhood can, politically, relate to notions of moral authority, legitimacy and blamelessness and as Gready (2011) argues, from the moral high ground, the 'victims license' can be claimed and sometimes granted, and under which the permanent victim is endowed with a moral authority that is permanently blameless and can do no wrong. By implication, the illegitimate and guilty 'other' sits outside the boundaries of victimhood. For the sociologist John Mack (1990: 125, cited in Rosland 2009: 296), this is 'the egoism of victimisation', 'the incapacity of an ethno-national group, as a direct result of its own historical trauma, to empathise with the suffering of another group'. The Northern Ireland case well illustrates that these contests frequently relate to the unresolved nature of the meta-conflict.

The dominant understanding of victimhood among unionist political elites and representatives of the security forces is a rigid and highly polarised distinction between 'innocent victims' and 'guilty combatants'. This perspective on victimhood rejects the inclusive Victims and Survivors (Northern Ireland) Order 2006 and the argument that there is a common experience of loss, suffering and need. For many interviewees, the Victims and Survivors (Northern Ireland) Order 2006 creates 'moral equivalence' between the actions of civilians and members of the security forces on one hand, and paramilitary activists on the other. The statutory definition of a victim or survivor of the Northern Ireland conflict and the associated critique of moral equivalence therefore challenges not only their claim to innocence and hierarchal understanding of victimhood, but their preferred reading of the past.

As this chapter has illustrated, contested understandings of victimhood can directly inform opposition to a formal truth process. For many unionists, the mechanics of a truth process have been interpreted as challenging their claim to innocent victimhood and have been perceived to deny and exacerbate the Protestant community's memories of loss and disproportionate victimisation (Hayward and Mitchell 2003). That an amnesty or limited immunity, as suggested by the CGP, may accompany a truth process is an obvious focus for many unionists, and the perceived implication of parity between members of the security forces (a number of whom who have privately supported an amnesty) and members of paramilitary organisations. Competitive and hierarchal notions of victimhood may also map onto a hierarchy of narratives on the past and a hierarchy of truths. In Northern Ireland, among unionist political elites at least, this has, at times, impacted on their willingness to receive the truths of the 'other' – those pertaining to the nationalist and republican community and has influenced their own calls for truth. Serving as a form of 'whataboutery', these dynamics do little to promote spaces for dialogue or true healing. Rather, competition over 'innocence' and 'guilt' and 'legitimate' and 'illegitimate' victims reflects the continuing and unresolved nature of the Northern Ireland conflict and unionists own relationship to that past. It is also, as explored in Chapter 4, related to their lack of trust in republican politicians and ex-combatants and the concern that a truth process would be used to 're-write' the past and discard unionist narratives of loss.

Notes

1 It should also be noted that an awareness of one's victimisation is a prerequisite. Due to a lack of access to public debate, the necessary social skills to make their voices heard or cultural and social stigmatisation surrounding sexual and reproductive violence, for example, victims routinely fail to articulate their experiences and so define themselves as 'victims' (Huyse 2003).

2 For a fuller exploration of the experience and needs of former paramilitaries in Northern Ireland see McEvoy *et al.* (2004), Shirlow and McEvoy (2008) and Jamieson *et al.* (2010).

3 A number of powerfully emotive positions on matters central to the Belfast Agreement, including the decommissioning of paramilitary weapons, the release of political prisoners and the reform of the RUC are also connected to this debate.

4 The Victims and Survivors (Northern Ireland) Order 2006. Available at: www.opsi.gov.uk/si/si2006/20062953.htm (accessed on 2 April 2009).

5 Victims and Survivors (Disqualification) Bill: Second Stage. Private Members' Business, Northern Ireland Assembly debates, 13 December 2010.

Brown (2012) argues that an implicit hierarchy of victimhood exists within republicanism. His study of Republican memory in east Belfast shows the privileging of paramilitary deaths, particularly where they relate to the purported 'oppression' of the British state, over civilians in commemorative space and narrative (Brown 2012). Civilian casualties are also more likely to be unnamed, even when killed by accident or in premature explosions caused by Republicans themselves (Brown 2012).

6 Victims and Survivors (Disqualification) Bill: Second Stage. Private Members'

Business, Northern Ireland Assembly debates, 13 December 2010.

7 Interview, Ian Paisley Junior, DUP, 12 September 2009.

8 Consultative Group on the Past. Private Members' Business, Northern Ireland Assembly debates, 2 February 2009.

9 Interview, Nelson McCausland, DUP, 3 April 2009.

10 Interview, Tom Elliott, UUP, 20 April 2009.

The DUP and UUP have both attempted to change the Victims and Survivors (Northern Ireland) Order 2006. Neither attempt was successful.

11 Members of the unionist and loyalist community who have been victims of loyalist violence have also criticised their elected representatives for not taking on their campaigns for truth and justice (Gallaher 2007). During a separate piece of research completed by the author, at least one representative of a victim's group based in the nationalist/republican community claimed that in cases where loyalist–security force collusion is alleged or suspected, members of the loyalist community have turned to them for help due to the failure of unionist political leaders to recognise and deal with these concerns. This project was entitled 'Assessing Support Initiatives for Victims of Terrorism in the UK and Spain: Lessons for the European Context' and was funded by the European Commission – Directorate-General Justice, Freedom and Security. See: http://victimsofterrorism.co.uk/ (accessed on 11 May 2013).

12 Interview, Dawn Purvis, 6 April 2009.

13 Interview, Dawn Purvis, 6 April 2009.

14 Interview, North Belfast community worker, 24 June 2009.

15 Interview, Eric McKee, UPRG, 18 June 2009.

16 The flipside to these arguments is that truth commissions can provide a powerful basis for challenging moral equivalence (Leebaw 2011). Finding, for example, that state forces were responsible for 93% of the violations documented in the report of the Guatemalan Commission for Historical Clarification (CEH), the Commission decisively rejected the 'theory of two devils', which had suggested that the state and resistance were equally accountable for devastating the country (CEH 1999).

17 Interview, Reverend John Dunlop, 17 June 2009.

18 This one off ex-gratia payment was modeled on the Irish Government's 'Remembrance Fund' and 'Acknowledgement Payment' of €15,000 to the surviving spouse or their children or to the parents of an individual who was either fatally injured in Ireland or who was resident in Ireland at that time (McDowell 2007).

19 Archbishop Eames reflected this point – 'It is a small gesture by our society to acknowledge the grief of the families left devastated by the last 40 years' (Tran 2009).

20 Consultative Group on the Past. Private Members' Business, Northern Ireland Assembly debates, 2 February 2009.

21 The IRA bombing of Frizzell's fish shop on the Shankill Road, 23 October 1993, killed nine Protestant civilians. This tragedy remains highly emotive and significant for members of the unionist community. One of the bombers, Thomas Begley, was also killed. His accomplice, Sean Kelly, survived.

Interview, Jeffrey Donaldson, DUP, 11 May 2009.

22 Dr Claire Moon, 19 May 2011, 'Refusing reparation: social suffering and social control in Argentina', School of Law, Queen's University Belfast. Seminar attended by author.

23 Interview, Maurice Morrow, DUP, 20 April 2009; Interview, Danny Kennedy, UUP, 5 May 2009. It should be noted that concern over the recognition payment was not exclusive to unionists. The SDLP and Alliance Party also

expressed misgivings, while SF MLA Gerry Kelly admitted that the proposal was a 'mistake' (SDLP 2009; Alliance Party 2009; BBC News 2009a).

24 Established in 1999, the purpose of this body is to obtain information, in strict confidence, which may lead to the whereabouts of the remaining 'Disappeared', the 17 victims who were abducted, killed and secretly buried between 1972 and 1986. See: www.iclvr.ie/en/ICLVR/Pages/Home%20Page (accessed on 5 June 2013).

25 See for example: News Letter (2008b) 'Victims' anger at 'amnesty for terrorists'', *News Letter*, 9 January 2008; Henry, L. (2008) 'Victims left outraged at amnesty plan for killers', *Belfast Telegraph*, 9 January 2008.

26 Interview, name withheld, UUP, 23 June 2009; Interview, Esmond Birnie, UUP, 19 May 2009; Interview, Tom Elliott, UUP, 20 April 2009; Interview, Maurice Morrow, DUP, 20 April 2009; Interview, Jim McDonald, RUC GC Foundation, 10 August 2009; Interview, Raymond White, NIRPOA, 19 May 2009. Reactions to this proposal also echoed those made in response to the controversial 'On-the Runs' legislation, which would have enabled the award of exemption from prosecution certificates for politically related offences committed in pre-Agreement Northern Ireland. Unionists opposed this legislation on the grounds that it gave a 'get out of jail free card' for suspects and equated those suspected of paramilitary offences with the actions of the security forces. See for example: Northern Ireland (Offences) Bill. House of Commons debates, Hansard, 23 November 2005.

27 Interview, Esmond Birnie, UUP, 19 May 2009; Interview, Archbishop Robin Eames, 23 October 2009; Interview, Denis Bradley, 8 October 2009; Interview, Lesley Carroll, 10 June 2009.

28 The UUP leader Mike Nesbitt has argued, 'The UUP supports the rule of law, and that means ensuring every evidential lead is taken up, and all possible prosecutions are pursued' (UUP 2012a).

29 There is also some difference of opinion among loyalist ex-combatants. Linked to their confidence to participate in a truth process, this factor is explored in full in Chapter 5.

30 Interview, Ian Paisley Junior, DUP, 12 September 2009. While beyond the scope of this research, Ian Paisley Junior identified similar tensions concerning the development of a centre for conflict transformation at the site of the former Maze prison, which, given its association with IRA hunger strikers, has been opposed by many unionists: 'I took the trouble to go round the Maze and look at it. For me as a historian, it was a fascinating place to see and I could see the merit in why a prison officer would want to tell his story about what it was like working under those circumstances, working with those people, but I would be bedeviled if I was to try to sell that aspect of it to my constituency or indeed certain of my political colleagues who say it would be a shrine'.

31 Interview, Denis Bradley, 8 October 2009; Interview, Lesley Carroll, 10 June 2009.

32 Stephen Nolan show, BBC Radio Ulster, 7 June 2012, author's recording. See also: Denis Bradley speech, 'The Past is Still Present', paper presented at 'The Past is Still Present: The legacy of the conflict: Where do we go from here' seminar, organised by the Committee on the Administration of Justice, 10 December 2010. Available at: www.caj.org.uk/files/2011/02/23/Denis_Bradley_Speech_December_2010.pdf (accessed on 18 January 2011).

33 Interview, Jim Allister, TUV, 20 March 2009.

34 Interview, Terry Spence, PFNI, 30 June 2009.

35 The DUP's Peter Weir alluded to this point – 'if we simply perpetuate a myth that in essence, suggests that, in some shape or form, we were all responsible

for what happened and that we are all victims in some shape or form, we will fudge the past'. Victims and Survivors (Disqualification) Bill: Second Stage. Private Members' Business, Northern Ireland Assembly debates, 13 December 2010.

36 See for example: DUP (2010c) 'Inquiries have created hierarchy of victims – Campbell', press release, 15 June 2010; Hutchinson, B. (2012) 'Why loyalism feels cut drift – Billy Hutchinson explains', EamonnMallie.com, 15 October 2012. Online. Available at: http://eamonnmallie.com/2012/10/why-loyalism-feel-cut-adrift-billy-hutchinson-explains/ (accessed on 17 October 2012).

37 Pat Finucane Case. Private Members' Business, Northern Ireland Assembly debates, 7 November 2011. This case is explored in full in Chapter 4.

38 According to Fealty (2005), 'Evasion may not be the intention but it is the obvious effect. It occurs when individuals are confronted with a difficult or uncomfortable question. The respondent retrenches his/her position and rejigs the question, being careful to pick open a sore point on the part of the questioner's 'tribe'. He/she then fires the original query back at the inquirer. Historical subjects can be the worst. Rational perspective disappears and opponents are forced to assume moral responsibility for their community's past sins. The substance of the issue is foregone for an emotional power play that comprises the solipsistic concerns of the participants, with little regard for fact or quality of argument'. Available at: http://sluggerotoole.com/2005/02/09/glossary_what_is_whataboutery/ (accessed on 23 May 2013).

39 The former Methodist president the Reverend Harold Good has also argued that 'We need to be careful lest in the sharing of our stories, we find ourselves indulging in the futile exercise of good old Ulster "whataboutery"' (Belfast Telegraph 2009b).

Chapter 4

Truth, trust and (re-)writing the past

> 'It is ultimately a question of trust, and clearly trust, like truth, is in short supply'.
>
> (UUP 2011b)

Introduction

Brewer (2010) argues that the 'facts' about the past are never neutral as 'memories' are as much interpretations as they are recollections of the past. Power is central to these negotiations whereby 'Victors rather than the vanquished write history and construct the way the past is supposed to be officially recalled' (Brewer 2010: 145). Truth processes have been implicated in this critique with the argument that not all parties to the conflict will openly participate and that the truth process itself and the information that is disclosed may be partial and used selectively (Wilson 2001; Hayner 2011). Cohen (1995: 47) argues that mediating this tension between 'control by opening, control by closing' the past is a major challenge for transitional states. Michael Ignatieff's (1996: 113) assertion that a truth process can 'narrow the range of permissible lies' and examine abuses on all 'sides' of the conflict has often been used to offset this critique. However, doing so requires a level of trust in the bona fides of the truth process itself and in the 'truths' of the 'other side' (Misztal 2011; Hunt 2004). That trust may be in short supply in the aftermath of violent conflict is not uncommon or unexpected and, as this chapter will argue, can directly impact on attitudes to truth recovery.

This chapter will argue that unionists' and loyalists' lack of trust in the motivations and intentions of republicans' calls for truth has been a significant influence on their opposition to truth recovery. In particular, they fear that republicans would seek to manipulate a truth process to 'rewrite' the past, justifying their own actions, while demonising those of the British state and security forces and marginalising unionists' narratives of loss. Such distrust is a legacy of the conflict, the nature of the peace process and the specific mechanisms of truth recovery that have been employed to date. The arguments that a truth mechanism would be 'nothing more than a "Brit bashing session" ' and a 'witch hunt of Protestants' typify this discourse (see for example: DUP 2003; UUP 2009a; McKittrick 2002; News Letter 2012b). They are traceable from 1998 when tentative discussion on the establishment of a formal truth process began through to the present day, indicating their longevity and the strength of this concern (DUP 2003, 2009a, 2011; UUP 2012c; EPIC 2004; NIRPOA 2008). This chapter will address four overlapping areas. First, the chapter will open with an exploration of the relationship between trust and truth-telling. This background will then be mapped on to the absence of trust that has characterised the Northern Ireland peace process. Next, this chapter will address two distinct areas of concern for unionists and loyalists in terms of dealing with the past. They are the 'state centricity' of current and prospective models of truth recovery and the argument that republicans cannot be trusted to provide the truth about their past actions. While exclusively referring to the Northern Ireland context, this chapter speaks to the broader challenge for transitional states – that while the aim of a truth process is to recover 'truths' on all 'sides' and contribute to a more complete historical narrative, without trust in the process of truth recovery and the truth-telling capacity of the 'other', there is little possibility for meaningful and comprehensive truth recovery.

Truth, trust and the past

As Simmel (1950: 326, cited in Newton 2001: 202) has suggested, 'trust is one of the most important synthetic forces within society'. At the most basic level, trust is interactional, implying reliance upon or confidence in some event, process or person (Golembiewski and McConkie 1975, cited in Hosmer 1995). Associated variables include civic-mindedness, political tolerance, the ability to compromise, honesty and, in Hosmer's (1995) opinion, an underlying assumption of an implicit moral duty (Newton 2001; Hetherington 1998). Trust, by definition, may therefore rest on a degree of uncertainty and vulnerability, potentially requiring a 'leap in the dark' by an 'individual [or individuals] making herself vulnerable to another individual, group or institution that has the capacity to do her harm or to betray her' (Booth and Wheeler 2008: 234–237; Levi and Stoker 2000: 476, cited in Horne 2012: 853). It is also inherently emotional, relating to identity and, in the aftermath of violent conflict, legacies of suffering (Fierke 2009). As discussed below, the notion of trust is particularly acute in the political sphere and according to Hetherington (1998), political trust between the governing parties and between the parties to the electorate is essential to the proper functioning of democracy. Sufficient levels of trust should help maintain peaceful and stable political relations (Hetherington 1998). Conversely, low levels of political trust have been linked to feelings of alienation, powerlessness and normlessness (Abramson and Finifter 1981). While political trust may be damaged by a 'one off' event or series of smaller events, a cultural theory of trust argues that trust in political institutions originates outside the political arena in long-standing and deeply seeded beliefs that are rooted in cultural norms and communicated through early life socialisation (Mishler and Rose 2001).

That trust is of particular importance in periods of uncertainty and transition has lent credence to the relationship between institutions of transitional justice and the fostering of trust/dismantling of distrust between previously opposing parties (Horne 2012). According to Lundy and McGovern (2008b), a key goal of truth-telling is the reconstitution of the social and political environment. While largely undertheorised in the literature, there are a number of potential ways in which transitional justice mechanisms and, in particular, truth recovery bodies can practically and symbolically foster trust (Horne 2012). For example, for victims, the capacity of a truth process to provide them with a voice with which to articulate their experiences can signal the new regime's commitment to non-violent means and recognition of past suffering (Wiebelhaus-Brahm 2010; Humphrey 2003). Likewise, for ex-combatants, engaging in truth-telling initiatives can provide an opportunity to explain their motivations and intentions, potentially aiding their return and reintegration (Waldorf 2010; Shaw 2007). At an institutional level, and as illustrated by the SATRC's examination of, among others, the medical, legal and business communities during apartheid, the process of revealing truth about the past can function as a mechanism to build trust in reconstructed government bodies and public institutions (Dyzenhaus 1998; Payne 2008). Finally and more broadly, efforts at truth-telling can increase confidence in the rule of law and democratic consolidation (Teitel 2000; Wilson 2001; Ensalaco 1994).

To facilitate these aims, the relationship between trust, truth and testimony is of particular importance. For societies moving out of violent conflict and/or mass human rights violations, where peace may be unfamiliar and ontologically strange, trust in the 'other' may not come easily (Brewer 2010; Dawson 2007). However, for the French philosopher Paul Ricoeur whose work is concerned with the ethics of 'remembering and forgetting', the public role of history and its place in the constitution and reconstitution of civil society and community, the ability of members of a given society to have 'confidence in the word of others' is a fundamental ethical and social goal because what it reinforces is not just the interdependence, but the shared common humanity of the members of a community' (Ricoeur 2004: 166, cited in Lundy and McGovern 2008b: 4). Likewise, Ricoeur (1999: 9) has argued that 'When I testify to something, I am asking the others to trust what I am saying is true. To share testimony is to exchange trust. Beyond this we cannot go'. Misztal (2011: 47) concurs, noting that trust is 'the lubricant of cooperation'. Two significant points for this chapter can be drawn from Ricoeur. First, as Misztal (2011) argues, the extension of trust in any particular setting depends on a reinterpretation and understanding of the contested nature of the past. Second, doing so not only entails challenging cultures of silence and mutually exclusive identities as discussed earlier in this book, but as the latter quote from Ricoeur suggests, to move from knowledge to acknowledgment of past events (Dawson 2007). According to Nagle (1989, cited in Cohen 2001), acknowledgement is what happens to knowledge when it becomes officially sanctioned and enters the public discourse. The public, by proxy, accepting of long-silenced facts has been considered vital to taking responsibility for past actions or omissions and recognising victims' experiences (Gormally 2006; Hayner 2011; Biggar 2003; Villa-Vicencio and Verwoerd 2000). Doing so relies on a degree of trust in, and acceptance of, the word of the other, leading Misztal (2003: 120) to conclude that 'in the final analysis, in our search for truth or what really happened, we rely on trust'.

However, as Ricoeur (1999, 2004) argues, the relationship between the giver and the receiver of testimony is also the point at which the tension between confidence and suspicion enters, resting on the balance between trustworthiness and untrustworthiness (Lundy and McGovern 2008b). For Lundy and McGovern (2008b: 46), the rise of suspicion creates a 'space of controversy' – the confrontation and/or assimilation between various testimonies as bearers of the truth of the past. Post-conflict truth-telling processes are designed to create this space (Phelps 2006; Tutu 2000). In those contexts marked by an absence of trust, it is possible that not all parties to the conflict will welcome the idea of a truth process as a 'space of controversy'. One reason, of particular concern to this chapter, is the perception that the process itself would become part of the conflict, characterised by one-sided participation and a selective recovery of 'truth' (Hayner 2011; Brewer 2010). The concern that powerful vested interests may seek to control what 'truths' are disclosed and that one party to the conflict may attempt to use a truth process to 'rewrite' the past, justifying and legitimising their actions is central to this critique. Foucault (1995) argues that this contest over the ownership of the past is related to the creation of 'regimes of truth' and the production of knowledge and power. As this chapter will illustrate, unionists' lack of trust in republican's commitment to truth-telling and the concern that they would use a formal truth process to 'rewrite' the past has been key to structuring their opposition to truth recovery in Northern Ireland.

Mistrust, loss and the republican agenda

That the Northern Ireland peace process has been characterised by an absence of trust has been well documented – 'At the heart of all the problems in Northern Ireland is mistrust. Centuries of conflict have generated hatreds that make it virtually impossible for the two communities to trust each other. Each disbelieves the other' (Mitchell 1996: 37; Peatling 2004; Dixon 2002; Aughey 2002). Trust relates to loyalty and is a product of socialisation. By implication, 'mistrust' accompanies 'disloyalty'. For many unionists and loyalists, given their empirical experience during the conflict, they have little trust in the actions and motivations of republican politicians and ex-combatants. A brief look at the statistical distribution of loss during the conflict sets out this case. As detailed in Chapter 1, the most up-to-date figures reveal that between 1966 and 2012, 3,739 people were victims of the Northern Ireland conflict (McKittrick and McVea 2012). Of this total, 2,167 were killed by republican paramilitary organisations (McKittrick and McVea 2012). Of these victims, 1,016 were members of the security forces – 305 RUC and RUC Reserve personnel; 206 members of the UDR and Royal Irish Regiment; and 505 members of the British Army (McKittrick and McVea 2012). While the figures are not directly comparable, the McKeown database reveals that republican paramilitary organisations were responsible for over 96% of these deaths.[1] Protestants living in the border counties of Northern Ireland, where there was a high concentration of casualties among members of the locally recruited security forces, and attacks on Protestant farms and businesses, experienced and continue to experience, a particularly pervasive sense of threat (Simpson 2009). In this highly symbolic region, IRA operations to undermine British control were interpreted as an attempt to 'drive' Protestants out and have since been described as a form of 'genocide' or 'ethnic cleansing' (Dawson 2007; Patterson 2013). It has also given rise to chronic insecurity and profound trauma. Making peace with republicans, therefore, politically and morally, involves a shift in perception many unionists and loyalists struggle to make (Dawson 2007).

As Dawson (2007) argues, rather than contributing to the rebuilding of trust and understanding, such memories tend to re-evoke distrust and suspicion that translate into more uncompromising positions in terms of peace processes. Reflecting a 'intense fear of a republican master-plan at work', there is an acute perception among many unionists and loyalists that the peace process and Belfast Agreement have disproportionately benefitted nationalists and republicans and have been structurally predisposed towards a nationalist/republican interpretation of the conflict (Southern 2007: 175; Hayes *et al.* 2005; Hayes and McAllister 2004; Dixon 2001; Hughes and Donnelly 2003; Aughey 2002; Patterson 2004; MacGinty 2004).[2] From a unionist perspective, key areas of opposition to the Belfast Agreement included the establishment of the power-sharing Assembly and inclusion of representatives of armed groups in government,[3] the release of politically motivated prisoners and the reform of the RUC (Hayes *et al.* 2005; Ryder 2000). Each was felt to benefit nationalists and republicans at the expense of the unionist community and to have shown the British government's willingness to accommodate republicans' demands (Hayes and McAllister 2004). The findings of the 2003 Northern Ireland Life and Times (NILT) Survey report, that, for example, 74% of self-declared Protestants felt they had not done as well as Catholics from the peace deal, only 18% thought the two communities were equal beneficiaries and none thought that Protestants had done better (NILT 2003). As a power-sharing or 'compromise' political agreement, defined by 'constructive ambiguity', whereby many of the main provisions of the Agreement were crafted in deliberately open-ended language to ensure maximum possible 'buy-in' from all parties, it is, in part, inevitable that some level of unease or distrust would result from the political negotiations (Brewer 2010; Bell and Cavanaugh 1998). Brewer (2010) argues this is because compromise post-violence societies have to contend with cultural differences of religion, ethnicity or national allegiance, which remain and are open to manipulation. Dixon (2002: 726) and Aughey (2002: 13) both argue that characterised by 'choreography and play acting', 'kite flying' and 'necessary fictions', the peace process has led to a mood of 'cynicism and resentment' among unionists. It is also the case that distrust and a sense of loss/lack of honour is partly instrumental, whereby, in a conflict marked by 'mutually exclusive identity categories', any 'concession' to the nationalist community or move away from the status quo, was interpreted as an attack on the Protestant community (Fierke 2009; Hughes and Donnelly 2003). When asked if he was confident the Belfast Agreement protected his cultural identity, the response of the Grand Master of the Orange Order Robert Saulters conveys this sense of loss:

> It does not protect my identity. Unionists have lost out since the Agreement in many ways, and it has been a process of give to nationalism and take by nationalism. I can't think of anything that Unionists have obtained through the Agreement [response to questionnaire, 15 July 2005, cited in Southern 2007: 169].

While space does not permit an exhaustive examination, in differing ways, unionists' reactions to the release of political prisoners and the reform of the RUC – both integral parts of the Belfast Agreement - serve as useful examples of their lack of trust in the peace process and the perception that it has furthered a 'republican' narrative of the conflict. The release of 453 eligible prisoners (199 loyalists, 242 republicans and 13 others) under the Northern Ireland (Sentences) Act 1998, was one of the most controversial aspects of the peace process (Dwyer 2007).[4] Paralleling release schemes in other transitional jurisdictions, advocates of the scheme argued that early prisoner releases were essential if paramilitary organisations and their political representatives were to sign up to the peace deal and that it would provide an incentive for such organisations to maintain their ceasefires

(McEvoy 2001). However, for unionists, on one level, the scheme represented a betrayal of law and order and an unprecedented interference with the operation of the criminal justice system (von Tangen Page 2006). More problematic was the fact that by supporting the early-release scheme, the British government appeared to acknowledge that the conflict was political, not criminal, and therefore had some grounds for justification – a long-standing republican demand (McEvoy 2001). Likewise, the reforms to policing recommended by the Patten Report were intensely problematic for unionists. As detailed in the introduction, Patten's recommendations included changes to the name, insignia, accountability mechanisms and composition of the RUC (ICP 1999). Given that the central function of the RUC was to defend the Northern Ireland state and union with Great Britain, for unionists, the Commission's recommendations not only challenged the identity and sacrifice of the RUC, but corresponded to republican's desire to undermine the legitimacy and organisational memory of the RUC, suggesting that reform was necessary because the RUC was, in some way, to 'blame' for the conflict (Mulcahy 2006; Ryder 2000).[5]

For many unionists and members of the security forces, there is therefore a profound sense that nationalists and republicans have been the overwhelming beneficiaries of the peace process, and, in doing so, have made considerable gains in 'rewriting' the history of the conflict. That the British state has been perceived to have acquiesced with republicans' demands has compounded their lack of trust in the direction of the peace process and associated conflict transformation initiatives (Southern 2007). As Dawson's (2007: 266) argument well illustrates, 'when such trust and confidence have been missing, or have ebbed or been eroded, then 'the past' is not experienced as being 'over' and 'passed' at all, but is lived as the continuing and on going present-day reality', this backdrop has been highly influential in regards to unionists' attitudes towards the truth recovery debate.

Controlling the past: State centricity and the focus of investigation

Speaking to the concern that a truth process may result in a 'selective' recovery of 'truths' or that truth may be a weapon with which to 'beat' the 'other side', one of unionists, loyalists and the security forces most well-rehearsed oppositional discourses to truth recovery is the argument that republicans would use such a process to 'rewrite' the history of the conflict, and ensure that only the State and its security forces are held to account (Brewer 2010; NIRPOA 2009; PFNI 2003, 2008a; DUP 2003, 2007, 2009a, 2011; UUP 2007b, 2012c; EPIC 2004). EPIC's (2004: 9–10) statement well captures this view:

> There is deep suspicion amongst loyalists about the high potential for a 'truth process' to be abused by republicans to suit their political agenda...the process will be a convenient instrument to blame the British state and 'its surrogates' for everything, providing justification for their war, thus allowing them to be let off the hook.

These arguments are directly related to unionist's lack of trust in the motivations and intentions of republicans and the themes of power, silence and the creation of historical narratives (Trouillot 1995). To attempt to rewrite the past is part of the battle for memory and social control, part of the process of 'control by opening, control by closing the past' (Cohen 1995: 47, 2001; Misztal 2003). Cohen (2001) argues that doing so, all societies use a selective transformation and/or eradication of memory. The Stalinist form of controlling the past – the deliberate suppression and distortion of history – is the classic type and the objective is to establish a version of history (a master narrative) to legitimate past actions and current practices (Scott 1992). By contrast, with the selective recovery of memory, the past is not deliberately obliterated or rewritten, rather, it is regrouped and reformed, merging into present practices (Scott 1992). In Northern Ireland, unionists believe republicans are actively trying to rewrite the past to justify and legitimise their armed campaign and believe that existing and prospective truth mechanisms have, and will, further this aim. Ian Paisley Junior well articulated this point:

> Telling history matters and if you tell it your way you may control the future. I think there will be an element of people who are clever enough to understand this is the version that has to go out, all our memory, all our records have to be balled towards that view and then that will justify what we did as terrorists. I don't think you have to be sophisticated to learn that and I think people have.[6]

Three distinct but overlapping centres of concern can be identified. The first two focus on the fact that public inquiries and the work of the OPONI has been 'state centric', while the third focuses on the disjuncture between the availability of documentation on the part of state services and paramilitaries. The resulting perception is that dealing with the past is imbalanced, anti-state and pro-nationalist. Each factor will be explored in turn below.

Public inquiries

Public inquiries have been the most visible and contested form of truth recovery in Northern Ireland to date. The largely 'state centric' focus of these investigations has been highly problematic for unionists, loyalists and members of the security forces and has had a decisive impact on their reading of the truth recovery debate. Alongside the Saville Inquiry into the events on Bloody Sunday, public inquiries have been held into the deaths of Rosemary Nelson, Robert Hamill and Billy Wright. A documentary review has also been held in the case of Pat Finucane. The allegation of collusion between British state agents and paramilitary organisations is central to each case and their establishment follows the recommendations of the Honourable Justice Peter Cory. Appointed by the British and Irish governments in May 2002, Cory was mandated to investigate the role of collusion in the deaths of Finucane, Nelson, Hamill, Wright, Chief Superintendent Breen, Superintendent Buchanan and Lord Justice and Lady Gibson (Requa 2007). Cory's findings were delivered to the British and Irish governments in October 2003. In all but the Gibson case, material that could be said to constitute collusion, defined as the state security services 'ignoring or turning a blind eye to the wrongful acts of their servants or agents or by supplying information to assist those servants or agents in their wrongful acts', was uncovered and public inquiries were recommended (Cory 2004a: 14). The Irish government published Cory's report into the deaths of Breen and Buchanan immediately and established the Smithwick Tribunal in accordance with Cory's recommendations. After some intense political pressure, Cory's reports on the deaths of Finucane, Hamill, Nelson and Wright were made public by the British government in April 2004 (McEvoy 2006). Public inquiries into the Nelson, Hamill and Wright cases and a documentary review into the Finucane case were subsequently established. By way of background, it is worth providing some detail on each individual case at this juncture.[7]

The first public inquiry to report on 14 September 2010 was that into the death of Billy Wright, a former leading loyalist and one time leader of the LVF, murdered in December 1997 in the Maze prison by republican inmates. Chaired by Lord MacLean, the inquiry opened in May 2007, following Justice Cory's (2004b) finding that potentially collusive acts by the prison authorities played a role in Wright's death. These acts included the transfer of Wright and other LVF prisoners to the C and D wings of H Block 6 at a time when INLA prisoners were housed in the A and B wings of the same block; the ignoring of warnings about the dangers of the above; and the standing down of the guard for the Observation Tower overlooking the A and B wings (Cory 2004b: 3.222–3.223).[8]

The report rejects the suggestion that collusion played a part in the death of Billy Wright – 'we were not persuaded…that in any instance there was evidence of collusive acts or collusive conduct' (MacLean *et al.* 2010: 642). Where failings in the conduct of prison authorities were identified, including the decision to allocate Billy Wright and the LVF to H Block 6 alongside INLA prisoners and that the RUC failed to communicate a major piece of intelligence, they were judged to be the result of negligence rather than intentional acts (MacLean *et al.* 2010: 642).[9] Billy Wright's father, David, was unconvinced by the findings, arguing, 'The inquiry adopted a narrow interpretation of collusion. Having considered the factual findings, it looks like collusion, it sounds like collusion and in my mind amounts to firm and final proof of collusion by state agencies in acts and omissions' (BBC News 2010a; Keenan and Hennessy 2010).

Rosemary Nelson was a human rights lawyer involved in taking cases against the RUC over their handling of nationalist protests against unionist Orange Order parades in the mid- to late-1990s. Her death was preceded by a range of threats to her life made by RUC officers and loyalist paramilitaries. In September 1998, for example, while giving evidence on human rights in Northern Ireland to an American Congressional Committee hearing, Nelson testified about her fears for her own safety.[10] Nelson was killed by a loyalist car bomb, March 1999, amid allegations the RUC colluded in her death. Among the acts and omissions on the part of the RUC and NIO that Cory determined as capable of giving rise to a finding of collusion include allegations that police officers chose to ignore threats made against Rosemary Nelson and encouraged others to attack her (Cory 2004a: 4.207, 4.208). In total, Cory outlined 17 potential instances that may be found to constitute collusive acts on the part of the RUC and NIO both prior to and after her murder (Cory 2004a).

Chaired by Sir Michael Morland, the Rosemary Nelson Inquiry was tasked with

> determining whether any wrongful act or omission by or within the Royal Ulster Constabulary, Northern Ireland Office, Army or other state agency facilitated her death or obstructed the investigation of it, or whether attempts were made to do so; whether any such act or omission was intentional or negligent; whether the investigation of her death was carried out with due diligence; and to make recommendations.[11]

The inquiry published its report on 23 May 2011 and found no evidence to suggest collusion between the security forces and loyalist paramilitaries in the death of Rosemary Nelson – 'There is no evidence of any act by or within any of the state agencies we have examined (the RUC, the NIO, the Army or the security services) which directly facilitated Rosemary Nelson's murder' (Morland *et al.* 2011: 465). A number of critiques of the RUC's and NIO's conduct were however made, including the assertion that 'we cannot exclude the possibility of a rogue member or members of the RUC or the Army in some way assisting the murderers to target Rosemary Nelson', that the conduct of some RUC members had 'the effect of legitimizing her as a target' and that the state 'failed to take reasonable and proportionate steps to safeguard the life of Rosemary Nelson' (Morland *et al.* 2011: 465, 466). While the Inquiry's findings were welcomed by the then NI SoS Owen

Paterson and the policing bodies, the interpretation of collusion as an act of 'commission' not 'omission' has been criticised by a number of parties, including Nelson's family and the human rights NGO's Amnesty International and the CAJ (Amnesty International 2011; CAJ 2011b).[12]

The investigation into the death of Robert Hamill, a young nationalist kicked to death by a gang of some 30 loyalists in Portadown, April 1997, with an RUC Landrover close at hand began formal proceedings on 6 January 2009. Chaired by Sir Edwin Jowett, its terms of reference were

> To inquire into the death of Robert Hamill with a view to determining whether any wrongful act or omission by or within the Royal Ulster Constabulary facilitated his death or obstructed the investigation of it, or whether attempts were made to do so; whether any such act or omission was intentional or negligent; whether the investigation of his death was carried out with due diligence; and to make recommendations.[13]

These issues speak not only to collusion, but also to institutional indifference on the part of the RUC (Cory 2004c). While the report was completed on 25 February 2011, at the time of writing, its findings have not been made public. This is due to ongoing legal action by the Public Prosecution Service against three persons who are to be charged in connection with this case (Belfast Telegraph 2010a).

The forth inquiry recommended by Cory concerns the case of Pat Finucane. Finucane, a solicitor was killed at home by members of the loyalist paramilitary group the UDA in February 1989. Collusion has been alleged between members of the UDA and the Army Force Research Unit, RUC Special Branch and MI5. Prior to the Cory report (2004d), the facts of the Finucane case had been the subject of three investigations by the former Chief of the Metropolitan Police Sir John Stevens. In the available summary of Stevens' third inquiry, it was concluded that Stevens had been obstructed in his previous inquiries; that Brian Nelson, a UDA member and Army Force Research Unit agent who co-ordinated the intelligence leading to Finucane's murder had been warned of his impending arrest by his army handlers; that the murder of Pat Finucane could have been prevented and was the result of collusion (Stevens 2003). While the Stevens Inquiries have now been largely superseded by the Cory reports, their conclusions are essentially the same, Cory (2004d: 1.293) concluding that 'there is strong evidence that collusive acts were committed by the Army (FRU), the RUC Special Branch and the Security Service'.

Despite Cory's (2004d) recommendation, a public inquiry has not taken place. First, a change in legislation – the Inquiries Act (2005), was strongly opposed by the Finucane family who insisted that they would not take part in an inquiry established under its terms. The Inquiries Act (2005) enables ministers to control the appointment and dismissal of an inquiry panel, set the temporal and substantive terms of the inquiry and control access to funding, evidence and the dissemination of findings (McEvoy 2006). As Justice Cory argued, by enacting the 2005 Act, the British government chose to 'change the ground rules' to better control information made public via public inquiries (Cory 2005: 50, cited in Requa 2007: 4). Requa (2007) argues persuasively that the Act was created specifically in response to Cory's recommendations on Finucane. As of May 2011, it was reported that the family were 'expecting a full inquiry' (BBC News 2011a). However, in October 2011, the Prime Minister David Cameron announced that Desmond de Silva QC would conduct an independent documentary review.[14] de Silva did not have the right to examine witnesses under oath and the Finucane family had no involvement in the process. This decision was widely condemned by the Finucane family and their legal and political representatives (see for example: BBC News 2011b; McDonald 2011a; Finucane 2011). de Silva reported in December 2012 and found 'no doubt that agents of the State were involved in carrying out serious violations of human rights up to and including murder' (de Silva 2012: 23). Those agents of the State included members of the RUC, Special Branch and Military Intelligence (de Silva 2012). de Silva (2012: 23) did however report that there was no 'over arching State conspiracy' to murder Pat Finucane. The family has rejected the report as a 'whitewash' and a 'sham' (Bowcott 2012).

That public inquiries have focused on the actions and inactions of state personnel and that the impetus for their establishment has been largely from the nationalist/republican community has contributed to the view among unionists and loyalists that public inquiries have been imbalanced at best and a 'witch-hunt' at worst.[15] The UUP leader Mike Nesbitt has been particularly clear on this point, arguing that

> The trouble is that, although each investigation in isolation may have some merit, when you put them all together, they add up to something else: a body of work that, in fact, represents the rewriting of history. That rewriting has the result that the state and its agents are consistently portrayed as the villains of the peace.[16]

Again, speaking during the Assembly debate that took place following the British government's decision to hold a documentary review into the Finucane case, Nesbitt explicitly emphasised the importance of the relationship between trust and truth-telling:

> We are rewriting history and we are doing so often in a way that portrays only the state and its agents as the villains. If we are to replace it with a complete process, it must be based on a trust that

> not only establishes the truth of what happened but does so in such a manner that individuals can accept that it is the truth.[17]

For Ricoeur (2004: 21), testimony constitutes the 'fundamental transitional structure between memory and history' (Novick 1999). "This is because testimony represents the articulation of memory' and, he argues, we have 'nothing better than memory to signify that something has taken place" (Ricoeur 2004: 162, cited in Lundy and McGovern 2008b: 46). If, as Ricoeur (2004: 21) suggests, there is a fundamental 'truth claim' of memory, tied to 'an ambition...of being faithful to the past', for those who are opposed to truth recovery, public inquiries have created the impression that a formal truth recovery process will aid the 'republican project' of rewriting the history of the conflict – one in which they had no option but to engage in a 'just war', and simultaneously erasing unionists' experiences from public memory.[18] Ian Paisley Junior alluded to this fear, commenting,

> There is the fact that the big atrocities in Northern Ireland were perpetrated against unionists – the Darkley massacre – all those sorts of things, Bloody Friday, no one is being held to account and none of those things are ever investigated. The question is why did so many Protestants die? I think that point is lost.[19]

While highly popular among interviewees, these arguments do, however, mask a number of important points that require further interrogation and offer useful insights when studying opponents of truth recovery in other jurisdictions. First, the establishment of public inquiries (and investigations by the OPONI) are not without legal reason and where the state may have violated its obligations in international law to protect its citizens, such inquiries should be carried out (Rolston and Scraton 2005). Second, it cannot be said that all public inquiries have investigated 'nationalist issues' in the manner in which the public inquiries detailed above have been construed. The inquiry into the death of Billy Wright is a case in point, and despite what I felt to be a lack of interest or enthusiasm when I raised this subject with interviewees,[20] its findings appear to have been welcomed by a number of unionists (BBC News 2010b). Nor can it be said that the findings from public inquiries have been overwhelmingly damaging for unionists and the security forces. This point was recognised at the time of interview by PSNI Assistant Chief Constable Alistair Finlay. Reflecting the much more open attitude to truth recovery displayed by senior members of the post-Patten policing structures discussed later in this book, Finlay argued that there had been 'no great smoking gun' and therefore no reason for such fear:

> I actually think we have got through some of this, we have come through those public inquiries, there have been people sitting there

> listening to what has been said and the various evidence and the newspaper headlines have not been full of great revelations if there was anything of interest they would have got to hear about it.[21]

Given that the Nelson and Saville inquiries have since reported and de Silva's documentary review of the Finucane case has been completed, it is arguable that Finlay's assertion remains largely correct. As noted above, the report of the Rosemary Nelson inquiry found no evidence of collusion and, indeed, was welcomed by the RUC GC F (Morland *et al.* 2011).[22] In other instances, for unionists, as a pro-state political ideology, the problem is partly structural (Bruce 1992b). In 2009, the head of the HET Dave Cox alluded to this point, arguing that while the HET has dealt with a number of high-profile cases that are critical of the IRA, the longevity, and anti-state nature of the IRA's campaign has meant that such investigations are 'not news' and consequently affect how the HET is seen to operate.[23] It is therefore difficult to find a firm basis for the DUP's David McIlveen's argument that the findings of public inquiries have been predetermined and detrimental to unionists and the security forces – 'we have to accept that these inquiries have become a push to get the answer that the instigator of the inquiry wants rather than to find the truth'.[24] Rather, such findings and conclusions should offer unionists some confidence and go some way to dissuading the claim that dealing with the past necessitates a 'witch-hunt' of former members of the security forces or is inherently anti-state.

Third, and most significantly, as made clear in the international literature on transitional justice and truth recovery, the very point of a truth process is to investigate abuses on all 'sides' of the conflict and to contribute to the creation of a more complete historical narrative (Hayner 2011; Smyth 2007). As Dawn Purvis, the only interviewee to openly recognise this argument noted, 'if you look at why people explore the need for a truth recovery process it is because they want the whole nasty truth out, it is because there is a crying need for that...it's about lifting the stone in every community to see what crawls out from underneath'.[25] To succeed and to be credible and legitimate, a truth process cannot engage in a partial examination of the past or act as a platform for a selective 'rewriting' of the past (Gibson 2006). In South Africa, for example, the SATRC did not engage in a 'witch-hunt' as alleged by some segments of the white Afrikaans speaking population but documented atrocities and attributed blame to *all sides* in the struggle over apartheid (Gready 2011). Kirk Simpson (2007: 329) has also emphasised this point, noting, 'those who seek truth recovery as validation or vindication for their actions or to 'concretize' their own predetermined and politicised version of the future, miss the point entirely'.

Fourth, I would argue that it is too simplistic to suggest that a truth process would merely 'rewrite' the past or play into republican cultures of victimhood. Dawn Purvis has in fact argued that SF's demand for an independent international truth commission is politically expedient – 'SF know that the chances of having a truth commission in Northern Ireland are pretty remote. So why not call for one anyway and be seen to be doing the right thing for your own community'.[26] A statistical breakdown of all deaths during the Troubles reveals that while the RUC and Royal Ulster Constabulary Reserve (RUCR) were directly responsible for 52 deaths, the PIRA alone is responsible for the loss of 1,771 lives (McKittrick and McVea 2012). There is therefore little for unionists to fear as regards the focus of a formal truth process and plenty of scope to investigate republicans' actions.[27] As detailed in Chapter 3, alongside the deaths of members of the security forces, significant collective tragedies for the unionist community include the La Mon House bombing, the Enniskillen Remembrance Day bombing, the Narrow Water bombing and the experience of Protestants in the border counties of Northern Ireland (Simpson 2008, 2009; Donnan and Simpson 2007).[28] The murder of approximately 227 Catholic civilians by republicans provides a further peg on which unionists could hang their calls for truth.[29] This is not to suggest that unionists have not called for truth (see for example: UUP 2012de; BBC News 2013b). It is however indisputable that efforts at truth recovery in Northern Ireland have, to date, been state centric and, in the absence of a formal truth process, it is likely that the piecemeal approach to the past will continue. Unionist's rejection of a truth process therefore consciously or unconsciously equates to a de facto acceptance of a continuing focus on the state in a context where non-state actors were responsible for 90% of deaths. Continuing this approach to the past effectively means letting non-state actors 'off the hook'.

Finally, and related to the above point, 'ugly truths' are likely to emerge or be confirmed by a truth process (Lawther 2013). Given their responsibility for the greatest loss of life, it is unlikely that republicans could comprehensively manage the sheer number of such 'ugly truths' to their own political advantage.[30] The HET report published in late December 2011 into the events at Loughgall, where, on 8 May 1987, a eight-man PIRA unit launched an attack on a local RUC base, but was ambushed by a British SAS unit who shot dead eight PIRA members and a civilian, for example, overturned republicans' long-held argument that the SAS opened fire first as part of a shoot-to-kill policy (Belfast Telegraph 2011b). Instead, the HET concluded that it was the IRA who opened fire, and that the SAS were within their rights to shoot dead those who were attacking them (Belfast Telegraph 2011b; McDonald 2011b). A formal truth process would provide a regulated space in which similar competing versions of history would be asserted and tested (McEvoy 2006). That these points have not been recognised is indicative of the absence of trust and, according to one interviewee, the 'paranoid frame of mind' generated by public inquiries.[31]

Office of the Police Ombudsman for Northern Ireland

Unionists' and the security forces' attitudes towards the OPONI, particularly under the direction of the first Ombudsman Nuala O'Loan, have largely mirrored the above arguments, indicating something of their depth. Historically, in Northern Ireland, the RUC investigated complaints against its own members – particularly problematic in a society in which a section of the population distrusted the police force and where there was a low substantiation rate for complaints (Hayes 1997; O'Rawe 2003). In November 1995, the former ombudsman Maurice Hayes was appointed to review the complaints system. Hayes' (1997) subsequent report 'A Police Ombudsman for Northern Ireland?' proposed the establishment of an independent Police Ombudsman with responsibility for investigating complaints made against the police. The OPONI was established in 2000 and is designed to provide an efficient, effective and independent police complaints system (Mulcahy 2006). According to Ellison (2007: 261), the OPONI has a 'dual mandate', taking on the role of a 'surrogate truth recovery vehicle' and launching a number of high-profile investigations into past RUC activities, alongside dealing with day-to-day complaints against the PSNI.[32] At the time of writing, the OPONI is dealing with over 150 historic cases in relation to deaths and other serious matters believed to have involved members of the RUC between 1969 and 1998 (Healing Through Remembering 2013).

While Prenzler and Ronkin (2001) state that dissatisfaction and unease is partly inevitable as any system dealing with police complaints has to run a fine line between maintaining public and police confidence in the process, it is arguable that, as regards the OPONI and the unionist/security force community, the perception that the Office has contributed to a 'rewriting' of the past and a blackening of the name of the RUC has been influential.[33] There have been a number of less-than-comfortable findings for members of the RUC. The investigation into the death of Eoin Morley, who was shot dead by the PIRA in April 1990, for example, found that the RUC failed to conduct a proper and thorough investigation into the murder (OPONI 2005). Critiques of the RUC's conduct included the lack of supervision of investigating officers, inadequate finger print audit systems and the lack of systems for the dissemination of information in Special Branch at the time (OPONI 2005). Paragraph 5.14 is clear in its critique:

> The failure by Special Branch to disseminate intelligence relating to the murder of Eoin Morley is unacceptable. There is nothing within the material examined by this office to justify or explain the rationale behind such a decision. This, together with the other evidence which was available, would have created significant investigative opportunities. These were significant failures.
>
> (OPONI 2005: 8)

Given some members of the security forces and unionist politician's ideological belief that the conduct of the RUC was never anything less than of the highest integrity, such findings have been interpreted as an overzealous and politically motivated search for evidence of collusion and corruption (NIAC 2005b: ev.63). A memorandum submitted by the NIRPOA to the NIAC provides some useful detail on this argument:

> There seems to be a culture within the Office of 'shopping' for cases to further increase the workload of the Office, also as part of the denigration process of past RUC operations…We have the perception that the Office is engaged in a witch-hunt against former members of the RUC in order to discredit them.
>
> (NIAC 2005b: ev.88)

Speaking to the close relationship between the security forces and unionist political elites, the memorandum submitted by the UUP closely mirrors these arguments. Critiquing the retrospective powers of the Police Ombudsman as amounting to a 'One-sided Truth Commission', it noted that:

> among broad unionism, the Ombudsman's office has been brought into disrepute and is viewed as being out to punish the security forces, RUC and Army and to rewrite history on behalf of republicanism…We believe that any proposal to allow the Ombudsman's office to interrogate elderly retired officers (some in their 70s and 80s) about events that took place perhaps 30 years before would confirm suspicions that an officially sanctioned witch-hunt into the security forces was taking place.
>
> (NIAC 2005b: appendix 12)[34]

As with public inquiries, the OPONI has therefore been regarded as providing a platform from which republicans can 'rewrite' the history of the conflict, provide 'evidence' to justify their activities and hold the state and its forces to account while evading examination of their own pasts. Moreover, the view that police officers 'went through and…still are going through a horrific experience at the hands of the Police Ombudsman's Office' has fed into and reinforced perceptions of how a formal truth recovery process would work (NIAC 2009: ev.287). A sense that the Legacy Commission proposed by the CGP or an alternative truth body would be both structurally predisposed towards believing allegations of collusion and provide a vehicle for the rewriting of history has consequently been compelling for many unionists.[35]

Documenting the past – A balanced equation?

Finally, and reinforcing the view that a truth process would provide a mechanism for republicans to put the 'state in the dock' is the matter of documentation on the past, specifically its availability.[36] Linked to the belief that the early prisoner release scheme has removed any incentive for ex-combatants to come forward with information, it has been argued that the inevitable disparity between documents and registration/regimental lists pertaining to the activities of the security forces and paramilitaries during the conflict would engender a highly one-sided process. With only a limited number of exceptions, this view was shared by unionists, representatives of the security forces and loyalist ex-combatants.

The Report of the CGP was a particular catalyst for these concerns. Punctuating the official pronouncements of politicians and representatives of the security forces during the Group's consultation period, the Report's recommendation that both the information recovery and thematic investigation units would have the power to compel the production of documents, and in the case of thematic investigations, the power to compel witnesses from Northern Ireland and Great Britain has been highly problematic (CGP 2009).[37] Professor Henry Patterson well explains this case and his remarks are worth repeating at some length:

> A remarkable feature of this 190-page report is that although it provides figures that show paramilitary groups were responsible for 90% of the deaths there is no attempt to deal with the problem of eliciting information from former republican and loyalist terrorists. This creates a profound imbalance in the mechanisms proposed … The report makes clear that the Commission will be looking at the documents collected by Stalker/Sampson inquiries into allegations of a police 'shoot-to-kill' policy in the 1980s and the three Inquiries by Lord Stevens into allegations of collusion. There is no consideration of how the Commission will be able to extract documents and witness statements from members of the IRA or UVF. Gerry Adams has already declared that republicans will not co-operate with a 'British appointed commission'. Pressed on this issue in interviews Denis Bradley admitted that while the Commission would have power over state agencies and members of the security forces it would have to rely on moral pressure from 'their communities' to ensure reciprocation from paramilitaries. This less than convincing response is symptomatic of the lack of intellectual and moral seriousness in the report.
>
> (Patterson 2009)

Combined with the existence of regimental numbers and registration lists of former service men (which could be used to identify persons to be compelled to testify), the disparity in documentation has caused many to argue that the balance of the Legacy Commission (or an alternative truth body) would be weighted towards those who committed violent acts and against the UK's 'legitimate' response to terrorist activity.[38] For those who are sceptical about republican's motives and intentions in a truth process, this 'accountability deficit' is best captured by Maurice Morrow's description of the Legacy Commission as 'another 'witch-hunt' and a dig and a drive against the RUC and UDR'.[39] That this perspective was shared by loyalist interviewees at first appears curious, given that many are ex-combatants themselves and are arguably in a similar position as regards documentation. However, as Bruce (1992b) points out, as pro-state terrorist organisations, they were easier to identify, infiltrate and hold to account. Much more detail on their activities during the conflict is therefore known and held by state authorities. The combined effect of these factors is a widespread perception that the only truth about the conflict that can be uncovered is that which focuses on the security forces and the state, furthering republican's aims of 'rewriting' the past.[40]

Members of the CGP were naturally keen to challenge these arguments.[41] Of particular importance are Lesley Carroll's comments on the Stevens Inquiries. As noted earlier in respect to the Finucane case, Sir John Stevens, the Deputy Chief Constable of the Cambridgeshire police force was appointed in September 1989 to head an investigation into allegations of collusion between the security forces and loyalist paramilitary organisations. Two subsequent investigations were carried out in 1993 and 2003. The full versions of the first and third Stevens Inquiries have never been published, and none of the second. As detailed above, the available summary of the third inquiry does however report that security force collusion with loyalist paramilitary killers led to a number of murders in Northern Ireland and that the death of Pat Finucane and student Brian Lambert could have been prevented if the security forces had not been involved in collusion (Stevens 2003). The details of these reports are therefore a source of considerable consternation for many members of the security forces and unionist politicians. However, during interview, Carroll posed a significant challenge to this perception:

> The Stevens material is all about, in people's minds, collusion, police, army collusion. I can say that the Stevens material will tell us as much, maybe more, about republican activity than it would tell us about security service activity, but even telling people that isn't enough. So there is something about trying to break in people's minds the view that the only truth that can be uncovered is truth about the state and its broad activities. Unless you can break that in people's minds, then they are going to understand it to be a kind of republican project.[42]

As demonstrated by Carroll, whether in respect to documentation, public inquiries or the OPONI, conditioned by a lack of trust, among unionists and loyalists, there is a widespread perception that the only truth about the conflict that can be recovered is that which focuses on the security forces and the state. In the opinion of Professor Henry Patterson, this has contributed to the feeling that they would be 'screwed over' in a truth process.[43] That such a view is inaccurate has been largely unrecognised and outweighs Ignatieff's (1996) argument that the objective of a truth process is to reduce the number of lies circulating unchallenged in public discourse. Again, this has stymied unionist's confidence in a truth process and their capacity to challenge republicans' narratives of the past.

Trust, truth-telling and the patterns of the past

Gready (2003: 2, cited in Dawson 2007: 5) and Granovetter (1985, cited in Hosmer 1995: 389) both make telling points about trust and political transitions, commenting, respectively, that 'Patterns from the past are often reconfigured rather than radically altered in transition' and that levels of trust in the past are directly correlated to levels of trust in the future. Against a backdrop of over 30 years of violent conflict and an uneven transition to peace, within unionism, there is a clear lack of trust in republican's commitment to truth-telling. As Phelps (2006) has argued, in other transitional jurisdictions, the absence of trust between previously warring sides has been a stumbling block to the establishment of a truth process. Leading unionists, the former UUP leader Tom Elliott and the DUP leader and First Minister Peter Robinson have affirmed that 'You just wouldn't get the truth' and 'What would be the purpose of having a Truth Commission when we know without a doubt that the terrorists will not be coming forward to tell the truth' (UTV News 2011; McAdam 2012). The following discussion will argue that two 'signal issues' have decisively informed unionist's opposition (Innes 2004). The first is the IRA's responsibility for the majority of 'the Disappeared', while the second concerns senior SF figures Martin McGuinness' and Gerry Adams' persistent attempts to silence and deny their past actions. Each will be explored in turn below.[44]

For many unionists and loyalists, the matter of the Disappeared exemplifies republican's commitment to truth-telling. As detailed in Chapter 3, between 1972 and 1986, 17 individuals were disappeared and secretly buried. Thirteen of those individuals have been acknowledged as killed and disappeared by the PIRA.[45] While primarily an expression of power and a demonstration of the ability to take control over life and deny the confirmation of death, forced disappearances leave unanswered questions of truth, justice, memory and closure for victims' families (Robins 2013; Edkins 2011). In an effort to concretise recovery efforts and in response to victims' demands, in 1999 a process was set in motion to facilitate the recovery of the remains of the disappeared. Under the Northern Ireland (Location of Victims' Remains Act) 1999 and the Criminal Justice (Location of Victims' Remains Act) 1999 (in the Irish Republic), the two governments established the ICLVR, the purpose of which is to obtain information, in strict confidence, which may lead to the whereabouts of the remaining Disappeared.[46] To date, ten bodies have been recovered.[47]

There have been a number of debates in the Northern Ireland Assembly regarding bringing truth and justice for the families of the Disappeared. For example, on 3 November 2008, Dominic Bradley (SDLP) moved the motion that 'this Assembly recognises the suffering of families of the Disappeared; believes that there has not been full disclosure on this issue; and calls on any individual or organisation with information which may lead to the remains of the Disappeared being returned to their loved ones for dignified burial, to bring forward that information without any further delay'.[48] The DUP's Lord Morrow's response conveys a sense of duplicity on the part of SF:

> This is an era in which we hear much about human rights. It is interesting to note that those who shout the loudest about such issues are strangely muted – to put it mildly – when it comes to the issues regarding the disappeared. If ever there was a violation of human rights, that is surely one of the greatest...There is a responsibility on Sinn Fein. It knows something. Society is crying out, and the families of the disappeared are turning to Sinn Fein directly for help...we are saying to Sinn Fein directly that it must give more. It knows more than it is telling those families, and it must give them assistance, and tell them exactly where their loved ones are. That is not too much to ask. Sinn Fein would demand it if the situation was the other way round.[49]

Again, in a more recent debate in April 2012, a clear overlap between unionists' attitudes towards republican's involvement in the fate of the disappeared and a formal truth process can be identified. As per Ricoeur (1999), UUP leader Mike Nesbitt identified a clear relationship, or lack of relationship, between testimony, trust and truth-telling,

> It is not just a question of acting in a civilised, humane and Christian manner. It is also a question of credibility – the credibility of any process of dealing with the past that involves those who took part divulging accurate information about what happened...How can we have confidence in dealing with the past when we cannot even satisfy four of the objective Ws? We know the who, we know the what and we know the when, but we do no know the where...As we look to deal with the past, we must have confidence not just in

> the truth but in it being delivered in a credible manner. It is not credible when we cannot even deliver the first four objective Ws.[50]

The disjuncture between republicans' calls for truth into cases of state violence and their reluctance to come forward with information in respect to the Disappeared has therefore been regarded as hypocritical and illustrative of the lack of integrity behind their calls for an independent international truth commission (UUP 2011c).[51] Writing in the wake of the SF 'Truth March' which took place in Belfast City Centre, August 2007, to highlight cases of alleged collusion, the UUP MLA for Fermanagh and South Tyrone Tom Elliott took up this case:

> Republicans have a blatant cheek asking for truth when they have consistently lied to the people of both Northern Ireland and the Republic of Ireland for the past four decades. If Republicans really want the truth to be told then a good starting point is to start with themselves. Let them tell the public the truth about Kingsmills, La Mon House, Enniskillen, Narrow Water.
>
> (UUP 2007b)

Adding further weight to these arguments are what I would argue have become two iconic reference points in unionists mobilisation against truth recovery – the conduct of senior SF figures – the Deputy First Minister Martin McGuinness and SF President Gerry Adams. Founded on the belief that the republican 'economy of truth' 'has served them very well', reference to these factors were made by the vast majority of interviewees.[52] They also continue to structure and inform many unionists' contributions to discussions on dealing with the past (UUP 2012ce). Martin McGuinness' evidence at the Saville Inquiry into the events on Bloody Sunday, 30 January 1972, is intensely problematic in terms of republican's commitment to, or capacity for, truth-telling. As the IRA's second-in-command in Londonderry at the time of Bloody Sunday, McGuinness was called to provide evidence to the Saville Inquiry in late-2003. When under cross-examination, McGuinness made frequent reference to a republican 'code of honour' – 'there is a code of honour that you do not disclose information about other IRA volunteers or about people who help the struggle for freedom in Ireland' – as a way to evade answering questions about the conduct or identity of other IRA members at that time.[53] Lord Saville subsequently concluded that McGuinness' 'duty of honour overrides the desire of the families for the Tribunal to discover the whole truth about the events of Bloody Sunday'.[54] McGuinness' conduct has since been held as an example par excellence of republican's duplicity around calls for truth recovery. Providing evidence to the NIAC, the remarks of Ann Boal, a representative of the Disabled Police Officers' Association well illustrate this point:

> All you have to do is look at the Bloody Sunday inquiry...I listened to statements made by Mr. McGuinness...He made it clear that the IRA take an oath of allegiance which forbids them from telling. Who are going to be the truth tellers and who are going to be the truth demanders?
>
> (NIAC 2005a: ev.141).

The continued denial of SF President Gerry Adams that he was ever a member of the IRA, despite compelling evidence of his senior position in that organisation provided by Coogan (2002), Bishop and Mallie (1987), Moloney (2002) and others, has also become a key marker of unionists' and loyalists' opposition to a formal truth process. For a number of interviewees, the demand that Adams admit he was once a member of the IRA was identified as the ideal starting point for a truth process. The DUP's Nelson McCausland for example remarked:

> The feeling is that the intent behind all of this is to keep creating grievances against the state whilst never subjecting yourself to any scrutiny. That view is reinforced every time Gerry Adams says I was never in the IRA. People conclude that if that is what he is still saying and if he is living in that world of denial about it, how could you ever believe anything that they would say in terms of truth recovery.[55]

Likewise, Billy McQuiston, a UPRG representative argued

> If there is going to be a truth recovery process, I think from the loyalist side the first thing they should do is call Gerry Adams and ask him was he ever a member of the IRA and if he says no, which he inevitably will do, then that will set the tone for the rest of it. You can then just forget about it.[56]

However, again, one notable exception to these sentiments was the former PUP leader Dawn Purvis. Responding to the author's suggestion that one of the main factors structuring unionists' and loyalists' opposition to a truth process is the credibility of nationalists' and republicans' calls for truth, Purvis called for a greater political maturity and ownership of the process of dealing with the past:

> That is unionism all the time. David Ervine used to say that unionism is clairvoyant and it is never good news. You are not going to know until you try...just because you feel that someone won't take part, is not an excuse not to have it or not to attend and I think people need to take responsibility for themselves rather than wonder what somebody else is going to do.[57]

Reflecting a firmly victim-centred approach to transitional justice rather than one that is entangled in political claims making, Purvis went on to argue that if people are genuine and sincere about helping victims, then there should be a commitment to being open and getting information out (Robins 2013).[58] Her remarks were, however, at some remove from the 'mainstream' unionist and loyalist view.

Unionists' and loyalists' views are entirely understandable[59] and it is inevitable that a formal truth process would scrutinise the role played by Adams and McGuinness during the conflict. It is however also arguable that Adams' position is based upon a number of practical legal reasons. For example, if Adams were to admit membership of the IRA, a criminal offence, it is possible that he could be prosecuted by the Public Prosecution Service, and, under the Terrorism Act (2000), serve a prison term of up to ten years. By contrast, Martin McGuinness, the SF Deputy First Minister, was able to admit that he was once a member of the IRA during the Saville Inquiry as he had served prison time for activities conducted during the conflict and because the Attorney General stipulated that during Lord Saville's inquiry, any written material or oral evidence provided by a witness could not be used to incriminate that witness in later criminal proceedings (McEvoy and Mallinder 2008). This was considered essential in order to reach the truth of what happened on Bloody Sunday (McEvoy and Mallinder 2008). As illustrated by the CGP's (2009) recommendation for a limited immunity, it is likely that as a matter of practicality, any future truth process would be accompanied by a similar measure.[60] Therefore, ironically, the only circumstances in which Adams would be able to admit membership of the IRA would be in a formal truth process. Unionist politicians have remained silent on this point.

Providing a further point of contrast is the suggestion that not only would regimental numbers and documents ensure that members of the security forces would be held to account, but also that their participation would be of a much more 'willing' and 'honest nature'. A number of interviewees advocated this point – a senior DUP advisor for example argued that 'state forces…are much more likely to be open and honest about their role' while on UTV Live's 'Search for Truth' recording Tom Elliott raised the question of 'why engage in it if you get *a better truth* from one section of the community than you would from another [author's emphasis]?'[61] These perspectives speak to competing perceptions around 'loyalty' and 'trustworthiness' and 'disloyalty' and 'untrustworthiness' (Connor 2007).

The assumption of a 'better' or more 'willing' truth from the security forces is not, however, entirely correct and, in itself, represents a stylised version of unionist social memory. Rather, powerful cultures of obfuscation can also be identified within the security forces. In Zerubavel's (2010: 36) opinion, such cultures of silence are often collective rather than individual affairs – 'it takes only one person to produce speech…it requires the co-operation of all to produce silence'. One of the best known and most controversial cases are the circumstances surrounding the investigation of Sir John Stalker, the former Deputy Chief Constable of the Greater Manchester Police, into the deaths of six men who were shot dead by the RUC in three separate incidents in November and December 1982. Stalker issued an apparently critical interim report that recommended 11 prosecutions (Lashmar 2003). Shortly afterwards, he was removed from the investigation following allegations of professional misconduct (McEvoy 2006). Stalker's (1988) memoirs reveal that throughout his investigation, working relations were characterised by a constant low-level friction that slowed down simple jobs and made progress difficult and extended to prevarication and obstruction. This included the Chief Constable Sir John Hermon's persistent obstruction of Stalker's efforts to obtain access to a MI5 tape or its transcript that was crucial to the investigation of the death of Michael Tighe, one of the six men (Stalker 1988). Stalker (1988) also records his belief that he was removed from the investigation for reasons of political expediency, motivated in part by the prospect that his findings would have caused huge political embarrassment and led to a number of resignations. These themes were repeated during the former Police Ombudsman Nuala O'Loan's 'Operation Ballast' investigation into allegations of collusion between loyalist paramilitary informers and members of the RUC.[62] O'Loan and her team of investigators encountered officers who, for example, gave evasive, contradictory and on occasion farcical answers to questions and senior officers, including two former assistant chief constables, seven former detective chief superintendents and two former detective superintendents who refused to assist the investigation (O'Loan 2010; Irish Independent 2007). The Ombudsman's report also exposed instances of the destruction of evidence, falsification of notes and the blocking of searches for paramilitary arms dumps (OPONI 2007).[63] While largely undiscussed or unacknowledged by unionist political elites or representatives of the security forces, cultures of silence are therefore not unique to republican politicians and ex-combatants (Winter 2010).

For unionists, the three examples given above are critical markers in the truth debate. At each, the conviction that republicans are neither committed to truth-telling or open participation in a truth process has been heightened. Again, this is regarded as part of the attempt to 'rewrite' history from a republican perspective and to marginalise unionists' narratives of loss (Trouillot 1995). Brewer (2010: 156) argues that 'If it is to serve its purposes…'truth' has to be perceived as plausible; if not, it is difficult to see what purpose it serves'. In this context of endemic mistrust, calls for participation in a formal truth process or the assertion, made by SF, that republican ex-combatants would be willing to participate in an independent international truth commission are little more than empty rhetoric for many unionists (Eolas 2003; BBC News 2009b; SF 2013).

Conclusion

This chapter has argued that the notion of trust is central to transitional justice debates and, in particular, the matter of truth recovery. Set against a context of personal and social trauma and cultures of denial and silence, trust is hard won and easily lost. If a truth process is to be established and function in a impartial and legitimate manner, there are at least three prerequisites: one, that all parties to the conflict can be trusted to participate; two, that the truth mechanism commands the support and trust of all parties; and three, that the 'truths' it recovers are perceived to be plausible.

For unionist political elites, calls for truth, primarily made by members of the nationalist and republican community, have been preceded by over 30 years of political violence, during which the greatest number of atrocities were committed by the PIRA and a peace process that is felt to be structurally biased against the unionist/loyalist community. As Sabel (1993, cited in Misztal 2003) argues, the extension of trust in any particular setting depends, in part, on 'the actors' reinterpreting their collective past in such a way that trusting cooperation comes to be a natural feature of their common heritage. Borne out of their empirical experience during the conflict and peace process, unionist's mistrust of the 'disloyal' 'other' has significantly influenced their attitudes towards truth recovery. As discussed above, their concerns centre around a number of themes – that truth recovery has and will be 'state centric', contributing to a process where the overwhelming emphasis is on the actions of the state during the conflict and that they cannot trust republican politicians or ex-combatants to honestly participate in a truth recovery exercise. The dominant perception among many unionists, loyalists and members of the security forces is that such actors would use a truth process to 'rewrite' the history of the conflict.

Unionists' lack of trust in the republican 'other' therefore presents a significant stumbling block to their further engagement with debates on dealing with the past and, as I have noted above, many of their concerns are well founded. However, as is also argued above, so great is their lack of trust in republicans that it has, at times, obscured the potential benefits of a truth process for the unionist community. This includes investigating questions of significance for unionist and loyalist communities and the overarching argument that an objective and respected source of truth narrows the capacity of politicians, ex-combatants, victims or other actors to assert partial or untrue versions of history (Ignatieff 1996; McEvoy 2006). As the Northern Ireland journalist Brian Rowan has argued, 'The past will only be a republican project and process if others allow it to be' (Rowan 2012a). The following chapter argues that alongside a lack of trust in the 'other', a lack of trust in self can also be identified among unionists and loyalists. Adding to their concerns that a truth process would marginalise their voices and experiences, this chapter will argue that bound up with notions of 'loyalty', unionists' and loyalists' lack of confidence in their historical narrative and how to present that narrative, is, at present, mitigating against their engagement with the truth debate.

Notes

1 McKeown Database of Deaths Associated with Violence in Northern Ireland. Available at: http://cain.ulst.ac.uk/victims/mckeown/ (accessed on 1 March 2013).
2 While beyond the scope of this book, it should be noted that the tendency to distrust the actions and motivations of nationalists and republicans has a considerable historical lineage (see for example: Farrington 2006; McAuley and Tonge 2007; McGladdery 2002; Spencer 2008).
3 This point was less problematic for loyalist paramilitaries who concluded as early as 1987 that the inclusion of SF in the devolved structures would be essential for success (Shirlow 2012).
4 Qualifying prisoners were defined as those convicted of a scheduled or terrorist offence before 10 April 1998; that s/he is not a supporter of an organisation not on ceasefire; that if released, the prisoner would not be likely to become a supporter of such an organisation; and, for life sentenced prisoners, if released immediately would not be a danger to the public (Northern Ireland (Sentences) Act 1998, s3 (2–7), cited in Dwyer 2007).
5 See Chapter 6 for a full exploration of narratives of betrayal and sacrifice among the policing family.
6 Interview, Ian Paisley Junior, DUP, 12 September 2009.
7 It should be noted that in the interests of clarity, this discussion is restricted to the cases of Hamill, Nelson, Finucane and Wright. Given its relevance to policing, the Smithwick Tribunal is explored in full in Chapter 6.
8 The INLA was formed in 1974, following a split in the Official IRA.
9 Both MacLean *et al.* (2010) and Morland *et al.* (2011) adopted a different definition of collusion than Justice Cory, concentrating on acts of 'commission' rather than acts of 'omission and commission'.
10 See: www.eire.dk/library/nelson_tale.html (accessed on 29 February 2009).
11 See: www.rosemarynelsoninquiry.org (accessed on 10 February 2010).
12 Rosemary Nelson Inquiry Report. House of Commons debates, Hansard, 23 May 2011: Column 644.
13 See: www.roberthamillinquiry.org/ (accessed on 10 February 2010).
14 Pat Finucane. House of Commons debates, Hansard, 12 October 2011. The reasons behind the government's apparent change of mind have been the subject of some speculation. Brian Rowan has suggested that it is 'Because of what might be shoveled to the surface, information and a pattern of dark activities that might challenge all of us to re-think the narrative of the past 40 years.' See for example: Rowan (2011), Belfast Telegraph (2012).
15 Interview, Esmond Birnie, UUP, 19 May 2009.
16 Dealing with the Past. Private Members' Business, Northern Ireland Assembly debates, 10 October 2011.
17 Pat Finucane Case. Private Members' Business, Northern Ireland Assembly debates, 7 November 2011.
18 Interview, Danny Kennedy, UUP, 5 May 2009; Interview, Sir Reg Empey, UUP, 17 April 2009.
19 Interview, Ian Paisley Junior, DUP, 12 September 2009. As explored later in this book, that the British government 'conceded' to republicans' demands by

funding public inquiries into so-called 'republican issues' has also led to further suspicion and hostility among some unionists.

20 The DUP's Jimmy Spratt, for example, emphasised that the inquiry was not an important matter for his Castlereagh constituents, while among the more sceptical, there was a feeling that the inquiry was simply a 'sop' to unionists and loyalists, inadequately designed to counteract the greater number of inquiries demanded by nationalists and republicans. Interview, Jimmy Spratt, DUP, 20 May 2009; Interview, Billy McQuiston, UPRG, 18 June 2009.

21 Interview, Allistair Finlay, PSNI, 4 August 2009.

22 'The RUC George Cross Foundation has welcomed the finding that there is no evidence of any act or omission by the RUC which directly facilitated Rosemary Nelson's murder…We hope this Report will once and for all put to rest the offensive and now discredited allegations of collusion with the people who carried out this despicable murder' (RUC GC F 2011).

23 Interview, Dave Cox, HET, 28 September 2009.

24 Dealing with the Past. Private Members' Business, Northern Ireland Assembly debates, 10 October 2011.

25 Interview, Dawn Purvis, 6 April 2009.

26 Interview, Dawn Purvis, 6 April 2009. See also: Rowan (2008) 'Purvis dismisses Truth Commission', *Belfast Telegraph*, 27 September 2008.

27 Again, Dawn Purvis acknowledged this point, commenting, 'There is going to be an imbalance in any truth recovery process because those who carried out the greater number of atrocities here are going to have the greatest amount of focus placed on them. At the minute that doesn't seem to be the case because the IRA were responsible for killing most of the people in Northern Ireland'. As the above discussion has demonstrated, her views were, however, outside the prevailing assumptions on this debate. Interview, Dawn Purvis, 6 April 2009. See also: Belfast Telegraph (2010b) 'Politicians must have honest conversation on Northern Ireland's violent past: Dawn Purvis', *Belfast Telegraph*, 22 February 2010.

28 In addition to 18 deaths at Narrow Water, these tragedies resulted in 12 deaths at La Mon and 11 at Enniskillen. All victims were Protestants and in each case the IRA was responsible. See also: Patterson (2011) 'People who risk being written out of history', *Belfast Telegraph*, 28 July 2011.

29 See: Sutton Index of Deaths. http://cain.ulst.ac.uk/sutton/index.html (accessed on 1 March 2013).

30 Despite expressing strong opposition to the idea of a formal truth process, EPIC's Tom Roberts also remarked that he had given some consideration to this idea, and argued that certain SF leaders would not be delighted about the prospect of full disclosure of their past activities. Interview, Tom Roberts, EPIC, 28 April 2009.

31 Interview, Professor Roy McClelland, 26 March 2009.

32 The difficulties of combining these two functions have been well documented and were clearly expressed by the former Police Ombudsman Al Hutchinson (OPONI 2011a; BBC News 2011c; Clarke 2011a).

33 See for example: News Letter (2007) 'Ombudsman 'pursued a witch-hunt against the RUC', *News Letter*, 6 November 2007.

34 Similar themes were expressed in light of the former Police Ombudsman Al Hutchinson's suggestion that former RUC officers should be compelled to provide evidence to the OPONI. DUP MLA Paul Girvan argued that these proposals were motivated by the desire 'to constantly have a witch hunt against those who served in the RUC' (UTV News 2012). At the time of writing, these proposals have not been taken forward.

35 Interview, Raymond White, NIRPOA, 19 May 2009; Interview, Jim McDonald, RUC GC F, 10 August 2009.
36 Interview, Nelson McCausland, DUP, 3 April 2009.
37 Consultative Group on the Past. Private Members' Business, Northern Ireland Assembly debates, 2 February 2009. Among the most critical was Maurice Morrow who argued that this recommendation revealed the 'real intent' behind the report – rewriting history in favour of a republican analysis of the past rather than truth and reconciliation. Interview, Maurice Morrow, DUP, 20 April 2009.
38 Interview, Raymond White, NIRPOA, 19 May 2009; Interview, Gregory Campbell, DUP, 12 May 2009.
39 Interview, Maurice Morrow, DUP, 20 April 2009.
40 Interview, Nelson McCausland, DUP, 3 April 2009.
41 Interview, Archbishop Eames, 23 October 2009; Interview, Denis Bradley, 8 October 2009; Interview, Lesley Carroll, 10 June 2009.
42 Interview, Lesley Carroll, 10 June 2009.
43 Interview, Professor Henry Patterson, 22 April 2009.
44 While each of these factors would be an important site of investigation for any truth process, it is important to note that they are not the sole cause of unionists' mistrust. Rather, as party political documentation makes clear, unionists have persistently called on republicans to make known the truth about a range of atrocities during the conflict – including, for example, the La Mon bombing and the Kingsmills massacre and their mistrust of republican's extends beyond Adams and McGuinness. However, the above topics have been, and were during interview, an enduring theme in unionist's discussions on truth. The emphasis here reflects this point.
45 www.iclvr.ie/en/ICLVR/Pages/TheDisappeared (accessed on 17 October 2007). The issue of 'the Disappeared' is one of the few actions committed by the IRA during the conflict that has been acknowledged by republican leaders as a 'human rights abuse'. Their response has included internal IRA investigations, the return of one body and the suggestion of a number of other sites where the authorities were able to begin digging (McEvoy 2006).
46 www.iclvr.ie/en/ICLVR/Pages/Home%20Page (accessed on 17 October 2007).
47 See: www.iclvr.ie/en/ICLVR/Pages/TheDisappeared (accessed on 17 October 2007). For full details on each of the disappeared see: http://thedisappeared ni.co.uk/ (accessed on 25 March 2013).
48 The Disappeared. Northern Ireland Assembly debates, 3 November 2008.
49 The Disappeared. Northern Ireland Assembly debates, 3 November 2008.
50 Disappeared Victims. Private Members' Business, Northern Ireland Assembly debates, 16 April 2012.
51 Interview, Martin Snodden, 3 April 2009; Interview, Jim Allister, TUV, 20 March 2009; Interview with Jim McDonald, RUC GC F, 10 August 2009.
52 Interview, Jim Allister, TUV, 20 March 2009.
53 Bloody Sunday Inquiry Transcript, Day 391, 5 November 2003. Available at: http://webarchive.nationalarchives.gov.uk/20101103103930/http://report.blood y-sunday-inquiry.org/transcripts/Archive/Ts391.htm (accessed on 11 June 2013).
54 Bloody Sunday Inquiry Transcript, Day 390, 4 November 2003. Available at: http://webarchive.nationalarchives.gov.uk/20101103103930/http://report.blood y-sunday-inquiry.org/transcripts/Archive/Ts390.htm (accessed on 11 June 2013).
55 Interview, Nelson McCausland, DUP, 3 April 2009.
56 Interview, Billy McQuiston, UPRG, 18 June 2009.

57 Interview, Dawn Purvis, 6 April 2009.
58 Interview, Dawn Purvis, 6 April 2009.
59 As detailed in the introduction, it should also be noted that the IRA did not meet with the CGP or give oral evidence to the Smithwick Tribunal, despite the Tribunal's assurance that safeguards would be put in place (Patterson 2008; BBC News 2013a).
60 See: http://blogs.qub.ac.uk/amnesties/ for an in-depth overview of this debate (accessed on 11 June 2013).
61 Interview, Richard Bullick, DUP, 25 March 2009; Interview, Terry Spence, PFNI, 30 June 2009; UTV Live, 15 June 2011, 'Search for Truth', author's recording.
62 This case in explored in full in Chapter 6.
63 A recent report by the current Police Ombudsman Michael Maguire into the death of three individuals, who entered a house known by the RUC to contain a IRA booby-trap bomb, also reports that the investigation was hampered by the failure of some retired officers to co-operate (OPONI 2013).

Chapter 5

Truth, confidence and loyalty

'They have a story to tell, it is a horrific story but they are still not convinced that it is a level playing field out there'.[1]

Introduction

In June 2010, the CVSNI (2010b: 36) reported that it 'is deeply concerned that there is a serious and profound confidence deficit in the unionist community concerning the concept of truth recovery'. That participants in a truth process may lack confidence in their ability to articulate their experiences is not uncommon, and in the transitional justice sphere the notion of confidence and its relevance to truth recovery is typically discussed in relation to gender representation, the security of victims and combatants and the importance of linking transitional justice and socio-economic transformation (Ni Aolain *et al.* 2011; O'Rourke 2013; Sriram *et al.* 2012; Waldorf 2012). This chapter draws on these themes, but also extends this analysis to explore how unionists and loyalists status as *loyal* pro-state actors has affected their confidence to participate in the truth recovery debate.

Loyalty is a social emotion that sits within 'a thick web of morally laden expectation. It is not just a feeling or a sentiment. It is demonstrated in our behaviour and our choices' (Rothstein 2001: 3). Denoting relationships, reciprocities and expectations, loyalty indicates how people should act in particular circumstances and enables others to predict responses to their actions (Connor 2007). This chapter examines the complexities of the term loyalty and how such a notion maps directly onto attitudes to truth recovery and contested understandings of the past. On one level, civic trust and citizens' loyalty to the state and nation are key to building stable democracies and can be fostered by transitional justice mechanisms (Mihr 2012). Yet, as this book has argued, for those who are loyal to the pre-transitional regime, truth and justice policies not only attack the raison d'etre or the legitimacy of that regime, but also challenge its supporters and the status quo (De Brito *et al.* 2001). As the quotation at the beginning of this chapter suggests, it is not the case that unionists and loyalists reject the idea of recovering truth about the past per se, or the importance of telling their story. Indeed, many interviewees spoke of their constituents' need to know what happened to their loved ones – 'they just want to know the truth, know why it happened', while a May 2012 editorial in the *Belfast Telegraph* ran under the heading of 'Unionists must realize it would do them good to talk' (Rowan 2012a).[2] Rather, this chapter argues that, as pro-state actors, unionist's and loyalist's sense of loyalty has impacted on their confidence to participate in a truth process, both in terms of how they can articulate their narratives of the past, and how to engage with the structural mechanics of such a body. Four sites of tension are identified and explored in turn: the notion of 'loyalty as silence'; the ability to 'sell' one's story; the impact of socio-economic alienation; and concerns over the structure of a truth process.

Explaining 'loyalty' and 'loyalism'

Connor (2007: 58) argues that loyalty 'embraces solicitude, unconditional love, personal loyalty and willingness to sacrifice for others'. Like anger, hatred, shame or guilt, loyalty is a social emotion that is often intensified by the experience of communal violence (Barbalet 2002; Brewer 2010, 2011). The signing of a peace accord does not necessarily assuage these emotional responses and peace processes often carry the effects of the emotional baggage of war well into the post-conflict period (Brewer 2010). Before looking at the relationship between truth recovery and loyalty, it is helpful at this juncture to explore in detail the sociology of loyalty and to illustrate how loyalty is a fundamental component of unionist's and loyalist's identity.

Connor (2007) has identified three aspects of loyalty that are relevant to this analysis: the relationship to identity, motivation to action and layering. Becoming 'loyal' is the result of socialisation and loyalty is engendered through shared experiences, collective memories, language, traditions and sentiments (Jollimore 2012). Signifying membership and a sense of belonging to a distinctive group, loyalty plays a role in the construction of the self and collective identities (Misztal 2003). Bound by a 'deep horizontal comradeship', this linkage of group membership and collective identity creates the imagined (political) community (Anderson 2006: 25, 26). For Fletcher (1993: 33), it is 'membership in a group competing with other groups' that is the hallmark of loyalty. Loyalty is therefore defined against an 'other' and to act outside the norms of one's familial, institutional or national group is to be 'disloyal' (Hirschman 1970).

As a marker of collective identity, loyalty also offers a sense of belonging and identification with particular people, causes, places and institutions (Connor 2007). In this sense, loyalty can be multiple, layered and overlapping (Connor 2007). Typical and potentially conflicting sites of loyalty include the family, religion and the nation. Different weightings may be attached to each element and the balance between sentiment and advantage in the making of loyalty may change subtly or dramatically over time and from place to place (Waller and Linklater 2003). Social, political, economic and cultural forces determine which layer is prominent and has the most influence on motivating action (Lamb 2010).

Third, as an emotional state, loyalty can provide justification for action, behaviour and cognition (Connor 2007). This may be particularly true in the case of ethnic conflict. As Ruane and Todd (2003) point out, much of the contemporary political science literature on ethnic conflict views ethnic and ethno-national communities as eliciting deep loyalty, intense attachment and resistance to change on the part of their members. Conflict therefore makes for more urgent loyalties and more insistent claims on actors 'to defend and work within the role' (Connor 2007: 50). For Anderson (2006: 224), 'it is this fraternity that makes it possible, over the past two centuries, for so many millions of people, not so much to kill, as willingly to die for such limited imaginings'. An element of reciprocity can also be detected, particularly where loyalty is contractual rather than natural (Fletcher 1993). Affective and effective, and marking the boundaries of inclusion and exclusion, loyalty is both a framework for social action and a vehicle for collective identity (Jollimore 2012).

In Northern Ireland, 'loyalty' has traditionally been associated with the Protestant unionist/loyalist pro-state community who remain 'loyal' to their communities, the British crown and the Northern Ireland state. The invocations of trust and support and the opposites of disloyalty, betrayal and mistrust levelled against the nationalist and republican community and the IRA's campaign of armed violence have been central organising features of political and cultural life (Barry 2003). The previous chapter clearly illustrated how this lack of trust influences attitudes to truth recovery. There are some subtle differences between unionists and loyalists. Connor's (2007) typology provides a useful framework within which to explore their views.

For unionists and the security forces, their loyalty is to the British crown, state and the union with Great Britain (Cochrane 1999). The following quotation by the DUP's Nigel Dodds (cited in Cochrane 1999: 44) well illustrates this ethos:

> ...the general principle of unionism, I suppose, is the maintenance of the union with Britain. My view is that at the end of the day, we have got to preserve a British way of life in Northern Ireland. That means seeking at all times to preserve the Union.

The discourse and actions of the security forces has, likewise, been replete with declarations of the 'utter dedication and commitment of the RUC' (PFNI 1999). The strongest practical manifestation of this discourse was the loss of 305 police officers who are presented as willing to pay the ultimate sacrifice – death – in the name of preserving peace and security (Ellison and Smyth 2000). Given the close relationship between unionists and the security forces, their loyalty is reciprocal, the former UUP leader Sir Reg Empey declaring, 'We will not allow the courage of the RUC, UDR, RIR and Regular Army to be besmirched by Sinn Fein orchestrated propaganda'.[3]

Loyalists have also expressed devotion to the British Crown and flag, the imagined political community of Ulster and to the Protestant working class and their local concerns (McAuley 2010). This attachment to a 'British way of life' is often constituted by loyalists as rational, irreproachable and intuitively natural and is offset by strong constructions of the 'disloyal' 'other' – those nationalists and republicans who challenged the legitimacy of the Northern Ireland state (McAuley 2010). The natural relation to a discourse of loyalty was that of defence – the motivation to action (Connor 2007). For both the UVF and UDA, defence of their communities against the threat of republican violence and to preserve the union between Northern Ireland and Great Britain was the primary aim. In total, loyalists were responsible for 996 deaths between 1969 and 2005, including 54 nationalist or republican activists and 712 Catholic civilians (Shirlow 2012). Moreover, reflecting Waller and Linklater's (2003) argument on the malleability of loyalty, their loyalty may be shifting. Spencer (2008), for example, argues that while loyalty was initially directed towards the British government and monarch, with the development of the peace process and the politics of 'new loyalism' – a more socially aware, inclusive and disproportionately working class politics – loyalty is now increasingly expressed in relation to the Protestant working class and their local concerns.

Truth, confidence and loyalty as silence

The first area of difficulty for many unionists and loyalists concerns the idea of loyalty as silence. This form of silence stems from the unconditional commitment and perseverance that is intrinsic to true loyalty, as, according to Lamb (2010: 999), 'Loyalty to group does not simply presume that the group is right, but that they care about the right things and make their judgements, even when they are mistaken, in terms of those shared values'. As pro-state actors, this sense of loyalty has affected unionists' and loyalists' confidence to participate in a truth process and, in turn, has informed their opposition to truth recovery. A number of manifestations can be identified and are explored in turn below. They concern unionist's reluctance to criticise the state and its institutions, a determination, at least on the part of loyalist ex-combatants, to differentiate themselves from nationalists' and republicans' calls for truth and, in terms of visibility and legal architecture, *who* pro-state actors should direct their questions to.

Unionists reluctance to criticise the state and its institutions or to support any political enterprise that would be considered tantamount to doing so is, as Bruce (1992b) has pointed out, a perennial problem for pro-state groups, as to speak against the state is to put oneself or one's organisation into immediate competition with the very state you claim to support.[4] Such silence may also be a strategic necessity. Cairns *et al.* (2003) for example report that throughout the Northern Ireland conflict, loyalist prisoners were dissuaded from speaking publicly about the conditions they experienced in prison.[5] Doing so was regarded as bolstering the nationalist and republican cause and as engaging in a nationalist and republican 'occupation'.[6] As reflected by a community leader in a loyalist area, loyalists were silenced by the need to preserve the binary opposition between 'them' and 'us':

> Anything that we did have, by way of a crisis, we quickly had to hide because we didn't want to show weakness. Showing weakness would have meant that the [Northern Ireland] state wasn't working. It would have been to say 'The state has failed' and that would have given credence to our enemies [as cited in Cairns *et al.* 2003: 26].

Ian Paisley Junior's involvement with the UDR Four (UDR4) campaign – a form of truth recovery itself – exemplifies some of these dynamics and is of relevance to the broader truth debate. This case involved four members of the UDR, a regiment of the British army, who had been convicted of murdering Catholic civilian Adrian Carroll in 1983 and, who, following their conviction in 1986, continued to proclaim their innocence and campaigned for their release (Parkinson 1998; McKittrick *et al.* 2007). The campaign therefore involved Protestant Ulstermen, serving in a regiment of the British Army, engaging in an unprecedented contest of a British courts legal decision (Parkinson 1998). As written by Paisley (1991: 1) at the time,

> These men have been caught between the devil and the deep blue sea. On the one hand they are Protestant, British and ex-soldiers who were part of the British way of life in Ulster. They detest the ideas of those who challenge the Northern Ireland system accepting that the police, army and courts were doing a job that had to be done. On the other hand, they are now precariously placed out on a limb, claiming that they were wrongly convicted by the system they supported.

Paisley's involvement and commitment to 'searching for truth' was problematic for many unionist onlookers and party members. The parallels drawn between his work and the Guildford 4, Birmingham 6 and Maguire family campaigns meant his efforts were interpreted as questioning the legitimacy of the state – an indicator of 'disloyalty'.[7] Erwin (1992: 405), for example, makes the point that 'A *really* loyal person subjugates (at least to some extent) his or her private interests to those of the object of loyalty' [author's emphasis]. During interview, the sense of sheer frustration conveyed to the author at the disjuncture between such mind-sets and what he considered a rightful and just course of action was palpable – "how could you be doing the same thing [as republicans] and are you questioning the legitimacy of the state by doing that?' No, I am searching for truth and in doing that search, this is the just outcome'.[8] As Fletcher (1993) argues, it is membership of the group that is the hallmark of loyalty and group members should act with partiality towards those to whom they are loyal (Lamb 2010). To speak against the state has therefore been interpreted as compromising unionists sense of 'we-ness' with the British state – a form of 'disloyalty' more readily associated with nationalists and republicans.

That loyalty is inseparable from unionists and loyalist's sense of collective identity immediately poses a challenge in terms of their willingness to support or participate in a formal truth process. As emphasised by Hayner (2011), for any truth recovery body to operate effectively, the participation of all parties to the conflict is imperative. In Northern Ireland, this would inevitably include the British state, which, as detailed in the introduction, is a point of contention in itself. For unionists, as supporters of the state, to engage in an initiative that would necessarily ask the 'hard' and 'difficult' questions of it and the security forces' conduct during the conflict is the antithesis of loyalty and an affront to their sense of imagined political community (Anderson 2006). The following comments by a member of the UPRG best capture this case: 'It is our state…it would be anti-state, it would be against everything that we stand for'.[9] As this interviewee suggests, maintaining a strategic silence on the past may therefore be a way of honouring and protecting their relationship with the British state.

As suggested above, a desire to differentiate themselves from nationalists and republicans also informed participant's responses, particularly among loyalist ex-combatants. Borne out of a defensive mentality, there was a sense among certain interviewees that 'war is war' and that combatants should be ready to accept the consequences of violent conflict (Rolston 2006: 664). To call for repeated reinvestigations of the past was consequently interpreted as breaking the conventions of military loyalty or diluting the 'warrior's honour' (Ignatieff 1998). Participant's responses also hinted at a complicated understanding of victimhood. As suggested in Chapter 3, this conceptualisation of victimhood did not automatically categorise ex-combatants as 'victims' and, in some cases, was quite critical of how the term 'victim' has been co-opted for political ends: 'Our view on it is you are involved in dirty old business, if you can't stand the heat get out of the kitchen…from a Protestant point of view we are not used to gurning, big boys don't cry' (see, for example, Brewer 2006; Brown 2011;

McEvoy and McConnachie 2012; Smyth 2009).[10] Moreover, these sentiments extended to discussion on the capacity of republican politicians and ex-combatants to meaningfully engage with a truth process. In particular, two interviewees attempted to link the 'military' nature of their campaign and the 'individual' nature of Protestant culture to a greater honesty over their past actions and compared this unfavorably with republican's 'political' campaign and more collective political culture (English 2003). For these interviewees at least, these structural differences were interpreted as a disadvantage for loyalists if a truth process were to be established:

> There is a different ethos in the Protestant community, murder is murder, it is wrong, the UDA, UVF or whatever, no doubt they knew it was wrong before they went out and did it, whereas the Catholic side, there is all the psychology – it isn't a human being you are killing, it's a uniform – what a load of bollocks.[11]

Further complicating these points is the question of *who* pro-state organisations should direct their questions towards. According to Bruce (1992b), during a conflict, from both a military and political perspective, anti-state organisations have a wide range of highly visible and 'legitimate' targets to pursue. Conversely, pro-state organisations have a much smaller target as members of anti-state groups tend to be much harder to find and keep themselves well protected within their communities (Bruce 1992b). Highlighting concerns of collusion between state forces and loyalist paramilitaries, in Northern Ireland, republican's calls for truth have been directed towards the visible architecture of the British state. Couched within the framework of international human rights law, these cases also have a resonance beyond Northern Ireland (Campbell and Ni Aolain 2003). Conversely, for unionists and loyalists, it is much harder to pinpoint and mobilise behind such readily identifiable causes – a point further complicated by the fact the Northern Ireland conflict took place in a liberal democracy (Campbell and Connolly 2012). Their relative silence and lack of confidence may therefore also stem from the fact that they do not have such easily accessible structures to pursue:

> They have a legitimate government to pursue, they have legitimate structures to pursue, they have real people who you know were in the British army, the RUC, they know all that...my community are not sitting on a level playing field because one side has got legitimate structures they can pursue and my community haven't, so even if we go into a truth recovery process, who do we bring to book, who do we get an inquiry into...who do you do it against?[12]

Truth, power and selling the story

Closely related to this sense of loyalty as silence is the argument that unionists have little confidence in the power of their arguments or, at least, that they will be able to articulate them persuasively in a truth process. As noted above, it is not the case that unionists do not wish to share their experiences of the conflict – as Ian Paisley Junior argued, it is important that they do so – 'I just think we have a huge story to tell and if we don't tell the vernacular of the story soon it will be lost'.[13] Rather, and as several interviewees acknowledged, the difficulty has been 'selling' that story:

> In the past we never sold our case, we didn't do it particularly well, we should be admonished for that, I think, as we look back...So we did miss a selling programme and we are now paying a heavy price for it.[14]

As Lundy and McGovern (2008b) note, the narratives available to different communities to explain the past to themselves and to others are not necessarily the same. In this case, a number of interviewees suggested that unionist's status as loyal pro-state actors and the nature of their structural relationship to the state and the balance of power may impact on their ability to develop an accessible narrative. By its very nature, a pro-state political narrative focuses on the story of the state and its apparatus (Bruce 1992b). In unionist terms, and according to one interviewee, the nature of this political tradition, concerned with a 'philosophy of modesty' based on continuity and a practical approach to governmental tasks is a more difficult narrative to convey than the 'complex, rich, emotional identity' of the anti-state project which is publicity generating and energetic in its attempts to overthrow the state (Brown 1985: 8, cited in Aughey 1989: 14; Peatling 2004).[15] Aughey suggests, 'it is easy to come up with good ideas when you are trying to shift something because you don't have any responsibility for it, whereas if you are trying to protect something, why would you come up with radical proposals?'[16] This view coincides with that of a senior UUP advisor who argued that as a British political culture, built around a weak interpretation of progress, parliamentary government, empire and economic prosperity, unionism is good at 'administering the state' but not the 'touchy-feely' aspect of politics.[17] As explored below, it is also the case that the pro-state orientation of loyalists has translated into a less-robust ideology than that of republicanism, as regards accommodation with a legacy of violence, imprisonment and post-conflict reintegration (Brewer *et al.* 2013).

These tensions can be seen in respect to how unionists and nationalists and republicans have used human rights discourse and, by extension, competing interpretations of how they can 'sell' their stories of loss and tragedy. The origins of the modern human rights movement can be traced to the Second World War and it has, by definition, focused on the activities of states (McEvoy 2003). As argued by Brett (1998), human rights laws are founded on the general principle that states are bound by international law (either by virtue of becoming party to a treaty or because the rule is recognised as a norm of customary international law) and the classic human rights view that governments, and only governments, can violate human rights. In Northern Ireland, given that human rights abuses are at the root of the conflict, competing loyalties and, in Connor's (2007) terminology, motivations to action, have provided both an obstacle to, and motivation for, engagement with human rights (Lamb 2010; Munce 2012; Livingstone and Murray 2005). This has led to a highly politicised perception of human rights concerns and the incorporation or rejection of human rights ideas for political ends (Lamb 2010). Unionists have historically had a difficult relationship with the concept of human rights and the NIHRC, which was established in 1999 (Munce 2012). In particular, they have criticised the NIHRC and other human rights NGOs, such as the CAJ, as being too focused on state violations of human rights, while ignoring the actions of non-state armed groups (Munce 2012). Structurally, and as explored above, given that their loyalty to the British state is based on a sense of commitment and acceptance of its actions, as the DUP's Arlene Foster (2003: 8) explains, it would also have been 'an anathema for grassroots members of unionism to challenge the state with a claim for their human rights'. By contrast, nationalist and republican political parties have a long tradition of expressing their political preferences and positions during the Northern Ireland conflict in the language of human rights, particularly relating to alleged human rights abuses by state authorities (Munce 2013; Livingstone and Murray 2005). For many interviewees, the application of the human rights framework was considered decisive in the ability of nationalists/republicans and inability of pro-state groups to develop outside support or 'coin a language' the world 'understood'.[18] This was very much the view of William Wilkinson, a former spokesperson from the unionist victims group Families Acting for Innocent Relatives (FAIR). He argued that in the 1960s, young and educated members of the nationalist community realised that if political progress was to be made, they needed to express their arguments in a language that had worldwide appeal.[19] The parallel timing of the civil rights campaign in the US was expedient and in Wilkinson's opinion:

> People didn't really know or care where Coalisland or the Bogside was but when someone stood up and said 'One man one vote', instantly students in Germany and France and people in liberal classes saw that as another example of right wing states putting down the working people and it fed in very very well.[20]

This backdrop has had a continued relevance in terms of dealing with the past and truth recovery, particularly regarding the availability of relevant legal frameworks and advocacy around cases of alleged state involvement in the deaths of members of the nationalist and republican community and other related injustices (Rolston 2000; Ni Aolain 2000). Inquests in the Coroners Courts, including those at the direction of the Attorney General and those taken in respect to Article 2 of the European Convention on Human Rights, and the work of the Criminal Cases Review Commission (CCRC), which investigates suspected miscarriages of justice, have largely, but not exclusively[21], focused on the victimisation of members of the nationalist and republican community or, in the case of the CCRC, where there are allegations that confessional evidence used during the conflict was obtained via the use of police torture or other abuses (see Healing Through Remembering 2013 for a comprehensive and up-to-date overview of these mechanisms). Such cases are not only damaging for the state and perpetuate the notion that truth recovery is inherently 'anti-state', but as noted above, they also draw from and are of relevance to rights advocates in other transitional or post-conflict societies and, more broadly, in respect to ongoing debates on the use of torture during the war on terror (Campbell and Ni Aolain 2003; Campbell and Connolly 2006; Dixon 2010). By contrast, and combined with a sense that they cannot criticise the state and a less-visible architecture to direct their grievances towards, the unionist story of the mechanics of the state is less easy to identify and to engage with. This point was well articulated by Lesley Carroll, a member of the CGP, and her remarks are worth repeating at some length:

> Sometimes I do get angry with people who work a lot with republicans, and I would be one, and therefore I get angry with myself, that we almost exist to flatter republicans and that in a way is understandable when you see people who were so far marginalised and live out of that experience and again, where is truth in this – how far were they marginalised, but nevertheless, their experience was that of being dominated and hurt and over looked and you kind of want to make it better, so you go into flatter mode, and then I catch myself on and I think wait a minute, nobody is going to flatter unionism because they are never going to be able to say we were hard done by in a way that people can understand.[22]

As Carroll suggests, there is a sense that unionists have struggled to develop an accessible narrative of their past and one that will have resonance beyond the confines of Northern Ireland politics. International humanitarian law, by which paramilitary organisations can be held accountable for their actions during an armed conflict, would provide a potential legal framework around which unionists could hang their calls for truth. It has, however, been similarly problematic. Unlike human rights law, international humanitarian law, founded on the 1949 Geneva Conventions, directly addresses armed situations where responsibility concerns all participants to the conflict (Mailhes 2005). It therefore automatically admits the political dimension of the conflict that makes the state not the victim of the conflict but an active participant as well (Mailhes 2005). Based upon the idea of 'legitimate' (state) and 'illegitimate' (civilian) targets, applying international humanitarian law to the Northern Ireland context could afford legitimacy to the actions of republican and loyalist paramilitaries (Brett 1998). Challenging unionist and security forces definitions of the conflict and the preferred organisational image of the RUC, this is not a course of action that is open to unionist political elites. Set against what many unionists perceive to be a greater 'sympathy' or 'acceptance' of republican versions of the past, this backdrop has inevitably affected their confidence to participate in a truth process (Phelps 2006).

Adding a further point of contention for many unionists and loyalists is the perceived power of republican politicians and ex-combatants propaganda and organisational skills. This has been a long-standing view throughout the conflict and, according to Dawn Purvis, the loyalist interpretation of a truth process as a republican 'Trojan Horse' is grounded in these concerns (Peatling 2004).[23] As a form of truth recovery itself, albeit one that has a single event focus, reactions to the BBC1 documentary on the 1983 Maze prison escape, aired in September 2008, illustrate these sentiments and how they feed into wider discourses on truth recovery.[24] Based upon contributions from some of those involved in the escape, including a prison officer, a BBC1 Northern Ireland spokesperson described the objective of the programme as 'to provide a detailed account of the Maze escape...to describe what happened in a fair and impartial manner' (Keenan 2008). Unionist politicians did not share this view. Descriptions of the programme as an attempt to glamorise and put the activities of republicans on a pedestal and to vindicate and popularise their actions are indicative of the suspicion that republicans would use a truth process as a propaganda platform (Keenan 2008).[25]

The absence of a quid pro quo in terms of a portrayal of Protestant voices and the perceived lack of interest in so doing has reinforced perceptions of a disjuncture between the capacity for, and interest in, republican articulations of their story and those of unionism and loyalism (News Letter 2008c; McDowell 2008). This view is entrenched in the argument that media coverage of the troubles has historically displayed sympathy with the nationalist/republican cause, over and above that of unionists and loyalists (Miller 1994; Curtis 1984). It has, for example, been argued that television documentaries on aspects of the conflict have been dominated by a 'non-unionist' agenda, prioritising miscarriages of justice, British military 'excesses', the hunger strikes and other 'humanitarian' topics, rather than, for example, the experiences of border Protestants (Parkinson 1998). The elevation of these subjects and nationalist's and republican's adoption of human rights issues has hence been critiqued by unionists as accounting for their greater difficulty in securing the support and endorsement of any significant audience external to Northern Ireland (Peatling 2004). Belying a circularity and self-perpetuity, Maurice Morrow argued that this has discouraged unionists and loyalists from telling their story.[26]

This backdrop has had a significant impact as regards the establishment of a formal truth process. Discussing this matter at the NIAC (2005a: ev.10), William Smith from EPIC made the point that 'The republican machine is adept at these things, they are better organised, they are long term organised, so the loyalists see inquiries as one-sided'. Likewise, a senior UUP advisor remarked that 'republicans have been ahead of the game on this particular issue and…have developed a very convincing narrative of the conflict'.[27] As these statements suggest, a sense that the republican movement is better prepared and equipped to deal with a truth process has engendered a sense of fear and perpetuated the notion that a truth process would be imbalanced and to the detriment of unionists and loyalists. While this perspective again overrides facts and arguments as to republicans' capacity to comprehensively manage a detailed expose of their past activities and the reality of how a truth process would operate, the perception among many unionists and loyalists is that

> if we are in this sort of position of having to appear in front of some sort of panel of a commission of some sort and you have got the international media there or some sort of international experts as Eames Bradley suggested, we would simply be outclassed in telling our side of the story relative to Sinn Fein,[28]

and, it is felt that 'if they [republicans] get into this, they will probably win again'.[29]

Truth, loyalty and alienation

As discussed above, loyalty is typically associated with inclusion, belonging and collective identity (Connor 2007; Jollimore 2012). The converse is exclusion, betrayal and alienation. 'Alienation', defined by Retzinger and Scheff (2000) as the result of the denial of emotion and a lack of knowledge of the motivations and intentions of the 'other', is commonly associated with members of the loyalist community in Northern Ireland. In particular, it is frequently used in reference to their relationship with unionist political elites and the British state – what Scheff (2011: 287) describes as 'bimodal alienation' and which he argues occurs between groups not only when there is 'isolation' between them, but also 'engulfment' within them. As explored below, the tension and constraints between loyalty, on the one hand, and, alienation on the other, has affected loyalists' attitudes to dealing with the past in a number of ways.

That loyalists have experienced socio-economic and political alienation in Northern Ireland has been well discussed. In addition to the political alienation detailed in Chapter 2 and characterised by low integration with institutional or political elites, socio-economic alienation, revolving around a perception of a lack of social capital and a weak and fragmented community infrastructure has been frequently associated with loyalist communities (Lundy and McGovern 2008b; Shirlow 2012). The Organisation for Economic Co-operation and Development's (1998) definition of social capital refers to 'the norms and social relations embedded in the social structures of society that enable people to co-ordinate action to achieve desired goals'. It is integrally related to other forms of capital, such as human (skills and qualifications), economic (wealth), cultural (modes of thinking) and symbolic (prestige and personal qualities). Putnam (2000, cited in Gribbin *et al.* 2005) argues that a community that has good social capital has networks, norms and social trust that facilitate co-operation for mutual benefit and is one where individuals feel safe, that they belong, have a voice and that their community can affect change, drawing on expertise and wider relationships. Similarly, the phrase community infrastructure refers to the resources a community has that enable it to deliver services to its members (Gribbin *et al.* 2005). Cairns *et al.* (2003) have found that a lack of social capital in loyalist areas has translated into a reluctance to engage in community development work, greater difficulty making funding applications than nationalist and republican community organisations and an 'apathy' towards and 'lack of confidence' in the ability of loyalist communities to deal with pressing social concerns (Cairns *et al.* 2003; Shirlow and McEvoy 2008). Gribbin *et al.* (2005) have also noted that the more fractured or fragmented nature of loyalist communities, the lower skill base of community organisations and the problematic relationship between loyalists and the statutory sector has affected both the actual and perceived effectiveness of local conflict transformation initiatives.

This backdrop has had an inevitable impact upon those loyalist ex-combatants who are now involved in conflict transformation work. As regards dealing with the past, and drawing on Retzinger and Scheff's (2000) argument that alienation is often linked to knowledge, several interviewees – particularly those involved in community work, argued that they do not have the skills or resources to educate community members about what a truth process would entail.[30] In the opinion of a senior member of the UPRG, Frankie Gallagher, this is a major impediment to involving his community in the truth recovery debate and he argued that given the distance between those 'on the ground' and political debate, it has reinforced a climate of fear and uncertainty towards the idea of dealing with the past:

> I don't think my community has engaged in dialogue even to understand truth recovery, they don't know it, they don't know what it means. It seems threatening in a way that it is a witch-hunt, it is not happening to the Catholic community, whereas the truth is they are probably better dealing with it because they address it. So we are in a bit of an impasse.[31]

In a more open approach to the truth recovery debate than that found among many unionists and security force personnel, at the time of interview, Gallagher's community organisation, Charter for Northern Ireland had just held meetings with the HET, CGP and Healing Through Remembering (HTR), a Belfast-based cross-community organization, which has conducted extensive work on how to deal with the legacy of the conflict. These grass roots meetings were designed to provide local people with an opportunity to find out what truth recovery would mean for them and to encourage the development of debate and dialogue. Again, it was argued that the problem is having the financial resources and personnel to sustain this type of work, particularly compared with the perceived efficiency and organisation of nationalist and republican communities – 'who is going to pay for that? Who is going to fund that'?[32] For this respondent, there was a fear that loyalists' voices would be at the margins of a formal truth process because of their social location and its lived effects, a point well made by Lundy and McGovern (2008b) who have argued that truth-telling cannot be divorced from the structural context in which it takes place. The following quotation well illustrates this point. It also speaks to broader themes in the transitional justice literature concerning the promotion of socio-economic transformation and the importance of building confidence and capacity in those most affected by violent conflict (see, for example, Waldorf 2012; Lambourne 2009; Laplante 2008):

> In terms of our community's engagement and attitudes towards this, I see it a bit in a way in terms of equity. We are all entitled to a slice of the cake, but my community, as opposed to the republican community don't even know where the cake is, they don't know how to get it but I'm sure if they were to get to that starting point, which would need political leadership as well by the way, then I think we would pursue that line.[33]

Political alienation, commonly linked to a sense of detachment from the peace process, and a lack of political integration with institutional or political elites has also impacted loyalist's confidence to participate in a truth process (Spencer 2008; Shirlow 2012). A number of complex and often competing arguments were put forward by interviewees, each of which illustrate how engagement and different collective capacities may be affected by a pro- or anti-state perspective (see also: Bruce 1992b). On one level, it was argued that the distance between loyalists and the truth recovery debate has left them susceptible to the negative rhetoric of unionist political elites. Frankie Gallagher's response is worth repeating at some length. It illustrates both a more nuanced understanding of what dealing with the past may mean on the part of the interviewee but also how, given an ethos of unswerving and uncritical loyalty, politics remains a zero-sum game and truth recovery is presented as an automatic loss for the pro-state community:

> Our community is prefixed on maintaining the status quo and that is because that is what our leadership tell them, they are not really open to change because change frightens them, change means a united Ireland, change means a dilution of their Britishness, whereas it actually doesn't, it means through me engaging, doing these things, I understand my Britishness better, I also feel stronger as a unionist and as a loyalist. My community don't know that, so when our leaders tell them to be cautious and not engage in these things, it reinforces a fear, that fear is like a siege mentality were we think our own British government is trying to sell us out and they are trying to put us into the hands of our enemies which are Irish republicans.[34]

However, there was also a sense that loyalist's relationship with unionist political elites – historically in Spencer (2008) and Cassidy's (2008) opinion – characterised by a culture of subservience and deference – has led to a reluctance to make their voices heard. The argument that 'the leadership has never led us in the direction of neediness' was also made during interview.[35] Frankie Gallagher's concern that loyalists lack the 'drive' for truth recovery displayed by members of the nationalist and republican community may therefore be part of the political culture of a 'protestant parliament for a Protestant people' which, on the basis of assumed loyalty, would look after their interests.[36] Cassidy (2008) has argued that it is hard to move people away from this mind-set. The resulting passivity and apathy has arguably both depressed the capacity of loyalists to look to their own community to resolve social and economic problems and has curtailed the development of strong positive community leadership (Gallaher 2007; Lundy and McGovern 2008b). This backdrop may have contributed to a lack of confidence in their capacity to deal with the issues raised by a truth process.

Yet, tempering this argument, virtually unanimous across all loyalist interviewees was the belief that unionist political elites do not want to see loyalist communities progress and develop their contribution to social and political life.[37] Spencer (2008) for example suggests that there has been a failure to instill confidence in the loyalist community by reinforcing the perception that there is no capacity for change and development (Shirlow 2012). The reluctance to support funding applications from loyalist community groups is part of this critique.[38] Alternatively, other interviewees suggested that unionist political elites fear their position in the community sector and are fearful of further revelations about their role during the conflict.[39] As discussed previously, the resulting perception is that loyalist's participation in a formal truth process would be discouraged and discounted, while also providing a further opportunity for unionist political elites to continue their alienation and demonisation.

Caught between these dynamics and illustrating Kemper's (1984, cited in Brewer 2011) argument that emotions are guided by three principles – reciprocity (or lack of), the principle of prior structural effects and devolution – the likelihood that emotional interactions that start well will decrease in positive effect as the interaction continues, 'loyalty' to unionist political elites has not provided loyalists with emotional certainty or security. Rather, socio-economic and political alienation has translated into the assumption that loyalist voices would be at the margins of a formal truth process. The result is 'they [loyalist ex-combatants] believe they have nothing to gain by engaging in the process'.[40]

Confidence and the structure of truth

The final area this chapter considers is how unionists' and loyalists' lack of confidence in the mechanics of a truth process has furthered their opposition to participating in such a body. These tensions are not uncommon internationally. The SATRC for example suffered significantly from public misconceptions concerning its role and limitations, which, at least in the short term, undermined public confidence and participation in the TRC (Posel and Simpson 2002). Likewise, in Sierra Leone, the issue of information sharing was particularly thorny, specifically concerning the question of whether the Sierra Leone Truth and Reconciliation Commission (SLTRC) would turn testimony and documentation over to the Special Court for Sierra Leone, therefore posing risks for perpetrators who chose to participate (Schabas 2003). While these fears were quickly put to rest – the SLTRC issued a press briefing in August 2002 stating that all information provided to it in confidence would remain that way, the fear of prosecution, at least initially, deterred many ex-combatants from testifying (Graybill and Lanegran 2004).

However, what I would argue is particularly significant about the Northern Ireland case is how unionists and loyalists 'loyalty' to, for example, the Northern Ireland state, their cause, the security forces and each other has had a direct and often negative impact on their confidence to engage with a truth process. Obvious points of contention concern the perception that dealing with the past will displace hierarchies of victimhood, that truth recovery has and will be 'anti-state' and that re-investigating the past undermines their commitment to, and sacrifice on behalf of, the British state. Given that these areas are explored in full in Chapters 3, 4 and 6, the discussion here is restricted to a focus on some of the more structural discussions that have taken place regarding the establishment of a formal truth process. That is, the claims that a truth process would be held in public, would 'name names' of those involved, the use of tenuous parallels between the SATRC and the Northern Ireland case, and, for loyalist ex-combatants, how they could safely participate in a truth process without fear of prosecution (Guelke 2008; McGarry 2001; Hamber 2003). Building on the analysis presented in the previous chapters and the recurring themes of denial and blame, I would argue that these concerns are indicative of a deep-seated fear that a truth process could only function to their disadvantage and are symptomatic of their lack of engagement with the truth recovery debate.

The prospect that a truth process would be held in public or that it would name names of those involved are of obvious concern to all parties to the conflict in Northern Ireland. However, the preponderance of these arguments have been from unionist sources and were cited by several interviewees as reasons why Northern Ireland should not have a truth process.[41] The importance of due process and the fear of violent recrimination often structured their responses. There is a lively international debate concerning these matters, both sides of which have been strongly argued by rights advocates. The first is that due process requires that individuals accused of crime be allowed to defend themselves before being pronounced guilty; the second is that telling the full truth requires naming persons responsible for human rights violations when there is clear evidence of their culpability (Hayner 2011). Only a small number of truth commissions have chosen to name perpetrators – El Salvador, Chad, the second commission of the ANC, the SATRC and the Liberian truth commission (Hayner 2011). Well-established international best practice standards also provide excellent guidance and outline essential safeguards (ICTJ 2013ab). Such resources could be well used by unionists. In any case, guarantees that the information recovery process would be held in private and would not name those responsible for past violations were all made in the Report of the CGP (CGP 2009). As a matter of practicality and given that the recommendations of the CGP were based on a period of public consultation, it is highly likely that any future truth process would include similar safeguards.

The comparison between the establishment of a truth process in Northern Ireland and the SATRC – itself stemming from the parallels that have been drawn between the two transitions, has also continued to dog discussions on truth recovery in Northern Ireland, particularly from a unionist perspective. While such comparisons are uncritical and do not stand up to sustained and rigorous scrutiny, there is considerable and understandable fear among unionists of being compared with the role played by white Afrikaners during South Africa's apartheid era (McGarry 2001; Guelke 2008). This linkage has furthered the perception that all efforts at truth recovery will be anti-state, pro-republican and rely on a heavy dose of quasi-religious and ethical moralising. Again, there are few concrete empirical facts to support this supposition. The Report of the CGP (2009) and statements made by British government officials have all stressed that any formal effort at dealing with the past in Northern Ireland would be a Northern Ireland response to a Northern Ireland problem (Paterson 2010).

In other cases, namely among ex-combatants, there are significant concerns regarding how a truth process would impact on their reintegration and return to community life, particularly in the absence of an amnesty. As has been pointed out in respect to ex-combatants in Sierra Leone and elsewhere, fears that they will face barriers to reintegration, social stigmatisation or scapegoating are not uncommon (Penal Reform International 2004; Gear 2002). That loyalist ex-combatants have experienced a more tenuous relationship with unionist politicians compared with the greater support networks and more positive attitudes towards imprisonment found within republicanism, illustrates further difficulties for pro-state actors (Shirlow and McEvoy 2008; Brewer *et al.* 2013). According to members of the CGP, some ex-combatants have suggested that they would be willing to participate in a truth process.[42] However, other interviewees argued that due to the early prisoner release scheme, there is little incentive for ex-combatants to come forward with information, while those whose crimes remain unaccounted for will hope to remain hidden.[43] Tom Roberts from EPIC spoke to some of these difficulties and his response belies an underlying lack of confidence in the notion of a formal truth process and its potential effects:

> In terms of being an ex-prisoner myself, there is no incentive that anybody could offer me to go and publicly disclose what I was involved in, given that what I was involved in was involuntarily exposed through the justice system and the treatment that ex-prisoners received having served time, so how much more venom would be directed to someone who would disclose details and then walk away?[44]

Some loyalist ex-combatants have linked their confidence to participate in a truth process with the issue of an amnesty or limited immunity from prosecution. The use of amnesty in return for truth-telling has been used in other transitional contexts as a confidence-building measure, providing a mechanism for ex-combatants to contribute to the creation of the historical narrative but also by providing a 'safe space' in which they can do so (Mallinder 2008). Sarkin (1999) suggests that the involvement of victims and perpetrators in a truth commission can also help foster a climate of reconciliation and may assist with re-integration (Roche 2005). The current leader of the PUP, Billy Hutchinson, has suggested some degree of willingness on the part of loyalist ex-combatants to respond to victims' questions, but that their capacity to do so is tempered by the need to provide adequate legal structures that remove the threat of prosecution: 'There are people out there who want to know what happened. That can't be done unless you give people [combatants] a safe way of doing it without persecution or prosecution'.[45] Not all loyalists agreed with this analysis however. By contrast, the UPRG's Billy McQuiston appeared to equate an amnesty or limited immunity with a 'get out of jail free card':

> If you are going to give people immunity if they go in and admit things then why just not give everyone an amnesty, just pull people through the front door and send them out the back door with an amnesty ticket in their back pocket? What is the point of it?[46]

As noted above, it is my view that loyalty, as a framework for social action and a vehicle for collective identity has been instrumental in shaping these concerns (Jollimore 2012). On one level, and as discussed throughout this book, unionists and loyalists are supporters of the Northern Ireland and British states. Their loyalty to the past, the present and their imagined future is challenged by the idea of truth recovery and unpacking the legacy of the past (Leebaw 2011; Anderson 2006). I would argue that what has, at times, been an automatic rejection of the truth recovery debate has precluded a deeper engagement with, and, consideration of some of the above challenges. Yet, as detailed throughout this chapter, dealing with the past poses distinct structural challenges for pro-state actors. The arguments that a truth process would 'name names' or be held in public, for example, arguably have a particular pique for unionists, loyalists and members of the security forces. For unionists and the security forces in particular, given the Northern Ireland state's rule of law status, the prospect that actions or inactions of state personnel would be publicly examined, facilitated, as noted in Chapter 4, by the availability of regimental lists and other documentation, is arguably particularly concerning (Campbell and Connolly 2012; Patterson 2009). By contrast, republican ex-combatants have strongly suggested that their approach to dealing with the past would be collective rather than individual (NIAC 2005a: ev.57–58; Smyth 2007). Given the state's legal and moral obligations, it is unlikely, however, that such an approach from the state or security forces would satisfy republican's demands for truth and justice. Structurally, unionists may therefore feel that they have more to 'lose'. Loyalist ex-combatants' difficult relationship with mainstream unionism has also raised problems concerning their confidence to participate in a truth process. With persistent fears of demonisation or stigmatisation and less political support for their actions during the conflict *vis-à-vis* their counterparts in republican paramilitary organisations, few interviewees felt comfortable or able to participate in a truth process (Shirlow and McEvoy 2008). For some loyalists, the use of an amnesty or limited immunity from prosecution is an essential confidence-building measure. I would therefore argue that while conflict may intensify one's sense of loyalty and galvanise the imagined community, in the post-conflict environment, loyalty may also mitigate against a re-engagement with that past (Connor 2007).

Conclusion

A common theme in the international literature on transitional justice is how mechanisms of truth recovery can provide participants with a 'voice' with which to articulate their experiences (Ross 2003; Phelps 2006; Hayner 2011). For many victims and survivors, this is one of the most attractive features of a truth process and statements such as 'I can tell my story. Therefore I am', have been well, if uncritically, rehearsed (Mbembe 2000, cited in Ross 2003: 327; McEvoy and McConnachie 2013). This chapter however has argued that rather than viewing a formal truth recovery process as an opportunity to present and gain acknowledgement of their narratives of the conflict, there is a profound lack of confidence among unionists and loyalists in the power of their arguments and in their capacity to participate in a truth process. I would argue that their status as 'loyal' pro-state actors has been highly influential. As Connor (2007) suggests, loyalty relates to identity and can shape and influence one's actions. The 'loyalty' of unionists, loyalists and the security forces is an enduring theme and central to their identity and collective memory. Motivating their response to the challenges posed by both constitutional nationalism and militant republicanism during the conflict, loyalty has also shaped their response to the truth recovery debate. Rather than offering confidence and security, as this chapter has argued, 'loyal' pro-state actors face particular difficulties in terms of not being able or willing to criticise the state – an inevitable part of any truth process and being able to 'sell' their story, while for loyalist ex-combatants, socio-economic alienation has impacted upon their confidence and capacity to engage in the truth recovery debate. At a structural or practical level, it has also given rise to concerns over the mechanics of a truth process. 'Loyalty' can therefore be a double-edged sword for such actors, and in the Northern Ireland case, but also of relevance to other pro-state actors in transitional regimes elsewhere, may lead to a preference for silence rather than an investigation of the past (Winter 2010). Moreover, as Bruce (1992b) points out, the tension between loyalty and betrayal is an inherent difficulty for pro-state groups. The following chapter picks up this theme.

Notes

1 Interview, Maurice Morrow, DUP, 20 April 2009.
2 Interview, Ian Paisley Junior, DUP, 12 September 2009.
3 Text of a speech by Sir Reg Empey to the AGM of the Ulster Unionist Council on 31 May 2008. Available at: http://cain.ulst.ac.uk/victims/docs/political_parties/uup/empey_050309a.pdf (accessed on 3 June 2008).
4 The DUP's Ian Paisley Junior articulated this point during interview, commenting: 'I think it is very important to remember the sort of community that unionists are'. Interview, Ian Paisley Junior, DUP, 12 September 2009.
5 Interview, Dawn Purvis, 6 April 2009.
6 Interview, Dawn Purvis, 6 April 2009.
7 Interview, Ian Paisley Junior, DUP, 12 September 2009. It is also interesting to note that Paisley worked alongside human rights groups such as the CAJ on this case, organisations he would otherwise have dismissed as displaying pro-Republican sympathies. The Guildford 4 and Maguire 7 were convicted in English courts in 1975 and 1976, respectively, in connection with the IRA Guildford pub bombing of October 1974. Their convictions were reversed in 1989 and 1991. The Birmingham 6 were sentenced to life imprisonment following the 1974 Birmingham pub bombings, believed to be the responsibility of the IRA. Their convictions were declared unsafe and unsatisfactory in 1991.
8 Interview, Ian Paisley Junior, DUP, 12 September 2009.
9 Interview, Billy McQuiston, UPRG, 18 June 2009. The former PUP leader Dawn Purvis disagreed with this point, arguing, 'I think exploration of conflict and what went on here would probably help a lot of people in their own sense of identity and probably question their own ideas and belonging to a particular tribe and what it means to belong to that particular tribe'. Interview, Dawn Purvis, 6 April 2009.
10 Interview, Billy McQuiston, UPRG, 18 June 2009.
11 Interview, Frankie Gallagher, UPRG, 11 June 2009.
12 Interview, Frankie Gallagher, UPRG, 11 June 2009.
13 Interview, Ian Paisley Junior, DUP, 12 September 2009.
14 Interview, Maurice Morrow, DUP, 20 April 2009; Interview, Lesley Carroll, 10 June 2009; Interview, Archbishop Robin Eames, 23 October 2009.
15 Interview, Arthur Aughey, 1 June 2009.
16 Interview, Arthur Aughey, 1 June 2009.
17 Interview, name withheld, UUP, 23 June 2009.
18 Interview, William Wilkinson, FAIR, 9 June 2009.
19 Interview, William Wilkinson, FAIR, 9 June 2009.
20 Interview, William Wilkinson, FAIR, 9 June 2009.
21 In early August 2013, the Attorney General John Larkin QC ordered the coroner John Leckey to proceed with a new inquest into the deaths of 10 Protestant workmen murdered by the IRA in the 1976 Kingsmill massacre. See: 'New inquest into Kingsmill murders', *BBC News*, 7 August 2013. Online. Available at:

www.bbc.co.uk/news/uk-northern-ireland-23609459 (accessed on 7 August 2013).

22 Interview, Lesley Carroll, 10 June 2009.

23 Interview, Dawn Purvis, 6 April 2009.

24 The 1983 Maze prison escape saw 38 PIRA prisoners escape from one of the highest-security and escape-proof prisons in Europe. As a result of the escape, one prison officer died and 20 others were injured. Amid British government embarrassment, the escape was a major propaganda coup for the IRA.

25 Commenting on the participation of SF minister Gerry Kelly in the programme, Jim Allister remarked, 'There he was, gloating that he had shot a prison officer in the head'. Interview, Jim Allister, TUV, 20 March 2009.

26 Interview, Maurice Morrow, DUP, 20 April 2009.

27 Interview, name withheld, UUP, 23 June 2009.

28 Interview, Esmond Birnie, UUP, 19 May 2009.

29 Interview, Archbishop Robin Eames, 23 October 2009.

30 Interview, Martin Snodden, 3 April 2009; Interview, Frankie Gallagher, UPRG, 11 June 2009.

31 Interview, Frankie Gallagher, UPRG, 11 June 2009.

32 Interview, Frankie Gallagher, UPRG, 11 June 2009.

33 Interview, Frankie Gallagher, UPRG, 11 June 2009.

Martin Snodden also echoed this point. Interview, Martin Snodden, 3 April 2009.

34 Interview, Frankie Gallagher, UPRG, 11 June 2009.

35 Interview, Frankie Gallagher, UPRG, 11 June 2009.

36 Interview, Frankie Gallagher, UPRG, 11 June 2009.

37 Interview, Dawn Purvis, 6 April 2009; Interview, Billy McQuiston, UPRG, 18 June 2009; Interview, Frankie Gallagher, UPRG, 11 June 2009; Interview, Martin Snodden, 3 April 2009.

38 Interview, Dawn Purvis, 6 April 2009.

39 Interview, Martin Snodden, 3 April 2009.

40 Interview, Martin Snodden, 3 April 2009.

41 Interview, Jim Allister, TUV, 20 March 2009; Interview, Nelson McCausland, DUP, 3 April 2009; Interview, name withheld, UUP, 23 June 2009.

42 Interview, Lesley Carroll, 10 June 2009.

43 Interview, Lady Sylvia Hermon, 3 April 2009; Interview, Terry Spence, PFNI, 30 June 2009; Interview, Dave Cox, HET, 28 September 2009. It is interesting to note that Dave Cox, the head of the HET, and therefore with considerable experience on the issue of truth recovery, did not think the Legacy Commission would get the necessary participation from ex-combatants.

44 Interview, Tom Roberts, EPIC, 28 April 2009.

45 Rowan, B. (2012a) 'Loyalist Billy Hutchinson on the play for the past', EammonMallie.com, 28 October 2012. Online. Available at: http://eamonn-mallie.com/2012/10/loyalist-billy-hutchinson-on-the-play-for-the-past/ (accessed on 17 July 2013).

46 Interview, Billy McQuiston, UPRG, 18 June 2009.

Chapter 6

Truth, sacrifice and betrayal

Introduction

The maintenance of life is one of the most sacred and universal values in human culture (Bar-Tal 2003). In turn, human loss intensifies social beliefs about patriotism, commitment, pride and loyalty towards the in-group and the country (Bar-Tal 2003). In response, these beliefs call for mobilisation and sacrifice and may demand a willingness to die for one's country (Bar-Tal 2003). As a tribute to these sacrifices, the killed and wounded are revered and memorialised, and the meaning of their death is often linked to societal beliefs about the conflict, including the delegitimisation of the opponent, the legitimisation of the self and support for claims to victimhood (Winter 1995; Hamber 2009). It is against this background that Michael Igantieff's (1998: 188) argument that in the aftermath of violent conflict there is a 'desire to keep faith with the dead, to honour their memory' underpins many of the conceptual and practical arguments made in this chapter. Drawing on the themes of sacrifice and betrayal, this chapter locates their importance to debates on transitional justice and truth recovery and will argue that transitional junctures and questions of how, or if, to unpick past actions (and inactions) can be interpreted as betraying the sacrifices that have been made during conflict.

Given that many members of the security forces and their unionist supporters have privileged a narrative of sacrifice – often by way of physical loss, and the parallel theme of betrayal many have associated with the peace process, their concerns are the major focus of this chapter. The first part of this chapter will explore the relationship between mechanisms of transitional justice and the importance of preserving memories of loss, paying particular attention to mobilisation against transitional justice and truth recovery. This backdrop will then be linked to the transitional period in Northern Ireland, and will illustrate the importance of the themes of sacrifice and betrayal for unionists, loyalists and members of the security forces. Third, this chapter will address the argument that the British government has historically 'used' the security forces in a politically expedient manner to 'appease' republicans' demands and has prioritised their calls for truth. Loyalists' concerns will also be explored at this point. Arguments as to the 'illusion of collusion' will then be critiqued. This discussion will focus on the argument that the suggestion of wrongdoing betrays the RUC's self-identification as the upholders of law and order and is part of a broader process of 'blaming' the security forces for much of the responsibility for the conflict. Fourth, the perception that the British government has failed to adequately recognise the sacrifice and service of the security forces and its impact on their attitudes to dealing with the past will be addressed. Finally, and in contrast to these points, the openness towards and commitment to 'doing' truth recovery that has been expressed at a senior level of the post-Patten policing structures - the PSNI, NIPB and OPONI, will be analysed and the relationship to honoring memories of loss explored. Drawing on these themes and others concerning the meaning of death, the recognition or betrayal of, and questions of a moral contract between citizens and states, this chapter raises complex questions that are of relevance beyond the Northern Ireland case study.

Transitional justice and keeping faith with the dead

Transitional justice processes generally involve a range of models that are aimed at helping a society come to terms with previous large-scale human rights abuses in order to ensure accountability for wrongdoing, and achieve justice and reconciliation for victims (McAlinden 2013). The drive to 'move on', reconcile and achieve closure has led to a number of critiques of the main mechanisms of transitional justice – particularly truth commissions – from a victim-centred perspective. One such critique is the use of easy and uncritical links between the assumed virtues of truth, reconciliation and healing (Hayes 1998; Moon 2008). Rather, hearing and telling the truth may be retraumatising and is often 'only one component of the victim's typically lengthy and painful healing process' (Hamber 2003: 161; Mendeloff 2004, 2009). Concerns as to the conflation of 'individual' and 'social' restoration have also been noted by Moon (2009) and Hamber and Wilson (2002). They argue that 'psychologizing the nation' mistakenly implies that individual and national processes of dealing with the past are concurrent and equivalent (Hamber and Wilson 2002). As they point out, to imply that individual and national 'healing' processes run in tandem can in itself be traumatic for victims and, more problematically, can mean subordinating individual needs to the broader objective of post-conflict reconciliation, exploiting victim's pain 'to publicly project the power of the state' (Humphrey 2003: 171, cited in Moon 2009: 83).

Also of significance but considerably less well explored in the literature is the impact of victims and survivors continuing bond with the dead on the establishment and reception of transitional justice institutions. As

Brewer (2010) argues, the emotions aroused in communal violence can be intense and widespread, since communal violence causes an emotional response in everyone touched by it. Moreover, the signing of a peace accord does not assuage these emotional responses, and peace processes often carry the effects of the emotional baggage of war well into the post-conflict period (Brewer 2010). Death itself is an assault on an individual's meaning system and when violent and large scale, destroys images of morality, kinship and belief and belonging in one's country (Butler 2006). Invisible pacts to achieve formal punishment or personal vengeance may be made as a way of respecting the person who has died and to make their death and memory meaningful (Hamber and Wilson 2002). Hamber (2009) suggests that this goes some way to explaining campaigns for truth, justice or reparations on the part of some victims and survivors or their involvement in self-help groups made up of others with similar experiences. Yet, the opposite is equally true – a process of transitional justice that seeks to 'deal with' or 'discharge' the past by truth telling, reparations or amnesty laws, for example, may be interpreted as a betrayal of victims' memory and sacrifice. This may be particularly the case where the meta-conflict is continuing and the nature or cause of their death remains contested, or, for those victims whose emotional legacy of the conflict is one of 'defeat', 'surrender' and 'humiliation', if not the cultural annihilation of the group (Scheff 1994; Brewer 2010). Hamber (2009: 88–89) captures this tension:

> we also need to be aware that it is through the social reality that the continuing bond with victims of political violence is renegotiated. This poses a myriad challenges to survivors because their ability to change the social and political context, and thus meet the obligations of the promises they made to their loved ones, is constantly under threat as societies in transition try to deal with the macro questions of doing justice, seeking accountability and making reparations for what happened.

The 'desire to keep faith with the dead, to honour their memory' has engendered opposition to post-conflict reconstruction and transitional justice in a number of settings (Ignatieff 1998: 188). The memory and sacrifice of those individuals or groups who make their 'victim identity' the focus of efforts to recover a moral contract between state and citizens has often become a potent weapon in this battle (Humphrey and Valverde 2008). The case of Argentina's Madres de la Plaza de Mayo is well known. Campaigning for the return of their children who were among the 8,960 'disappeared' during the military regime of 1976 to 1985, the Madres have consistently opposed the offer of state-sponsored reparations (Guembe 2006). They argue that this is an attempt to buy their silence, arrest the truth recovery process and to avoid bringing perpetrators to trial (Moon 2012). As Suarez-Orozco (1991: 496) explains,

> The Mothers argue that any such bureaucratic intervention requires them to psychologically become their children's executioners; they would first need to psychologically kill and bury their children before proceeding with the legal route. And this is too costly, much too guilt inducing. It is as if giving up hope is betraying their children.

Similarly, the offer of amnesty to aid former combatants demobilisation and reintegration or to incentivise truth recovery – as in South Africa, for example – is often one of the thorniest post-conflict debates and has been interpreted as a sacrifice of justice and a negation of victims' experiences (Mallinder 2008). South African apartheid victim Duma Khumalo spoke for many victims when he protested, 'We have been betrayed. The previous government gave the killers golden handshakes and the present government gave them amnesty. [But] the victims have been left empty handed' (Hamber and Wilson 2002: 67). In other instances, it has been argued that in transitional societies and those in the midst of violent conflict, including South Africa, Guatemala and Israel/Palestine, to begin to unpick past actions (and inactions) betrays the sacrifices that have been made during the conflict and fails to do justice to such acts (Payne 2008; Isaacs 2010; Dudai and Cohen 2007).

As Bar-Tal (2003) points out, violence increases the emotional involvement of the parties engaged in intergroup conflict and the use of language such as 'sons', 'motherland' and 'family' is designed to encourage a sense of belonging and closeness. In political conflict, this means ownership of the dead is often collective and shared (McEvoy and Conway 2004). This arguably gives further depth and strength to the notion of sacrifice and, by extension, the invisible bonds between the living and the dead. While, as discussed above, maintaining these bonds may find expression, on the part of some victims and survivors, in lobbying for truth, justice or reparations for example, the need to preserve the sacrifice and memory of those who died can also translate into opposition to transitional justice and truth recovery. Challenging communities of memory and often the significance and meaning of loss, this chapter highlights the significance of these debates to unionist's opposition to truth recovery in Northern Ireland.

Northern Ireland, transition and the betrayal of sacrifice

Samson (2006: np, cited in Lamb 2010: 1006) and Dudai and Cohen's (2007) arguments that 'when new forms of thought and action must struggle with old ones, there has to be a sacrifice' and that the feeling of betrayal is one of the strongest in personal and political lives in general, are particularly relevant to post-conflict societies and the establishment of transitional justice mechanisms. The Northern Ireland case study well bears out this case, where, for the pro-state community, the themes of sacrifice for, and betrayal by, the British state are strongly associated with the conflict and period of conflict transformation. Tracing these narratives and linking them to Hamber and Wilson's (2002) suggestion that the trauma and confusion that accompanies violent death not only shatters cognitive assumptions about the world, but is exacerbated when the markers of that past are destroyed or rendered invisible, the following discussion provides much of the backdrop against which unionists', loyalists' and the security forces' opposition to truth recovery is structured.

As detailed in Chapter 5, 'loyalty' is central to the identity and collective memory of unionists, the security forces and loyalists. One of the most visible manifestations of their loyalty was their willingness to defend the Northern Ireland state and union with Great Britain, often by way of physical loss and sacrifice. A discourse of sacrifice is particularly clear in the organisational memory of the RUC, specifically relating to the 305 police officers murdered during the course of the conflict and those who were injured. As Mulcahy (2006: 53) has argued, 'By drawing on the flesh and blood costs endured by its officers, the RUC's official discourse cast the force as a long-suffering and heavily victimised organisation' (Mulcahy 2000). Members and supporters of the RUC have used a number of mediums to practically and symbolically emphasise the importance of their sacrifice. This has included the use of *Police Beat* (the organisational magazine), Annual Reports, the environment surrounding the funerals of security force personnel and physical memorials found in police stations (Mulcahy 2006). For commentators such as Ryder (2000), the emphasis on the sacrifice offered by the RUC is no less overt. 'Motivated by a limitless admiration for the valiant men and women of the RUC', Ryder's (2000: xv) text is infused with eulogising statements on the bravery and loyalty of the RUC. The strongest of these narratives were expressed in the post-ceasefire period, when the infallible moral claim was made that officers' sacrifice directly contributed to peace. As the then Chief Constable suggested,

> They gave their lives and suffered injury in the just cause of peacekeeping. The loss to the bereaved families and the suffering of the maimed can never be fully assuaged but they can draw solace and meaning from the sure knowledge that peace was only made possible because of such sacrifice (Chief Constable's Annual Report for 1994: 11, cited in Mulcahy 2000: 77).

The image of willing sacrifice has therefore been core to the RUC's collective memory and self-image (Switzer and Graham 2009). It has also been used to establish an ethical dimension to their activities and the sacrifice of the physical body has been used to embed moral authority and legitimacy (De Soucey *et al.* 2008).

In practical terms, alongside the daily reality of policing in Northern Ireland and its associated dangers for members of the security forces, the close knit nature of the 'policing family' also meant that the losses sustained and their impact were closely felt. This idea is founded upon the unionist conception of the RUC as 'one of our own' and as 'their police' and is reinforced by the service tradition within the unionist community (McGarry 2000: 180; Ellison and Mulcahy 2001). It has also extended to encompass the family members of those in the security forces, many of whom had other relatives in the RUC. The policy of 'Ulsterisation' whereby from 1975 onwards the British government transferred responsibility (and therefore the human cost) for law enforcement to the local population of Northern Ireland further heightened this relationship (Neumann 2003). It was also common for members of the unionist political parties to either be former members of the security forces themselves or for family members to be involved. These links were real, not imagined or theoretical, and the losses and their impact were acutely felt. During interview, the UUP's Danny Kennedy captured something of this relationship:

> There is a strong view within the unionist community that these are *our honoured dead*, and look around, (gesturing at walls), I have pictures of the RUCs sacrifice, it strikes a chord because I knew some of those individuals, I know the extended family of many of them, I know and worked with the families of those who are pictured here.[1]

The theme of sacrifice is equally important among loyalists and can be traced to loyalist's involvement in the First and Second World War, the battle of the Somme in particular playing a visible part in loyalist murals and other forms of memorialisation (Graham and Shirlow 2002). Like members of the security forces, the natural relation to their loyalty was defence or, in Connor's (2007) terms, motivation to action. For both the UVF and UDA, defence of their communities against the threat of republican violence and to preserve the union between Northern Ireland and Great Britain was the primary aim (Taylor 1999). Their 'sacrifice' found physical expression in the deaths of members of loyalist paramilitary organisations and in the prison sentences many served and the often negative consequences for their family lives and life chances (Shirlow 2012). Their 'crimes' were therefore those of 'loyalty' and reflective of their paradoxical relationship with the British state in which 'loyalists have to stand up to them [the British] for the right to be them and, on the other hand, fight for them' (cited in Graham and Shirlow 2002: 892; Wood 2006).

The flipside to these narratives of loyalty and sacrifice is a discourse of betrayal. Presupposing a 'social contract' – the belief that when one party provides something to another party, the second party is expected to give something in return, the expected return on unionists and loyalists imagined relationship with the British state was support, commitment and protection (Rousseau 1995, cited in Restubog and Bordia 2006). William Wilkinson, a former representative of the unionist victims group FAIR alluded to this point – 'you put yourself in harm's way because you believe that that state will see you right'.[2] Yet, in much of the literature on the psychology of betrayal, it is argued that a form of betrayal occurs when the agents of protection cause the very harm they are entrusted to guard against, breaching the basic assumptions and expectations about the relationship or social contract (Rousseau 1995, cited in Restubog and Bordia 2006; Koehler and Gershoff 2003). That the peace process and many of the main markers of transition have challenged unionists and loyalists understanding of their social contract with the British state was well articulated by Wilkinson:

> There is a protestant unionist concept around the idea of a contract that individuals in society and government enter into and there are certain expectations that flow from that, that crime will be punished, that they will be protected, that the state will look after their interests...Unfortunately many of their working principles have been fractured and abused over the past decade, that so many traditional points of reference, even 'crime is crime is crime' have been absolutely eroded by the way in which political status has been given and that practically translated into prisoner releases and all manner of erosion of very fundamental principles.[3]

Ben-Yehuda (2001) argues that the study of loyalty and betrayal brings forward matters of social and moral boundaries as well as notions of power. For unionists, loyalists and members of the security forces, and as suggested above by Wilkinson, that the peace process involved the early release of political prisoners, the inclusion of former armed groups in government and the reform of the RUC, was a fundamental betrayal of their loyalty and sacrifice and an exercise of power over their social and moral boundaries: 'our crime was loyalty. For we were always loyal and we got nothing' (McAuley 2010: 140; Rolston 2006). The perception that the British government was willing to prioritise republicans' demands over and above the loyalty and service of the pro-state community is typified by Ian Paisley's declaration that the RUC was 'to be offered as a final sacrificial lamb, to appease Roman Catholic Republican murderers and their nationalist fellow travellers' (DUP Press Release, 9 September 1999, cited in Mulcahy 2006: 159; McAuley 2004). Reflecting Connerton's (1989: 2) argument that 'our experience of the present very largely depends upon our knowledge of the past', the argument that the attendant erosion of trust not only alters understandings of the past but also shapes readings of the future is directly reflected in unionists' and loyalists' attitudes towards a formal truth process (Jones and Burdette 1994, Reina and Reina 1999, cited in Restubog and Bordia 2006; Shackleford and Buss 1996).

Truth, betrayal and appeasing 'the other'

That transitional justice may involve uncomfortable trade offs between the need to preserve the memory of the past and construct a new imagined political community has been well established (Huntington 1991; Wilson 2001; Teitel 2000; Leebaw 2011). For certain parties, part of this discomfort may stem from the perception that their opponents have been 'bought' into the transitional process via a series of concessions or more lenient treatment. In South Africa, for example, Ramphele (undated, cited in Boraine and Levy 1995) warned that for some victims and communities, the TRC could be interpreted as a process of 'appeasing the past' rather than confronting and dealing with it meaningfully. Stanley (2002) has similarly critiqued truth commissions on the grounds that for those who wish to retain their status, truth telling can be an opportunity to construct new democratic identities, embolden claims to legitimacy and consolidate economic, political and social power. As in Argentina and Uruguay, for example, government-initiated reparation programmes may also be interpreted as an attempt to placate demands for formal prosecutions and keep powerful political interests on side (Guembe 2006; Minow 1998). In each of these cases, for certain victims, their demands for truth, justice and acknowledgement of wrongdoing appeared to be negated by the politics of transition.

In Northern Ireland, the argument that during the peace process and post-conflict phase, the British government has too readily 'appeased' or been willing to meet republicans' demands is one of the strongest manifestations of the discourse of betrayal among unionists and members of the security forces. The DUP's Maurice Morrow, for example, declared that, 'they have been shamefully treated by a government that was more interested in political expediency than doing what was right'.[4] As regards dealing with the past, a major oppositional narrative in unionist and loyalist discourse is the argument that the British government has and will continue to prioritise republicans' demands for truth concerning state abuses to the neglect of hurt and loss within their communities (NIRPOA 2008; PFNI 2008a; EPIC 2004).[5] For many, as detailed in Chapter 4, this is typified by the fact that the British government has supported a documentary review into the murder of Pat Finucane and public inquiries into the deaths of Robert Hamill and Rosemary Nelson – all members of the nationalist/republican community and whose deaths are linked to allegations of British security force collusion with loyalist paramilitaries. Speaking after the publication of the Saville Report, Maurice Morrow appeared to suggest that this imbalance was, in fact, inevitable:

> The outcome was doomed from the start…The sad truth is that, yet again, the Protestant community was resigned from the start to the inevitability of the outcome going against its views of the events. Such resignation stems from past experience of government policy over the last two generations, which has been to appease those who shout the loudest and to acquiesce in the views of those who could prove the bigger threat. The harsh reality is that the predictability of the findings is further proof of the extent to which successive Governments and the establishment at every level have incessantly pandered to those who are contemptuous of the rule of law in the United Kingdom…This had absolutely nothing to do with truth and justice. Purely and simply, this was an attempt to appease the unappeasable.[6]

More recently, and speaking to wider concerns over the dominance of law and the threat of post-conflict prosecution, loyalists' concerns have been levied against the HET, the independent police body that is re-examining 3,268 deaths attributable to the conflict between 1968 and 1998 (McEvoy 2007). As of March 2011, the unit had made 72 arrests – 70 loyalists and two republicans. Of the 70 loyalists, 65 were arrested in connection with 'Operation Ballast'. This case was originally investigated by the OPONI (2007) and concerned the activities of a UVF gang in North Belfast who were alleged to have been involved in serious organised crime and paramilitary murders, including collusion with members of the security forces. The case was passed to the HET as a matter of public interest. One of the most significant outcomes of the investigation was the loyalist 'Supergrass trial', which sat between September 2011 and January 2012. This trial centered on the evidence of two former members of the UVF who, in return for reduced sentences, testified against a further 14 alleged members of the organisation. The accused faced a total of 97 criminal charges, including murder (Rutherford 2011).

While 12 of the 14 accused were found not guilty on the basis that the evidence was 'infected with lies', the fact that the first Supergrass trial to be held in Northern Ireland for over 25 years concerned the activities of loyalists has 'given the impression that the HET is part of the witch hunt against loyalism' (McDonald 2012).[7] The statistical record issued by the HET in February 2013 does not support this allegation – it reveals that having reviewed 1,700 cases, the HET had passed 39 of these to the PSNI for criminal investigation and that of these cases, 26 concerned republicans and

13 concerned loyalists (Nolan 2013). However, the depth of the Operation Ballast investigation and the high media profile afforded to the Supergrass trial has translated into a perception of a biased and partial approach to the past. Loyalist's anguish has been further compounded by the assertion, made by some, that in 1998, the former Northern Ireland Secretary of State Mo Mowlam offered an undeclared amnesty to anyone involved in the conflict (Belfast Telegraph 2010c).[8]

Given that unionists, members of the security forces and loyalists have historically prided themselves on the expectation that the state will look after its loyal citizens, for many, the expected 'return' on their sacrifice was a commitment, on the part of the British state, to uphold law and order and to seek justice, through criminal convictions where possible (Rolston 2006). That the British state has appeared willing to act upon republicans' calls for truth and accountability in cases of state/security force wrongdoing, while the 'dust of neglect' is gathering on the unsolved files of more than 200 police officers who were murdered during the conflict is therefore a fundamental betrayal of their loyalty.[9] There is also a sense, on the part of the security forces at least, that their sacrifice has been subsumed by the demands of political expediency: 'The lack of activity regarding the murders of our colleagues is a sad indictment of this government who seem only too happy, for reasons of political expediency, to pump millions into the deaths of a select few' (PFNI 2003). Likewise, for loyalists, in the absence of a visible quid pro quo in terms of investigations into the actions of republicans and the perception of an overzealous focus on their past, their experience of truth recovery has also been one of betrayal, giving way to 'a seething anger, defeat to an intense sense of humiliation' (Todd 1987: 17). Their frustration can be keenly felt:

> If you look at any of the inquiries that have been going on and all these things they have been looking at, about people crying out for truth, it is all from the republican side so that doesn't give any confidence to the Protestant community that this is going to be for both sides. There is a mural on the Shankill Road about the McArdles bar, Fridells fish shop, the Balmoral showrooms, the Mountain View Tavern and the Four Step Inn and it says on it 'where are our inquiries?' That is the way people feel. A republican was killed at three o'clock in the morning going for a bottle of milk, don't know where he was going to find a shop open at three o'clock in the morning to get a bottle of milk but there was an inquiry into it. But you can bomb a bar on the Shankill Road and kill 10 people and nobody gets an inquiry into that.[10]

It is however interesting to note that alongside recommending public inquiries in the Hamill, Nelson, Finucane and Wright cases, Justice Cory also called for a public inquiry into the deaths of Chief Superintendent Breen and Superintendent Buchanan (Cory 2003). Breen and Buchanan were serving RUC officers murdered by the PIRA in March 1989 as they returned from an informal meeting with senior Garda officers. The car they were travelling in was unmarked. As with the above cases, Cory found evidence to suggest that their deaths were the result of Gardaí collusion with the IRA (Cory 2003). Established in March 2006, the terms of reference for the Smithwick Tribunal are to investigate 'suggestions that members of An Garda Siochana or other employees of the State colluded in the fatal shootings of RUC Chief Superintendent Harry Breen and RUC Superintendent Robert Buchanan'.[11] In his opening statement, Judge Smithwick further confirmed that his investigation would not be limited by a narrow definition of collusion, but that it would be 'examined in the broadest sense of the word', including acts of commission but also acts of omission or the failure to act.[12]

Given the nature of this investigation and Smithwick's wide terms of reference, one would have thought that it would be a source of considerable interest for unionists and members of the security forces. It should also go some way to counteracting the perception of an imbalanced approach to the past. However, the fieldwork on which this book is based and continued documentary analysis does not present a wholly persuasive picture. Unionists have certainly supported the inquiry and, as it has progressed, several have given evidence and the decision to extend Smithwick's timeframe has been welcomed.[13] However, during interview, several more negative or dismissive arguments were made. This included the argument that the profile of the Smithwick Tribunal is so low, that it has no impact on the general population, while for others, their views were subsumed within a broader framework of opposition to the financial costs of public inquiries and the concern that inquiries raise more questions than they can reasonably answer.[14] For the UUP's Tom Elliott, in 2009 at least, the fact that the inquiry was not one of a series focused on republican activists was problematic:

> I think the problem there again is they are not dealing with a recovery into republican terrorists. What they are doing is still dealing with state issues and we believe that is the way it will continue to be, that you will get most of the information and recovery from the state but you wouldn't get it from the terrorists.[15]

Elliott's argument may be informed by a lack of understanding of Smithwick's remit or the view that the inquiry is a token gesture or 'sop' to appease unionists and the policing family.[16] If it is the latter, this is suggestive of a deep hostility towards truth recovery and a continuing perception that republicans are continuing to benefit from historical investigations. On the basis of evidence presented in this book, I would support this assertion and argue that against this backdrop, unionists and loyalists have mapped their perception of a biased and partial approach to public inquiries on to their opposition to a formal truth process.

For some interviewees, the language and concepts associated with the truth recovery debate has also been linked to a sense of betrayal. Key concerns that arose during the work of the CGP and, particularly in respect to the matter of amnesty/immunity, are likely to be raised in opposition to any further discussions on a truth process, include the prospect that the conflict would be redesignated a 'war', amnesty/immunity proposals and the Recognition Payment (NIRPOA 2008; PFNI 2008ab, 2009). Uniting these issues was the claim that the British government had allowed republicans' demands to come to the fore, legitimising their conduct and implicitly supporting the vilification of the name and conduct of the RUC. The controversy over the suggestion that an amnesty may be offered to encourage truth recovery bears out these arguments. As noted above, the equation of an amnesty with the appeasement of former perpetrators is not uncommon in other transitional jurisdictions (Mallinder 2008). In Northern Ireland, unionists have also argued that offering an amnesty would create 'moral equivalence' between the actions of the security forces and former paramilitaries, compromising their identity and claim to innocent victimhood. The acute sense of betrayal is readily identifiable in the PFNI's (2008a: 3) submission to the CGP:

> An amnesty would be a betrayal of the professional service of over 30,000 police officers, their families and every citizen all of whom were capable of distinguishing between the legitimate institutions and instruments of a democratically elected government and ruthless terrorist organisations lacking a democratic, legal, moral or even historical mandate.

As part of the broader architecture of the truth debate, unionists' opposition to these factors, alongside the prospect of further investigation into their past, is symptomatic of their sense of betrayal by the British state (Anderson 2006). This is manifested in the argument that there has been a lack of commitment to investigating unionists' and loyalists' narratives of loss and a prioritisation of republicans' calls for truth and justice. For many interviewees and other members of the unionist/security force elite, there is an acute sense that the British government has been persuaded by republican's claims, in fact or for reasons of political expediency. As discussed at length in Chapter 3, unionists in particular have adhered to a hierarchal understanding of victimhood and a static conceptualisation of the terms victim and perpetrator. The British government's 'failure' to prioritise the deaths of members of the security forces may therefore be interpreted as challenging their claim to innocent victimhood. Doing so would be a fundamental rejection of their loyalty and commitment (Ben-Yehuda 2001).

Moreover, probing all aspects of the past, a truth process would inevitably raise some of these most challenging questions for unionists. As Cherry (2000: 140) notes, 'The issue of betrayal is probably the most difficult of all to confront and this is the reason why truth commissions have trodden carefully around it rather than forced communities and individuals to face the truth'. This leaves unionists in a double bind – their perception of truth recovery has to date, been one of a one-way process in favour of republicans and it is a process that, for many, appears to have the support of the British state. The truth recovery debate has therefore challenged their sense of identity and belonging and has compromised their notion of a 'social contract' with the British state (Rousseau 1995, cited in Restubog and Bordia 2006; Koehler and Gershoff 2003).

The 'illusion' of collusion

An inevitable feature of any truth process established in Northern Ireland will be further investigation into allegations of security force collusion with loyalist paramilitaries. Other problematic policing practices including claims of 'shoot-to-kill' policing and the torture of police suspects would also feature in such an investigation of the past. Evidence of collusion, found by, for example, Sir John Stevens, Justice Cory and the OPONI, has been strenuously denied by members of the security forces and unionist politicians by way of a four-pronged defence: outright denial – literal denial; ascription to a tiny percentage of 'bad apples' who were immediately dealt with – isolation; the argument that the conditions of the time means their actions cannot be judged retrospectively – contextualisation; and by way of reference to the role of the RUC in upholding the law and defeating terrorism – an advantageous comparison (Cohen 2001).[17] Based on fieldwork with unionist and security force elites, it is my view that allegations of collusion are interpreted as a betrayal of the memory and sacrifice of the RUC. Two themes informed interviewee's responses – the argument that the suggestion of wrongdoing betrays their self-identification as the upholders of law and order and, second, that it is part of a broader attempt to 'blame' the RUC for much of the responsibility for the conflict. The 'legacy' of betrayal engendered by previous investigations into allegations of collusion and the prospect of further investigation in the future is therefore a major element in their opposition to a formal truth process.

Allegations of collusion have been investigated by Sir John Stevens, Justice Peter Cory, which led to the public inquiries detailed in Chapter 4 and the OPONI. Several highly significant results have been returned. Sir John Stevens published the first official definition of collusion in 2003. Including 'serious acts and omissions', Stevens' (2003: 16) definition of collusion consisted of a list of actions – 'Collusion is evidenced in many ways. This ranges from the wilful failure to keep records, the absence of accountability, the withholding of intelligence and evidence, through to the extreme of agents being involved in murder'. Stevens (2003: 16) concluded, 'My three Enquiries have found all these elements of collusion to be present'.

The Cory collusion inquiries worked to a similarly broad definition of collusion. Justice Cory (2003: 2.59) argued that:

> the definition of collusion must be reasonably broad...That is to say that army and police forces must not act collusively by ignoring or turning a blind eye to the wrongful acts of their servants or agents or by supplying information to assist those servants or agents in their wrongful acts or encouraging others to commit a wrongful act. Any lesser definition would have the effect of condoning, or even encouraging, state involvement in crimes, thereby shattering all public confidence in these important agencies.

The importance of including acts of omission and commission is clear in Cory's report into the death of Robert Hamill. Discussing, for example, the actions of 'Reserve Constable B', accused of advising a chief suspect to destroy the clothes he wore on the night of the attack, Cory (2004c: 2.231) notes that:

> If established are capable of being found to constitute the most flagrant type of collusion. His actions did not constitute the simple turning of a blind eye. Rather they could be found to be carefully planned and premeditated actions taken to frustrate a murder investigation and to protect or exonerate an individual who might have been guilty of murder.

Following the completion of de Silva's documentary review into the case of Pat Finucane, the existence of 'shocking levels of collusion' was acknowledged at the highest level of the British government (McDonald and Bowcott 2012). Prime Minister David Cameron declared that 'On behalf of the government and the whole country, let me say again I am deeply sorry' (BBC News 2012b). As explored in Chapter 4, many unionists have dismissed such findings as an attempt to 're-write' the past in favour of a republican narrative of the conflict and as a 'witch-hunt' of the security forces.

The OPONI has also played a prominent and highly publicised role in investigating cases of alleged collusion, notwithstanding the controversy that engulfed the Office in mid-2011 and is explored in full below. The investigation into the death of Raymond McCord Junior is arguably one of the most significant and high-profile cases taken on by the OPONI. A young Belfast man, McCord Junior was murdered by the UVF, amid allegations of collusion between British government agents and police informers. It was also alleged that the informant involved in this case and others had been protected from prosecution for serious crimes for years. Mr McCord Senior had expressed misgivings about the adequacy of the police inquiry into the circumstances surrounding his son's death and following initial enquiries, the then Police Ombudsman Nuala O'Loan estimated that intelligence strongly indicated the involvement of informants, mostly from the UVF in several murders and serious crimes between 1991 and 2003 (OPONI 2007). The terms of the investigation were subsequently widened to include not only the investigation of Mr McCord's son's murder but also the police handling and management of identified informants, and information received by and about them over the 12-year period (O'Loan 2010). The subsequent report 'Operation Ballast' was published in January 2007. Clear evidence of collusion between loyalist paramilitary informers and members of the RUC Special Branch was reported (OPONI 2007). Crucially, this was not only the case in respect to Raymond McCord Junior, 'Informant 1', the suspect, being described as 'a well known terrorist and criminal', but also in a number of other cases:

> There is no reason to believe that the findings of this investigation are isolated. Indeed, given that many of the failings identified in the course of the investigation were systemic, this is highly likely and the implications of this are very serious.
>
> (OPONI 2007: 140–1)

'Grave concerns about the practices of police officers' that were uncovered included: arresting informants suspected of murder, then subjecting them to lengthy sham interviews at which they were not challenged about their alleged crime, releasing them without charge and withholding intelligence from police colleagues, including the names of alleged suspects, which could have been used to prevent or detect crime (OPONI 2007). The cumulative effect of these activities was to protect Informant 1 and other informants from investigation. O'Loan concluded that 'this was collusion by certain police officers with identified UVF informants' (OPONI 2007: 13).

As a self-professed 'law-bound, disciplined, visible public service, in order to protect life and property', the findings of Stevens, Cory and the OPONI stand in direct opposition to police narratives of impartiality, legitimacy and professionalism (NIRPOA 2009: 19; Ellison and Smyth 2000; Ryder 2000). Instead, it speaks to a force that is the antithesis of these values and challenges the core of the organisational identity.[18] While many of those interviewed for the purposes of this research were unswerving in their dedication to the RUC and refuted any suggestion that collusion extended beyond the proverbial 'bad apple',[19] a senior UUP advisor acknowledged that it is extremely difficult and indeed dishonourable to countenance the thought of wrongdoing by the security forces (Cohen 2001).[20] He argued that given unionists 'emotional commitment' to the security forces, 'you feel this visceral attachment to these guys who put themselves in harm's way for us; rightly or wrongly we stand by them'.[21] Loader and Mulcahy (2003) argue this is particularly the case in divided societies where the police can become a force of the imagination, protecting 'us' from 'them' and are believed to be capable of delivering order and security to a world experienced as changing, dangerous and unstable. Under such conditions, the police be may be mobilised as a 'primal shelter' for the insecure (Loader and Mulcahy 2003). This statement is also a prime example of how keeping faith with the dead – in this case those individuals who lost their lives while on duty, and the broader memory of the RUC, is to continue to remember, respect and uphold their values in the face of challenge (Ignatieff 1998; Dawson 2007). As Willie Frazer (cited in Dawson 2007: 281) points out, it also requires a certain fixity of memory – 'If I go back on my opinion and change what they believed in, I'd be degrading their memory'. While not written in respect to Northern Ireland, Ignatieff's (1996: 118) sentiments echo this point: 'To discover that their heroes were guilty of war crimes is to admit that the identities they defended were themselves tarnished'. Thus, as argued by the DUP's Jeffrey Donaldson, for the policing family, allegations of collusion have been interpreted as 'a betrayal of the brave men and women who served in the security forces'.[22] Given that any truth recovery process will inevitably explore allegations of collusion, this backdrop has had a major influence upon attitudes to truth recovery among representatives of the RUC and unionist politicians.

For others, allegations of collusion have been framed within the broader perception that the security forces have been used as a convenient scapegoat for much of the responsibility for the conflict and that the British government has participated in this process.[23] As Girard (1972, 1989, cited in McEvoy and McConnachie 2013) reminds us, such efforts to locate blame in the 'other' absolves 'us' of any semblance of guilt or responsibility. Again, this challenges the forces' organisational memory and identity. Symmetry in narratives can be identified from the police reform debate through to the truth recovery debate. For example, speaking at the PFNI Annual Conference, June 1997, the then Chairman of the PFNI, Les Rodgers argued,

> Over the years the RUC has held this community together when at times it would almost have disintegrated under the pressures of civil disorder. We have stood firm in an unenviable and isolated position doing our best to keep communities from each other's throats. At all times we have worked to bring communities together in support of the rule of law. We are now being portrayed by our enemies as part of the problem of Northern Ireland rather than its essential protective binding.
>
> (Rodgers 1997, cited in Ryder 2000: 484–5)

The reaction to the work of the CGP mirrored this opinion and demonstrates the enduring salience of the themes of loyalty and betrayal. Writing in respect to public inquiries, but of broader relevance to this discussion, the NIRPOA's (2008) submission to the CGP illustrates how many within the security forces view truth recovery as a process through which they will continue to be blamed for the conflict. Cautioning the CGP against further inquiries, their concern is palpable:

> ...their remits unfortunately, are strongly reflective of the agendas of certain pseudo human/legal rights' groups intent on pedalling theories of alleged State conspiracies and institutionalised collusion as being a major factor in the deaths of many victims of the troubles.
>
> ...the most likely outcome being that they will create a new raft of scapegoats to be further victimised, or worse still, held vicariously liable for the political, administrative and organisational failures surrounding matters over which they had little or no influence.
>
> (NIRPOA 2008: 3)

However, it is significant to note that resistance to allegations of collusion have not been universally shared among rank and file officers. Former members of the security forces, including Fred Holroyd, Colin Wallace and former Special Branch members Alan Barker (2004) and Jonty Brown (2005) have come forward and alleged that, in certain circumstances, there was close co-operation between loyalists and the security forces in the murder of members of the nationalist and republican community (Holroyd and Foot 1989, cited in Rolston 2005). Their claims provide a tacit acknowledgment that collusion was happening, that many ordinary police officers were outraged by the activities of Special Branch in particular and that the otherwise disputed findings of Stevens, Cory and the OPONI are essentially correct (Brown 2005). Indicating the level of betrayal, the authors of these revelations have been dismissed as 'whistle-blowers', 'fantasists' and 'liars' by their former colleagues (Rolston 2005: 195; Zerubavel 2010).[24]

Truth and sacrifice in service

As detailed above, there is a long tradition of sacrifice among the security forces in Northern Ireland, and during the conflict, members of the RUC were presented as willing to pay the ultimate sacrifice – death – in the name of preserving peace and security (Ellison and Smyth 2000; Mulcahy and Ellison 2001). The death and sacrifice of RUC members therefore had wide social repercussions and was an assault not only on the individual, but also on the collective (Bar-Tal 2003). However, and in keeping with the twin themes of sacrifice and betrayal explored throughout this chapter, for many members of the security forces and their unionist supporters, there is a sense that while throughout the peace process the British government has been only too willing to make 'concessions' to republicans, security force members and their families feel they have been forgotten, and their sacrifice and service unappreciated. For many, it has also called into question the meaning of their death. In particular, while many officers believed the post ceasefire period provided an opportunity to acknowledge their achievements, the 'indecent haste' with which suggestions for reform were made was interpreted as an insult to the memory of the force (Mulcahy 2006: 92; Ryder 2000; Barker 2004; Holland and Phoenix 1996).[25] Latterly, it was argued that the Patten Report itself failed to pay due regard to their sacrifice and bravery.[26]

The strength of this community and their lived experiences has therefore provided a substantive bulwark against which anything perceived to threaten the memory and sacrifice of the security forces is resisted and this backdrop has had an inevitable impact upon their attitudes to truth recovery. The following memoranda made by the Disabled Police Officers Association Northern Ireland to the NIAC (2005a: ev.125) provides a way into this thinking:

> Members of the Police Family feel totally betrayed by this government. How can our members who were cut down, many in the prime of their lives, be expected to look forward and consider Peace and Reconciliation when they are being treated so shabbily by a government who does not give due recognition to the sacrifices that the men and women of the RUC made and also to that of their families who bore the wrath of 'both' communities in this province?

A number of procedural and substantive concerns can be identified which link to a betrayal of their physical sacrifice and organisational memory. Paralleling the above note on the 'dust of neglect', it has, on one hand, been argued that the differential between what are viewed as a small selection of politically motivated inquiries, complete with vast resources and the 211 unsolved murders of members of the security forces is indicative of the governments lack of regard for their sacrifice (Helin and Lindstrom 2003; David and Choi 2009).[27] As is also outlined above, to achieve justice – typically retributive justice – or some form of reparation or other acknowledgement of wrongdoing is often a central demand from victims in the aftermath of violent conflict (Teitel 2000; Gready 2011; CVSNI 2012). For many members of the policing family, the perceived failure to effectively deliver any of these variables – particularly retributive justice – has doubly exacerbated their trauma and dissatisfaction with the current approach to the past. This tension can be clearly seen in respect to the announcement in July 2012 that British soldiers involved in Bloody Sunday are to be questioned by the PSNI as part of a murder investigation into the events of that day, with a view to prosecutions (Rayner 2012). While the PFNI Chairman Terry Spence has publicly stated that the Federation supports the view that if there is sufficient evidence of criminality by police officers or army personnel, prosecutions should follow, the Federation's press release points to competing notions of fairness and hierarchies of investigations – 'Why are police resources already under enormous pressure to be devoted to a particular event when the unsolved murders of 211 RUC GC police officers are being investigated along with over 2000 civilian unsolved murders through the HET?' (PFNI 2012). It continues, 'The law must take its course but it should also be used equitably on behalf of all people bereaved or injured as a result of terrorism who have yet to see justice' (PFNI 2012).

For other representatives of the RUC, a discourse of sacrifice betrayed has been expressed in light of the 'burden' placed on former members to provide evidence to historical investigations.[28] If a truth process were to be established, as has been repeatedly emphasised in Northern Ireland and elsewhere, the participation of all parties to the conflict would be required (CGP 2009; McEvoy 2006; Hayner 2011). However, Raymond White, a representative of the NIRPOA, has argued that former members

> are now almost on call, as it were, as unpaid public servants to be at the beck and call of whoever wishes to revisit the past. This is our fear, that in respect of the Legacy Commission this is yet another imposition...when do retired police officers actually get retired in the same fashion as other members of the public?
>
> (NIAC 2009: ev.26)

Given the volume and uncoordinated nature of historical investigations – involving public inquiries, the HET, OPONI and inquests in the coroner's courts, there are a considerable number of processes requiring the input of former members of the security forces. This is both time-consuming and disruptive to family life. It may also be retraumatising:

> It is not a paper exercise as far as our members are concerned; it takes them back to dark corners of their past that they do not wish to visit again. It may have been 20 years ago and they have come to some degree to terms with it, but if you spend 2 or 3 hours on a reinvestigation and you are walking through inquest photographs and investigative processes, that is real live memory recall as far as those officers are concerned.
>
> (NIAC 2009: ev.26; Mendeloff 2009)[29]

The above sentiments are indicative of the view that to ask former officers to revisit the past is to betray the service they have provided and erodes what should be a well-earned retirement.[30] However, and more problematically, given as noted in Chapter 4, that some former members of the security forces have failed to provide historical information to the OPONI, whether this is because such officers have genuinely left the past behind or because a degree of culpability is involved, remains to be seen (Cohen 2001; Payne 2008).

At a more substantive level, investigating or unpicking the past is associated with the implication of wrongdoing. As argued throughout this book, members of the security forces have consistently resisted the suggestion that their actions explicitly or implicitly played a role in the conflict (Lawther 2010, 2013). Among other techniques of denial, a discourse of sacrifice, in which the security forces are presented as willing to die in the name of peace and stability has been used as shield of legitimacy (Lawther 2010, 2013; Cohen 2001).[31] To call aspects of the past into question therefore challenges their identity and organisational memory, and calls into question the meaning of their death (Cohen 2001; Dawson 2007). As explored at length in Chapter 4, calls for truth recovery have also been interpreted as part of the attempt to re-write the past:

> Republican terrorism cost the lives of 336 of our members and we had to support their families when others forgot them. We will not let their memory die. We must ensure that history is not rewritten to blacken those of them who served in the security forces because that would be an utter travesty.
>
> (*Antrim Times* 2012)

Still others have argued that the perceived lack of political will to sanction investigations into the deaths of members of the security forces is because the British government is embarrassed by its association with the RUC and would prefer not to have attention drawn to their relationship.[32] This argument again coalesced around the disjuncture between the resources allocated to the small number of public inquiries and the high number of unsolved murders of members of the security forces. As expressed by the former Chairman of the PFNI, Irwin Montgomery,

> There are endless resources devoted to tracking down the murderers of Pat Finucane and Rosemary Nelson and to exploring the events of Bloody Sunday through the Saville Inquiry. My members do not begrudge the effort made to bring their murderers to justice or to find the truth behind horrific events. We just cannot accept that the plight of our colleague's widows and families should be treated like some kind of lingering embarrassment which time will erode from the social landscape.[33]

A number of points can be deduced from this argument. First, is the fear that 'the UK Government may be tempted to view a Truth and Reconciliation Commission as providing a tidying up opportunity on the past, a way of writing and closing a last chapter on a book' (PFNI 2008a: 6). As explored above, this concern links to the argument that the British state has failed to honour unionists and loyalists commitment and sacrifice and has bypassed their calls for truth and justice. More problematic is O'Rawe's (2003: 1072) argument that the British state is 'still clinging valiantly to any myth which allows it to distance itself from identification as a player in the conflict'. Calling for the establishment of a formal truth recovery process, Ni Aolain (2002: 588) similarly asserts that 'unresolved cases represent an enormous accountability gap for the state. The story about these cases is a missing narrative about the role of the state during the conflict itself'. It is thus arguable that in the quest to compartmentalise the horror of the past, the perceived willingness of the British state to acquiesce with republicans' demands and to disassociate itself from the RUC, may be part of an attempt to shield its own past from scrutiny. These difficulties for the state were highlighted during the UTV Insight documentary on collusion aired in May 2013, during which the journalist Brian Rowan made the point that 'if you put Special Branch in the dock, Special Branch will put the State in the dock'.[34] The continuation of the 'piecemeal' approach to the past may therefore suit the state by preventing a fuller examination of the conflict. As part of a broader effort to control the investigation of the past, the examination of the losses incurred by the RUC may fall within this accountability gap.

Professionalism, the Police Service of Northern Ireland and breaking with the past

Grounded in broader trends of post-conflict identity transformation, a difference of opinion on the need for a truth process and the associated variables of sacrifice and betrayal can, however, be found with those at elite managerial levels of the post-Patten policing bodies – the PSNI, NIPB and the OPONI (Arthur 2011; Orde 2005; Irish News 2007). The following discussion will argue that alongside speaking to broader themes in the transitional justice lexicon – those of 'healing', 'closure' and 'accountability', for example, this greater openness to dealing with the past is linked to questions of identity – in this case 'professional' identity and the need to 'break' with the past. The objective of such efforts is to allow the PSNI to become a modern and effective force that is forward-looking rather than burdened by or dependent on constructions of the past to legitimise its conduct.

This is not, however, to suggest that the OPONI or HET have been entirely free of controversy as regards their involvement in historical investigations.

In 2011, critical reports published by the CAJ (2011a) and the CJINI (2011) questioned the effectiveness, efficiency and operational independence of the OPONI. Among other concerns, the reports pointed to a lack of a clear or consistent definition of collusion, inconsistencies in the investigation process and evidence that reports into historical cases were being rewritten to exclude criticism of the police (CAJ 2011; CJINI 2011). The resulting controversy led to the suspension of historical investigations, the resignation of the then Police Ombudsman Al Hutchinson, his replacement by Dr Michael Maguire and a period of internal reform (BBC News 2011d, 2012c). Major changes include an increase in funding to deal with historical cases and the establishment of a new Historical Investigations Directorate within the OPONI, with a revised structure and processes to deal with historic cases (OPONI 2011a). The Unit is designed to be severable from the OPONI should an overarching body for dealing with the past be established (OPONI 2011a). Historical investigations re-started in January 2013, after a follow-up review by the CJINI found evidence of substantial progress (CJINI 2013). Dr Maguire has also confirmed that the OPONI will return to utilising the same definition of collusion as drawn up by Justice Cory and was previously deployed by Dame Nuala O'Loan during her tenure.[35] As detailed above, O'Loan's approach to investigating historical cases was frequently uncompromising and was often greeted with a hostile reception from former members of the RUC and the main unionist political parties.

Professor Patricia Lundy (2009ab, 2012) has also questioned the independence and effectiveness of the HET, particularly in regard to its structural relationship to the PSNI and staffing policies. Some of Lundy's (2009ab, 2012) findings include the involvement of former long-serving RUC officers, including ex-Special Branch members, at each stage of the HET process and inequalities of treatment in cases where state agencies and personnel are involved, compared with cases involving non-state or paramilitary suspects. Following Professor Lundy's final report, a review of the HET by HMIC was commissioned. The HMIC reported in early July 2013 and found that the HET's approach to cases involving the state was inconsistent with the European Convention on Human Rights, specifically Article 2 – the right to life and the requirement that if life is taken by the use of state force, the state must properly investigate the circumstances and, if the death was unlawful, bring the perpetrator to justice (HMIC 2013). PSNI Chief Constable Matt Baggott has accepted the HMIC's recommendations in full and confirmed that all military cases will be re-examined (BBC News 2013c). The NIPB however has declared that it has no confidence in the leadership of the HET (NIPB 2013).

While serious difficulties remain with police-led truth recovery in Northern Ireland, I would however argue that there remains a commitment to 'doing' truth recovery and to a broader truth process. An effort has been made on the part of the PSNI to attempt to address victims' needs and respond to their unresolved questions. Energised by the former Chief Constable of the PSNI Sir Hugh Orde, the HET was established with this objective in mind. Aiming to 'assist in bringing a measure of resolution to those families of victims affected by deaths attributed to the troubles in the years 1968–1998 and to re-examine all 3268 deaths attributable to the troubles', much of the language surrounding the HET reiterates the ideals of 'closure', 'resolution' and a 'family focus' (NIAC 2008: 10; HET undated). The emphasis on these objectives reflects one of the most lauded values of truth recovery in the aftermath of violent conflict – the ability to bring victims' families much-needed information (Hayner 2011). In some cases this may be the difference between knowledge and acknowledgement; in others it may be a simple detail family members have spent years searching for (Hayner 2011). For other victims and survivors, the fact that there is an interest in their case may, in itself, be enough. Orde's argument, detailed below, is clearly founded on these points:

> success for me is not the number of prosecutions; success for me is have we allowed some people to move on in their lives to a degree that they would not have been able to move on if HET had not existed and given them that interaction and opportunity to ask questions they have never had before.
>
> (NIAC 2008: ev.82)

Orde repeated these points following the publication of the HMIC (2013) report and stressed that while the HET was never designed to be a comprehensive truth recovery mechanism, it was 'a genuine attempt to try to make a difference for a small number of people who had no voice at all at that time'.[36] It is also interesting to note that while the HMIC (2013) report makes a number of serious criticisms of the HET, it also notes that among the 180 people it interviewed during the course of the investigation, there was an 'almost universal desire' for the unit to be retained, subject to operational improvements (HMIC 2013: 101).

Among senior managers in the PSNI, this commitment to truth recovery extends to a more-positive attitude to the work of public inquiries and inquests than is generally associated with the representative bodies of the RUC. As explored throughout this book, resistance to such investigatory work is predicated on allegations of betrayal, that it provides a vehicle for republicans to reshape the history of the conflict and that it undermines and erodes the legitimacy of the RUC and its memory. During interview, a senior member of the PSNI challenged this critique. Instead, his emphasis lay on prioritising accountability and acknowledging wrongdoing:

> Some people may perceive that if you look at the world through certain optics but I don't think that is the case. I think it is about

> government seeking to be open and if things have gone wrong acknowledge them...We are saying ok, what lessons can we learn from that, how can we have that examined and brought forward so that we either acknowledge previous failings or let's seek to demonstrate that as far as possible, we did everything that we could.[37]

Framing Assistant Chief Constable Allister Finlay's arguments was a full and open acknowledgment of the legal (and moral) obligations of a liberal-democratic state:

> There is an expectation that government and agents of government will actually operate within the law...and it is not unreasonable that people come up and say 'well in actual fact you were not playing by the rules'...The public inquiries and the inquests are now examining that, it is more detailed than that, but basically you didn't play by the rules. Is that unfair? It might be, but then the manifestation of the state is that you will play by the rules...and if people don't play by the rules then there is a framework there to hold them to account.[38]

These arguments not only mark a radical transition from the approach of the RUC and its supporters, but involve a tacit acknowledgement that the history of policing in Northern Ireland is not as wholesome as many would like to suggest. Pragmatism over the question of former officers having to provide evidence to inquests and inquiries was also associated with this perspective – 'I don't think morally you can hold those positions and walk away'.[39]

Despite this commitment to existing mechanisms of truth recovery, senior representatives of the PSNI, NIPB and OPONI have maintained that a formal truth process is required. In part, their arguments are couched within broader international trends of transitional justice. Reiterating a common demand of transitional societies, the former chairman of the NIPB, for example, called on the British government to establish a truth commission as a vital part of the move to 'reconcile the losses of the past and embrace the future' and argued that this matter 'must be given the priority it deserves' (BBC News 2004). Likewise, the need to move away from polarised narratives of the past to a more-complicated greyscale has been recognised and articulated at a senior level of the PSNI (Leebaw 2011). As one senior officer remarked,

> That is where Eames Bradley I think becomes the catalyst of acknowledging that you can have various versions of the truth out of one set of circumstances, it doesn't say that is wrong...There is more to it than going through files...So a formalised process would bring more people into it than us, get other peoples' perspectives

> because I think with just us involved it becomes very easy to say 'yes they did' or 'no they didn't'. It needs a richer experience than that.[40]

In a similar vein, Sir Hugh Orde has advocated a broader approach to the past than is available through the current patchwork of measures and has expressed dissatisfaction that the recommendations of the CGP, including the proposal to subsume the HET within the 'Review and Investigation' unit of the Legacy Commission, have been sidelined.[41] During interview in 2009, Dave Cox, the director of the HET also expressed openness to this recommendation.[42] Likewise, the former Police Ombudsman Al Hutchinson consistently argued that the current 'piecemeal' approach to the past is destabilising and used the controversy over the Office's operational independence in mid-2011 to reiterate his call for the establishment of an overarching truth body (Bell 2003; NIAC 2008: ev.15–23; OPONI 2011b; Clarke 2011a).[43] At this time, the respected *Sunday Times* journalist Liam Clarke asserted that 'Unless a body is established to handle the legacy of the twentieth century divisions, they have the capacity to destroy institutions needed to deal with twenty first century problems' (Clarke 2011b; BBC News 2011e). The potential damage to public confidence in the PSNI has been well recognised (McEvoy 2006; NIAC 2013).[44] Collectively, these points speak to an overarching process of professionalism and a managerial drive to provide a service that enjoys maximum confidence and 'buy in' from the community.

For others, broader public sector trends of 'new public management' and social market approaches for improving efficiency and effectiveness have been influential (McLaughlin *et al.* 2001; McEldowney 2003). Having filtered down into policing practices, Reuss-Ianni and Ianni (2005) argue that the 'managers' of twenty-first century policing are 'intended to make the "business" of policing more productive or efficient', their remits shaped by objectives, strategies, management and accountability (Bayley and Shearing 2005). In regards to the efficiency and effectiveness of service delivery within the PSNI, a number of reasons have been put forward in favour of a formal truth process. Chief among these is the burden investigating the past puts on the organisation in terms of personnel and time constraints. As argued by Mr Peter Sheridan, a former Assistant Chief Constable of the PSNI, for those officers investigating events related to the Troubles, they are 'not looking at preventing last night's events…So in terms of researching and assessing current intelligence, a proportion of their time is spent researching intelligence from the past rather than trying to prevent next week's robbery or next week's murder' (NIAC 2009: ev.86).[45] The NIAC (2008) report 'Policing and Criminal Justice: the Cost of Policing the Past' has also found the high financial cost of historical investigations is 'financially unsustainable' and compromising the PSNI's ability to police the present, while as detailed earlier in this book, there has been sustained financial pressure on the HET. While acknowledging the benefits for victims' families, as Bayley and Shearing (2005) point out, these themes are in keeping with the drive to modernise and streamline public policing in line with international best practice standards.

Thus, while O'Rawe (2003: 1026) is critical of what she terms the 'can't and won't change dialectic' of policing in Northern Ireland, arguing, 'All is fixed on "building for the future" without realising that a past not properly laid to rest will provide a very unsteady foundation for the new project', it is clear that the arguments in favour of truth recovery discussed here are at variance with this analysis. As the remarks of Orde, Hutchinson, Rea and others have demonstrated, for those at the elite levels of the new policing structures, particularly those who are not tied to the RUC, the past requires examination if the police service is to function in a modern and effective manner. It is my view that these differing stances speak to a broader identity tension between those who can be termed 'traditionalists' or, using O'Rawe's (2003) term, the 'old guard' – the staunch supporters of the RUC in the PFNI and the RUC GC F, for example, and 'modernisers' – the new managers and professionals associated with the PSNI, NIPB and OPONI. For 'traditionalists', it is imperative to keep the flame of the RUC's loyalty, sacrifice and courage alive and so 'secure the past'; for modernisers, the PSNI is a modern police force, outward-looking and reflective of twenty-first century values and practices (Lawther 2010). A debate over the 'ownership of the past' within the policing family, and one that speaks to competing notions of sacrifice and corporate memory on one hand, and professional identity and rule of law compliance on the other, is therefore reflected in their differing opinions on the need for a formal truth recovery process (Lawther 2010).

Conclusion

In the aftermath of conflict, the memory and legacy of violent death provokes strong feelings of anger, hurt and loss among survivors, as well as a sense of obligation to keep faith with the dead, to honour their memory and to justify their sacrifice (Brewer 2010; Scheff 1994; Ignatieff 1998). As this chapter has argued, this backdrop can negatively impact upon victims' attitudes to transitional justice mechanisms, including truth recovery projects. This is particularly the case where such processes are interpreted as betraying victims' memory and the significance and meaning of their physical loss (Hamber 2009).

The concept of sacrifice has had a historical longevity for unionists, members of the security forces and loyalist ex-combatants. It is, therefore, unsurprising that a sense of betrayal has informed their attitudes to existing and prospective truth recovery mechanisms. As argued above, there are three elements to this discourse. Illustrating how the politics of transition may appear to be a process of 'appeasing the past' rather than confronting its legacy, there is a clear sense among unionists and loyalists that the British government has prioritised republicans' demands for truth and justice to the neglect of their sacrifice. This also links to the argument that establishing a truth process fails to pay due recognition to the sacrifice and service of the security forces. That a truth process would be likely to conduct further inquiries into allegations of collusion has also been problematic, betraying a fundamental component of the RUC's identity and organisational memory. By contrast, a greater openness to truth recovery can be detected at senior levels of the post-Patten policing structures. In this case, the importance of responding to victims' needs and developing operational effectiveness and a professional identity were privileged over the memory and sacrifices of the past.

This contest readily illustrates how victims and survivors continuing bond with the dead can be reflected in their reception or rejection of transitional justice mechanisms. On one level, the importance of preserving victims' memory and sacrifice may translate into opposition to truth recovery and the emotional and practical 'unpicking' of the past that such a process would entail. Second, holding fast to the memory of loss and sacrifice is also about 'securing the past' (Lawther 2010). As this chapter has illustrated, the elevation or neutralisation of a discourse of sacrifice and suffering may be part of the post-conflict battle for legitimacy and political agency. Critically interrogating contested understandings of the past, a truth process would challenge at least some of these narratives.

Notes

1 Interview, Danny Kennedy, UUP, 5 May 2009; Interview, Jim McDonald, RUC GC F, 10 August 2009.
2 Interview, William Wilkinson, FAIR, 9 June 2009.
3 Interview, William Wilkinson, FAIR, 9 June 2009.
4 Interview, Maurice Morrow, DUP, 20 April 2009.
5 Interview, Maurice Morrow, DUP, 20 April 2009; Interview, Lady Sylvia Hermon, 3 April 2009.
6 Bloody Sunday Inquiry. House of Lords debates. Hansard, 13 October 2010, vol. 721, part 46, col. 570.
7 Interview, Frankie Gallagher, UPRG, 11 June 2009.
8 There is no official confirmation that such a deal was made.
9 Interview, Lady Sylvia Hermon, 3 April 2009.
10 Interview, Billy McQuiston, UPRG, 18 June 2009.
11 www.smithwicktribunal.ie/smithwick/HOMEPAGE.html (accessed on 1 May 2013).
12 Smithwick argued, 'I intend to examine whether anybody deliberately ignored a matter, or turned a blind eye to it, or to have pretended ignorance or unawareness of something one ought morally, legally or officially to oppose'. www.smithwicktribunal.ie/smithwick/HOMEPAGE.html (accessed on 1 May 2013).

13 The UUP's Tom Elliott argued, 'The truth may well be inconvenient, embarrassing and shocking, but the truth must be revealed and it must not be time limited' (UUP 2012f).
14 Interview, Jim Allister, TUV, 20 March 2009; Interview, Nelson McCausland, DUP, 3 April 2009; Interview, Peter Weir, DUP, 27 April 2009; Interview, Jimmy Spratt, DUP, 20 May 2009; Interview, Jeffrey Donaldson, DUP, 11 May 2009.
15 Interview, Tom Elliott, UUP, 20 April 2009.
16 Interview, Peter Weir, DUP, 27 April 2009.
17 Interview, Jim McDonald, RUC GC F, 10 August 2009; Interview, Terry Spence, PFNI, 20 June 2009; Interview, Raymond White, NIRPOA, 19 May 2009; Interview, Jeffrey Donaldson, DUP, 11 May 2009; Interview, Trevor Ringland, One Small Step Campaign, 21 May 2009.
18 Interview, Lesley Carroll, 10 June 2009. As argued by an RUC Chief Inspector (cited in Mulcahy and Ellison 2001: 398), 'The RUC are what I like to call the 'thin green line' – it's a phrase I have used many times – and it sums up quite well what I perceive the role of the RUC to be in this community. Basically, we try and maintain some semblance of order and stability until the politicians can agree on a solution. The force has no interest in the politics of the situation – we are just the umpire holding the ring'.
19 See Chapter 3 for a discussion on techniques of denial.
20 Interview, name withheld, UUP, 23 June 2009.
21 Interview, name withheld, UUP, 23 June 2009.
22 Interview, Jeffrey Donaldson, DUP, 11 May 2009; Interview, Jim McDonald, RUC GC F, 10 August 2009.
23 Interview, Professor Henry Patterson, 22 April 2009; Interview, Maurice Morrow, DUP, 20 April 2009. Reflecting the discussion in Chapter 4, for members of the security forces, claims and investigations into allegations of collusion were also seen to play to republican propaganda whereby the repeated association of the security forces and the term collusion becomes synonymous with adverse images and are eventually seen as factual statements.
24 It is interesting to note that during an interview, Lesley Carroll, a member of the CGP, raised this precise issue and suggested that an organisational approach to truth recovery could be beneficial. Interview, Lesley Carroll, 10 June 2009.
25 By contrast, O'Rawe (2003) argues that claims of sacrifice not only provided a reason in itself to resist change, but also acted as a smokescreen with which to counter such demands.
26 Interview, Lady Sylvia Hermon, 3 April 2009. A Grand Orange Lodge of Ireland press release, for example, stated, 'These changes are clearly designed to besmirch the gallant memory of those who have served their country, many paying the supreme sacrifice, in defeating terrorism against the state' (Grand Orange Lodge of Ireland 1999).
27 Similar arguments were made by the many former and serving police and prison officers at the public consultation evening held by the CGP in Bangor, January 2008, attended by the author. At this public meeting, participants laid particular emphasis on their disgust at the disjuncture between the cost of public inquiries and the lack of social welfare provision that has been made available for former members of the security forces. A £20 million 'gratuity payment' was however paid to former members of the RUC Part-Time Reserve in 2011 and was designed to recognise their service during the conflict (BBC 2010c).
28 Interview, Jim McDonald, RUC GC F, 10 August 2009.
29 Interview, Jim McDonald, RUC GC F, 10 August 2009.

30 Interview, Raymond White, NIPROA, 19 May 2009; Interview, Jim McDonald, RUC GC F, 10 August 2009; Interview, Lady Sylvia Hermon, 3 April 2009.
31 Parallels may be drawn to East Timor, where Kent (2011) argues the East Timorese political leadership has attempted to construct the past, particularly that of the role of the Armed Forces for the National Liberation of East Timor, as a story of sacrifice and has attempted to give meaning to suffering and death by writing individual's painful stories into the broader narrative of the liberation of the nation. She argues that in doing so, and in shaping the past to buttress political legitimacy during the formative nation-building period, certain complex and less palatable truths were suppressed (Kent 2011).
32 Speech by Irwin Montgomery, Chairman of the Police Federation for Northern Ireland, 31st Annual Conference, 2003. Copy on file with author.
33 Speech by Irwin Montgomery, Chairman of the Police Federation for Northern Ireland, 31st Annual Conference, 2003. Copy on file with author.
34 UTV Insight. (2013) 'Live and Let Die'. 7 May 2013. Author's recording. Special Branch was an elite and highly powerful section of the RUC. It had responsibility for counter-insurgency activities and was widely viewed as a force within a force.
35 Speech by Dr Michael Maguire, Committee on the Administration of Justice Annual General Meeting, November 2012. Attended by author.
36 UTV Live. (2013) 'Interview: Hugh Orde'. 4 July 2013. Author's recording.
37 Interview, Allister Finlay, PSNI, 4 August 2009.
38 Interview, Allister Finlay, PSNI, 4 August 2009.
39 Interview, Allister Finlay, PSNI, 4 August 2009.
40 Interview, Allister Finlay, PSNI, 4 August 2009.
41 UTV Live. (2013) 'Interview: Hugh Orde'. 4 July 2013. Author's recording.
42 Interview, Dave Cox, HET, 28 September 2009.
43 Hutchinson argued: 'One of the most significant challenges facing this Office is dealing with historic cases, with each involving a disproportionate amount of time, effort and media attention…there is not enough time or resources to deal adequately with each case in a timely fashion. The Office is essentially standing as a proxy to deal with an issue, which has not been resolved through politics or within civil society…It is critically important that society finds an accepted and alternative way of dealing with the past' (OPONI 2011b: 5).
44 Interview, Al Hutchinson, OPONI, 19 August 2009.
45 The NIPB has been similarly unequivocal on this matter, arguing, 'It is the view of the NIPB that the efficiency and effectiveness of the police service in preventing and detecting crime should not be compromised by dealing with the various commitments to historical inquiries' (NIAC 2008: ev.110).

Chapter 7

Conclusion

Truth, transition and political responsibility

Transitional justice and truth commissions attempt to mediate between what Cohen (2001: 6) terms the competing 'forces of denial and acknowledgement'. In essence, the field and its central institutions grapple with the clamour for truth, justice and reconciliation after mass atrocity on one hand, and the desire to bury and silence the past on the other. 'Dealing with the past', often through the recovery of truth about past human rights violations, is now a frequent demand and expectation post-conflict (Hayner 2011). While the scholarly literature reflects this emphasis, less well-explored are those sites where a formal truth process – which would explore the causes, context and consequences of a period of political violence, has been rejected or remains hotly contested some time after the cessation of violence and the signing of peace accords. Northern Ireland is one such site. Focusing on unionist, loyalist and security force opposition to a formal truth process, this book has sought to develop a fuller understanding of the political, sociological and ideological objections to truth recovery.

The conclusions speak to the global and the local. Leebaw (2011) argues that transitional justice projects must render decisive judgements that define a break between past wrongs and present values. Such efforts to deal with a legacy of political violence and human rights violations require not only a response to the harms suffered by individual victims, but also entail the pursuit of political change (Leebaw 2011). The central theme that runs throughout this book is how the contested nature of the past can directly map onto and structure opposition to a formal truth process. In this contest, there is often little desire to 'break' with the past and its unpacking, or the prospect of, may signal a 'crisis of memory', defined by Terdiman (1993: 3, cited in Misztal 2003: 43) as people's experience of 'the insecurity of their culture's involvement with its past, the perturbation of the link to their own inheritance'. Rather, competing interpretations of legitimacy, identity and the politics of memory are marshalled in the attempt to 'secure' the past (Lawther 2010).

This book has identified five themes that can structure opposition to truth recovery. Each thematic area is overlapping and is designed to move the debate forward from opposition or critiques of formal truth recovery projects on, for example, practical – but no less important grounds – such as the potential for political instability or retraumatisation, or procedural and technical concerns, including the use of data recording equipment or whether hearings should be held in public or private. Starting with an examination of denial, blame and blamelessness, this book has illustrated how a vision of the 'past perfect' will conflict with the objective of challenging the distortions and irregularities of the past and creating a 'new' imagined political community (Booth 2001; Teitel 2000; Leebaw 2011; Anderson 2006; Cohen 2001). Chapter 3 has demonstrated how a starkly polarised conception of past wrongs can translate into a sharp delineation between 'innocent' and 'guilty' victims and a hierarchy of victimhood. Any deviation – real or perceived – from these categories, by, for example, attempting to recognise the complexity of the term victim or to give equal weight to all narratives of the past can readily give rise to a hierarchal understanding of truth and the critique of creating moral equivalence between victims and combatants and negating levels of loss (Bouris 2007; Gready 2011; Enns 2012). The importance of preserving historical accounts closely links to a lack of trust in one's political opponents and their intentions as regards truth recovery. Chapter 4 points to the difficulty of truth recovery without trust in the available mechanisms and in the other's capacity for truth telling (Horne 2012; Brewer 2010). Often compounding the concern that a truth process would be used to 're-write' the history of a conflict in a partial and politically self-serving manner is a lack of confidence in one's ability to 'sell' one's story. Particular challenges for pro-state actors can be identified and for whom 'loyalty' to the state and pre-transitional regime is a key marker of their identity (Connor 2007; Bruce 1992b). In such contexts, a particular understanding of loyalty may mitigate against engagement with a truth process and engender silence rather than voice (Lamb 2010; Winter 2010). Yet loyalty is often linked to sacrifice and its converse – betrayal. Chapter 6 has illustrated how examining and investigating the past – particularly the past of those who 'sacrificed' during the conflict may be interpreted as a betrayal of their memory and the meaning of their death. Individually and collectively, these themes broaden out our understanding of why political elites may oppose a truth process and contribute to a fuller understanding of the tension between truth and denial.

As regards Northern Ireland, it remains a country that is 'obsessed' by the past, a society demarcated by a 'conflict calendar in which every day is an anniversary' (Rowan 2012c; McBride 2001; Graff-McRae 2010; Pine 2011; Dawson 2007). Over the course of writing this book, the past has never been far away. The establishment and Report of the Consultative Group on the Past, the completion of four public inquiries, one documentary review, the supergrass trial, crisis and controversy within the OPONI and HET and continued public and political tensions over commemoration and memorialisation have formed the backdrop to much of my work. Brian Rowan's (2012c) argument that 'The present is being pulled under the swamp that is the past; into that quagmire that is the unanswered questions relating to decades of conflict, and not just one sides questions but all sides' has frequently rang true. As I write this conclusion, the push-pull of the past and the future and the latent tensions between could not be more apparent. In one quarter of the political sphere, the DUP leader Peter Robinson has just announced a dramatic turnaround on the party's support for the development of a centre for peace and conflict resolution at the site of the former Maze prison, citing an absence of consensus on how the centre would be used and demanding a change of attitude by Sinn Fein towards victims of the IRA (Robinson 2013). In another, as noted earlier, all-party talks, chaired by the former US envoy to Northern Ireland Richard Haass are being convened, and tasked with bringing forward a set of recommendations by the end of 2013 on dealing with the past, parades and protests, and flags, symbols and emblems. The dealing with the past debate looks set to continue for some time and will inevitably involve further discussion on establishing a formal truth process. Its challenges and controversies and Haass's recommendations are likely to provide the context in which this book is published.

Given the weaknesses and shortcomings of the current methods of truth recovery detailed in chapter 1 and elsewhere throughout this book, it is difficult to resist the logic that some revisiting and examination of the past is required if the legacy of the conflict is to be put to rest, society allowed to move forward and the lessons of the past learnt (McEvoy 2006; CGP 2009; Smyth 2007; CVSNI 2010b). The international context and phenomena of 'post-transitional justice' – the recent 're-irruption' of attempted prosecutions of past human rights violations in Latin America, is also instructive (Collins 2010a). The explosion of 'memory politics' in Spain, facilitated, for example, by the exhumations of civil war victims carried out by the Association for the Recovery of Historical Memory, the passage of the Law on Historical Memory and the creation of the Historical Memory Document Centre has led Aguilar (2008) to conclude that while policies aimed at victims of human rights violations can be sidestepped for a time, no institutional arrangement can guarantee that their demands and their memory will not irrupt onto the political agenda once democracy has established itself. In terms of post-transitional justice, in Argentina for example, despite being several decades after the transition and coming on the back of earlier efforts to hold former government officials accountable, during his presidency (2003–2007), Néstor Kirchner introduced measures calling for greater scrutiny of the past, most notably by declaring the 'full-stop' and 'due obedience' laws as null and void, as well as reopening trials for human rights abuses, particularly relating to the perpetrators of forced disappearances (Kovras 2013). Likewise in Chile, there is a reemergence of contestation over human rights violations associated with the 1973–1990 military dictatorship following years of silence (Collins 2010b). These and other cases point to the idea that demands for truth, justice and accountability are unlikely to simply melt away, and strongly suggest that 'truth will out'.

As I have argued throughout this book, there is significant opposition from unionist political elites, loyalist ex-combatants and representatives of the security forces to many of the mechanisms of truth recovery currently in operation and to the establishment of a formal overarching truth process. As regards a formal truth process, at the time of writing, the Report of the CGP has provided the focal point for their concerns. Their opposition has been informed by a rejection of any ownership or responsibility for the conflict; a polarised and hierarchal understanding of victimhood; a fundamental mistrust of republican's and a conviction that truth recovery is 'anti-state'; the tension between loyalty and how to participate in a truth process; and the importance of preserving the sacrifice and memory of the security forces. Individually and collectively, and challenging their memory and identity, these five thematic areas pose significant stumbling blocks to the establishment of a formal process and unionists' participation in the truth debate (Lawther 2010, 2011, 2013). Yet, the past is not past and neither is the discussion on best to deal with the legacy of that past. I would argue that in this evolving context, unionists *should* engage in the truth debate. This point was also made by CGP member Lesley Carroll during interview and her words are worth highlighting at this point –

> I don't think that within the broad unionist community there is yet a greater vision of the future than a dominance of the past…It would be really, I think, liberating for this society if that community were to do a little bit, it wouldn't take a whole lot. It would unplug a real stalemate I think.[1]

Cohen (2001: 4) argues that challenging or acknowledging dishonest denial entails losing the relative 'comfort' of 'living within the lie' and 'risking vulnerability'. His sentiments sit in direct opposition to what, in Northern Ireland, as elsewhere, is at times a reified vision of the past and an unbending and partial sense of collective memory. It is true that dealing with the past means confronting uncomfortable details, acknowledging 'truths' rather than 'truth' and broadening responsibility for past violence and its transformation (Biggar 2003; Boraine 2000; Hayner 2011; Payne 2008). But, I would argue that these objectives should not be manipulated or understood as a series of binary oppositions with identity, memory and victimhood on one side and moral equivalence, betrayal and 're-writing' the past on the other. Nor should engaging with a truth process be interpreted as tantamount to ceding ownership of one's identity or collective memory.

Rather, engaging in a truth process should be seen as an opportunity for unionists to truly take 'ownership' of the past – and the future. For example, at the most obvious level, and to re-cap on the arguments made in chapter 4, truth recovery has, to date, focused overwhelming on the actions of state actors and has fitted with a narrative that puts the unlawful and inhumane deployment of state power at the root cause of the conflict (Dawson 2007). Yet, republican paramilitaries bear responsibility for the greatest loss of life during the conflict. Without a formal truth process, truth recovery will continue to be conducted through the coroner's courts, OPONI and the HET – essentially a state-centric approach, despite the fact non-state actors were responsible for 90% of deaths. Likewise, as emphasised in chapter 2, the objective of a truth process is to challenge the denial of past wrongs – a thickening of the historical narrative that encompasses the actions of *all* parties to the conflict (Ignatieff 1996; Cohen 2001). For loyalist ex-combatants who fear scapegoating and criminalisation, engaging in a truth process could provide an opportunity to contextualise and complicate their involvement in the past (Shirlow and McEvoy 2008). Similarly, to deal with the past is not to forget or silence its victims but to remember and to honour their experiences (Minow 1998). A truth process offers an opportunity to indelibly write those names, dates and places into the historical record. In response to the question of 'where are our inquiries', for those victims who want to know the truth about what happened to their loved ones, a formal truth process could provide some answers, and for many victims, more answers than are available at present (CVSNI 2012).[2]

For the security forces, as many interviewees argued, there is frustration and anger over continued calls to investigate allegations of collusion and other aspects of policing during the conflict (Lawther 2010). This is twinned with a sense that their retirement is marred by the threat of, or having to provide evidence to historical investigations (Lawther 2010). A formal truth process could provide a forum for a definitive examination of these issues and ultimately draw a line under historical investigations. If such a body was accompanied by an amnesty or measure of limited immunity, and which according to members of the CGP, is in fact supported by former members of the RUC, it would not only remove the threat of prosecution, but allow former members of the security forces to tell *their* experiences of policing during the conflict, and contribute to a fuller understanding of the environment in which they worked. As Minow (1998: 131) reflects, 'The asking and the telling unwind something more than complicity; a complicated process of identification and implication in the past must be confronted as part of building a new relationship between all citizens and the state'.

This book ends with a call for greater creativity and political responsibility on the part of pro-state actors in Northern Ireland as regards truth recovery and dealing with the past. At various junctures in Northern Ireland, risk and political generosity have pushed the peace process and political landscape forward. Greater moral, social and political responsibility could break the stranglehold of the past on the present and the future. Lesley Carroll has argued that 'unless we can look each other in the eye and see each other as moral human beings, who maybe did immoral things, but nevertheless as ordinary human beings, there is no chance we can be reconciled'.[3] For Bankowski (2002, cited in Schapp 2005: 131), this demands 'a willingness to live through the consequences of the past in the present'; for Porter (1996: 15), it is about opening 'creative possibilities for the future'. Taking political responsibility does not mean shouldering the 'blame' for the past, diminishing hurt or pain or sanitising the most heinous of crimes. Rather, as Bankowski (2002, cited in Schapp 2005: 131) eloquently argues,

> it means acknowledging one's implication in wrongdoing as a consequence of one's entanglement in history. In its world-delimiting moment, political responsibility enjoins us to care for and preserve the fragile web of human relationships that constitute the world. But, in its world rupturing moment, political responsibility means engaging with our former enemy in collective action in order to change the circumstances in which we find ourselves. It means assuming the risk of politics in the hope that this world will be disclosed in its commonness.

One of the main ways by which the conflict was sustained in Northern Ireland was through the reproduction of competing and partial historical narratives. Post-conflict, these contests have continued through other means and have structured the acceptance and rejection of many of the new institutions and efforts at conflict resolution. As yet, there has been little space or opportunity to create a shared understanding or recognition of these competing histories. The transition between truth and denial, between silence and acknowledgement, the past and the future is incumbent on such a process.

Notes

1 Interview, Lesley Carroll, 10 June 2009.
2 Interview, Billy McQuiston, UPRG, 18 June 2009.
3 Interview, Lesley Carroll, 10 June 2009.

Appendix

List of interviewees

Interviewees are listed alphabetically, showing their organisational affiliation or the position they held at the time of the interview, the date of interview and its location. Two interviewees asked not to be identified.

Allister, Jim, Traditional Unionist Voice, MLA and party leader, Belfast, 20 March 2009.

Aughey, Professor Arthur, University of Ulster, Professor of Politics, Belfast, 1 June 2009.

Birnie, Esmond, Ulster Unionist Party, advisor, Parliament Buildings, Stormont, 19 May 2009.

Bradley, Denis, Consultative Group on the Past, Co-chair, Londonderry, 8 October 2009.

Bullick, Richard, Democratic Unionist Party, advisor, Parliament Buildings, Stormont, 25 March 2009.

Campbell, Gregory, Democratic Unionist Party, MP, Parliament Buildings, Stormont, 11 May 2009.

Carroll, Lesley, Consultative Group on the Past, panel member, Belfast, 10 June 2009.

Cox, Dave, Historical Enquiries Team, Director, Lisburn, 28 September 2009.

Donaldson, Jeffrey, Democratic Unionist Party, MP, Parliament Buildings, Stormont, 11 May 2009.

Dunlop, Reverend John, former moderator of the Presbyterian Church, Whitehead, 17 June 2009.

Eames, Archbishop Robin, Consultative Group on the Past, Co-chair, Hillsborough, 23 October 2009.

Elliott, Tom, Ulster Unionist Party, MLA, Parliament Buildings, Stormont, 20 April 2009.

Empey, Sir Reg, Ulster Unionist Party, MP and party leader, Belfast, 17 April 2009.

Finlay, Allister, Police Service of Northern Ireland, Assistant Chief Constable, Belfast, 4 August 2009.

Frazer, Willie, Families Acting for Innocent Relatives, Leader, Armagh, 6 April 2009.

Gallagher, Frankie, Ulster Political Research Group, spokesperson, Belfast, 11 June 2009.

Garland, Roy, The Union Group, group member and newspaper columnist, Belfast, 8 June 2009.

Hamber, Professor Brandon, Healing Through Remembering/International Conflict Research Institute (INCORE), University of Ulster, Director of INCORE and Chair of Healing Through Remembering, Jordanstown, 18 May 2009.

Hermon, Lady Sylvia, Ulster Unionist Party, MP, Bangor, 3 April 2009.

Hutchinson, Al, Office of the Police Ombudsman for Northern Ireland, Police Ombudsman, Belfast, 19 August 2009.

Kennedy, Danny, Ulster Unionist Party, MLA, Parliament Buildings, Stormont, 5 May 2009.

McCausland, Nelson, Democratic Unionist Party, MLA, Belfast, 3 April 2009.

McClelland, Roy, Professor Emeritus of Mental Health at Queen's University Belfast, former Chair of Healing Through Remembering, Belfast, 26 March 2009.

McDonald, Jim, Royal Ulster Constabulary George Cross Foundation, Chairperson, Belfast, 4 August 2009.

McKee, Eric, Ulster Political Research Group, member, Belfast, 18 June 2009.

McQuiston, Billy, Ulster Political Research Group, member, Belfast, 18 June 2009.

Morrow, Maurice, Democratic Unionist Party, MLA, Parliament Buildings, Stormont, 20 April 2009.

Mullan, Greg, Office of the Police Ombudsman for Northern Ireland, Director of Research, Belfast, 19 August 2009.

Name withheld, Ulster Unionist Party, advisor, Parliament Buildings, Stormont, 23 June 2009.

Name withheld, Ulster Political Research Group, representative, Belfast, 24 June 2009.

Nesbitt, Dermott, former member of the Ulster Unionist Party, Belfast, 24 March 2009.

Paisley, Ian (Junior), Democratic Unionist Party, MLA, Parliament Buildings, Stormont, 12 October 2009.

Patterson, Professor Henry, University of Ulster, Professor of Politics, Jordanstown, 22 April 2009.

Purvis, Dawn, Progressive Unionist Party, MLA and party leader, Belfast, 6 April 2009.

Ringland, Trevor, One Small Step Campaign/The Union Group, Belfast, 21 May 2009.

Roberts, Tom, Ex-Prisoners Interpretive Centre, Director, Belfast, 27 April 2009.

Snodden, Martin, Conflict Trauma Resource Centre, Director, Belfast, 3 April 2009.

Spence, Terry, Police Federation for Northern Ireland, Chairman, Belfast, 30 June 2009.

Spratt, Jimmy, Democratic Unionist Party, MLA, Belfast, 20 May 2009.

Weir, Peter, Democratic Unionist Party, MLA, Parliament Buildings, Stormont, 27 April 2009.

White, Raymond, Northern Ireland Retired Police Officers Association, Chairperson, Belfast, 19 May 2009.

Wilkinson, William, Families Acting for Innocent Relatives, project co-ordinator, Armagh, 9 June 2009.

Bibliography

Abramson, P. and Finifter, A. (1981) 'On the Meaning of Political Trust: New Evidence from Items Introduced in 1978', *American Journal of Political Science*, (25)2: 297–307.

Aguilar, P. (2001) 'Justice, Politics and Memory in the Spanish Transition', in B. de Brito, G. Enriquez and P. Aguilar (eds.) *The Politics of Memory. Transitional Justice in Democratizing Societies*, Oxford: Oxford University Press.

Aguilar, P. (2008) 'Transitional or Post-Transitional Justice? Recent Developments in the Spanish Case', *South European Society and Politics*, (13)4: 417–33.

Aiken, N. (2010) 'Learning to Live Together: Transitional Justice and Intergroup Reconciliation in Northern Ireland', *International Journal of Transitional Justice*, (4)2: 166–88.

Alliance Party (2009) 'Ford welcomes Woodward move to stop Eames-Bradley payments', Press Release, 25 February 2009.

Amnesty International (2011) 'Northern Ireland: Amnesty response to findings of Rosemary Nelson Inquiry', Press Release, 23 May 2011.

An Phoblact (2009) 'Adams calls for republicans' participation in truth process', *An Phoblact*, 8 October 2009.

Anderson, B. (2006) *Imagined Communities: Reflections on the origin and spread of nationalism*, rev. ed, London: Verso.

Annan, K. (2004) *The Rule of Law and Transitional Justice in Conflict and Post-Conflict Societies. Report of the Secretary-General.* UN Document No. S/2004/61. Online. Available at: www.unrol.org/files/2004%20report.pdf (accessed on 27 March 2013).

Anthony, G. and Mageean, P. (2007) 'Habits of Mind and 'Truth Telling': Article 2 ECHR in Post Conflict Northern Ireland', in J. Morison, K. McEvoy and G. Anthony (eds.) *Judges, Human Rights and Transition: Essays in Honour of Stephen Livingstone*, Oxford: Oxford University Press.

Antrim Times (2012) 'History must not be rewritten – Hume', *Antrim Times*, 11 July 2012.

Ardoyne Commemoration Project (2002) *Ardoyne: The Untold Truth*, Belfast: Beyond the Pale. Online. Available at: http://cain.ulst.ac.uk/issues/victims/ardoyne/ardoyne02a.htm (accessed on 23 October 2007).

Arendt, H. (1968) *Men in Dark Times*, New York: Harcourt Brace Jovanovich.

Arthur, P. (2011) *Identities in Transition. Challenges for Transitional Justice in Divided Societies*, Cambridge: Cambridge University Press.

Aughey, A. (1989) *Under Siege: Ulster Unionism and the Anglo-Irish Agreement*, Belfast: Blackstaff Press.

Aughey, A. (2002) 'The Art and Effect of Political Lying in Northern Ireland', *Irish Political Studies*, (17)2: 1–16.

Bachman, R. and Schutt, R. (2001) *The Practice of Research in Criminology and Criminal Justice*, London: Pine Forge Press.

Baines, E. (2007) 'The Haunting of Alice: Local Approaches to Justice and Reconciliation in Northern Uganda', *International Journal of Transitional Justice*, (1)1: 91–114.

Barbalet, J. (2002) 'Introduction: Why emotions are crucial', in J. Barbalet (ed.) *Emotions and Sociology*, Oxford: Blackwell.

Bar-Tal, D. (2003) 'Collective memory of physical violence: Its contribution to the culture of violence', in E. Cairns and M. Roe (eds.) *The role of memory in ethnic conflict*, Houndmills, England: Palgrave Macmillan.

Barker, A. (2004) *Shadows: Inside Northern Ireland's Special Branch*, Edinburgh: Mainstream.

Barry, J. (2003) 'National identities, historical narratives and patron states in Northern Ireland', in M. Waller and A. Linklater (eds.) *Political Loyalty and the Nation-State*, London: Routledge.

Bayley, D. and Shearing, C. (2005) 'The Future of Policing', in T. Newburn (ed.) *Policing: Key Readings*, Cullompton, Devon, UK: Willan.

BBC News (2004) 'NI commission "could heal wounds"', BBC News, 18 February 2004. Online. Available at: http://news.bbc.co.uk/1/hi/northern_ireland/3499613.stm (accessed on 1 July 2008).

BBC News (2007) 'Inquiries 'money-sucking' – Orde', BBC News, 1 December 2007. Online. Available at: http://news.bbc.co.uk/1/hi/northern_ireland/6254863.stm (accessed on 19 May 2008).

BBC News (2009a) 'Northern Ireland Troubles Payment is "Mistake"', BBC News, 16 February 2009. Online. Available at: http://news.bbc.co.uk/1/hi/northern_ireland/7891478.stm (accessed on 16 February 2009).

BBC News (2009b) 'Adams' call over Northern Ireland truth process', BBC News, 7 October 2009. Online. Available at: http://news.bbc.co.uk/1/hi/northern_ireland/8294850.stm (accessed on 7 October 2009).

BBC News (2010a) 'Wright's father claims report is "proof of collusion"', BBC News, 14 September 2010. Online. Available at: www.bbc.co.uk/news/uk-northern-ireland-11303364 (accessed on 14 September 2010).

BBC News (2010b) 'Reaction to inquiry into the death of Billy Wright', BBC News, 14 September 2010. Online. Available at: www.bbc.co.uk/news/uk-northern-ireland-11303038 (accessed on 14 September 2010).

BBC News (2010c) '£20m gratuity scheme for police part-time reserve announced', BBC News, 8 November 2010. Online. Available at: www.bbc.co.uk/news/uk-northern-ireland-11710888 (accessed on 12 May 2013).

BBC News (2011a) 'Pat Finucane family "expecting full inquiry"', BBC News, 13 May 2011. Online. Available at: www.bbc.co.uk/news/uk-northern-ireland-13392299 (accessed on 13 May 2011).

BBC News (2011b) 'Mansfield slams government over Finucane "travesty"', BBC News, 13 October 2011. Online. Available at: www.bbc.co.uk/news/uk-northern-ireland-foyle-west-15286179 (accessed on 13 October 2011).

BBC News (2011c) 'Hutchinson debate flags up other questions of the past', BBC News, 5 September 2011. Online. Available at: www.bbc.co.uk/news/uk-northern-ireland-14794191 (accessed on 5 September 2011).

BBC News (2011d) 'Police Ombudsman Al Hutchinson to Stand Down In January', BBC News, 21 October 2011. Online. Available at: www.bbc.co.uk/news/uk-northern-ireland-15386227 (accessed on 21 October 2011).

BBC News (2011e) 'Hutchinson debate flags up other questions of the past', BBC News, 5 September 2011. Online. Available at: www.bbc.co.uk/news/uk-northern-ireland-14794191 (accessed on 5 September 2011).

BBC News (2012a) 'Amnesties should be an option in Northern Ireland: Al Hutchinson', BBC News, 12 February 2012. Online. Available at: www.bbc.co.uk/news/uk-northern-ireland-17002545 (accessed on 12 February 2012).

BBC News (2012b) 'Pat Finucane Murder', BBC News, 12 December 2012. Online. Available at: www.bbc.co.uk/news/uk-northern-ireland-20697856 (accessed on 12 December 2012).

BBC News (2012c) 'Dr Michael Maguire to be new Northern Ireland Police Ombudsman', BBC News, 4 April 2012. Online. Available at: www.bbc.co.uk/news/uk-northern-ireland-17616976 (access on 4 April 2012).

BBC News (2013a) 'Smithwick Inquiry: Former IRA members refuse to testify', BBC News, 1 February 2013. Online. Available at: www.bbc.co.uk/news/uk-northern-ireland-21283776 (accessed on 1 February 2013).

BBC News (2013b) 'Birmingham pub bombings: Peter Robinson backs inquiry calls', BBC News, 10 May 2013. Online. Available at: www.bbc.co.uk/news/uk-england-birmingham-22488960 (accessed on 22 July 2013).

BBC News (2013c) 'Historical Enquiries Team treats state cases with "less rigour"', BBC News, 3 July 2013. Online. Available at: www.bbc.co.uk/news/uk-northern-ireland-23161353 (accessed on 5 August 2013).

Beetham, D. (1991) *The Legitimation of Power*, Basingstoke: Macmillan.

Belfast Telegraph (2007) 'Inquiries, lawyers and bank balances', *Belfast Telegraph*, 7 June 2007.

Belfast Telegraph (2009a) 'Government axes £12k for victims of troubles', *Belfast Telegraph*, 25 February 2009.

Belfast Telegraph (2009b) '"Day of Acknowledgement" needed in Northern Ireland', *Belfast Telegraph*, 10 August 2009.

Belfast Telegraph (2010a) 'Three face charges over Robert Hamill murder', *Belfast Telegraph*, 21 December 2010.

Belfast Telegraph (2010b) 'Politicians must have honest conversation on Northern Ireland's violent past: Dawn Purvis', *Belfast Telegraph*, 22 February 2010.

Belfast Telegraph (2010c) 'Mo Mowlam loyalist terror amnesty claim', *Belfast Telegraph*, 23 March 2010.

Belfast Telegraph (2011a) 'Paterson: Truth body will not work for Northern Ireland's Troubles Legacy', *Belfast Telegraph*, 5 October 2011.

Belfast Telegraph (2011b) 'SF can't accept any other version of war', *Belfast Telegraph*, 3 December 2011.

Belfast Telegraph (2012) '"Mystery intervention" against Pat Finucane inquiry', *Belfast Telegraph*, 14 January 2012.

Bell, C. (2003) 'Dealing with the Past in Northern Ireland', *Fordham International Law Journal*, (26)4: 1095–1147.

Bell, C. (2009) 'Transitional Justice, Interdisciplinarity and the State of the "Field" or "Non-field"', *International Journal of Transitional Justice*, (3)1: 5–27.

Bell, C. and Cavanaugh, K. (1998) '"Constructive Ambiguity" or Internal Self-Determination? Self-Determination, Group Accommodation, and the Belfast Agreement', *Fordham International Law Journal*, (22)4: 1345–71.

Bell, C. and Keenan, J. (2005) 'Lost on the Way Home: The Right to Life in Northern Ireland', *Journal of Law and Society*, (32)1: 68–89.

Bell, C., Campbell, C. and Ni Aolain, F. (2004) 'Justice Discourses in Transition', *Social and Legal Studies*, (13)3: 305–28.

Ben-Yehuda, N. (2001) *Betrayals and Treason: Violations of Trust and Loyalty*, Colorado: Westview Press.

Ben-Ze'ev, E., Ginio, R. and Winter, J. (2010) *Shadows of War. A Social History of Silence in the Twentieth Century*, Cambridge: Cambridge University Press.

Biggar, N. (2003) *Burying the Past. Making Peace and Doing Justice after Civil Conflict*, Washington DC: Georgetown University Press.

Birnie, E. (2009) *Evaluation of the Report of the Consultative Group on the Past – Eames Bradley*, Copy on file with author.

Bishop, P. and Mallie, E. (1987) *The Provisional IRA*, London: Heinemann.

Blakely, G. (2005) 'Digging Up Spain's Past: Consequences of Truth and Reconciliation', *Democratization*, (12)1: 44–59.

Blom-Cooper, L. (2006) 'Bloody Sunday: Was the NICRA march Illegal or the Ban on Marches Unlawful?', *The Political Quarterly*, (77)2: 227–37.

Braithwaite, J. (2002) *Restorative Justice and Responsive Regulation*, Oxford: Oxford University Press.

Booth, J. (2001) 'The Unforgotten: memories of justice', *American Political Science Review*, (95)4: 777–91.

Booth, K. and Wheeler, N. (2008) *Security Dilemma: Fear, Cooperation and Trust in World Politics*, Basingstoke: Palgrave Macmillan.

Boraine, A. (2000) *A Country Unmasked: Inside South Africa's Truth and Reconciliation Commission*, Oxford: Oxford University Press.

Boraine, A. and Levy, J. (1995) *The Healing of a Nation?* Cape Town: Justice in Transition.

Borer, T.A. (2003) 'A Taxonomy of Victims and Perpetrators: Human Rights and Reconciliation in South Africa', *Human Rights Quarterly*, (25)4: 1088–1116.

Borneman, J. (2005) 'Public Apologies as Performative Redress', *SAIS Review of International Affairs*, (25)2: 53–66.

Bouris, E. (2007) *Complex Political Victims*, Bloomfield, Conn: Kumarian.

Bourke, R. (2003) *Peace in Ireland: The War of Ideas*, London: Pimlico.

Bowcott, O. (2012) 'Pat Finucane's widow calls de Silva report "a whitewash"', *The Guardian*, 12 December 2012.

Boyce, D.G. (1979) '"Normal Policing": public order in Northern Ireland since partition', *Eire-Ireland*, 14: 35–52.

Boyd, D. and Doran, S. (2006) *The Viability of Prosecution Based on Historical Enquiry. Observations of Counsel on Potential Evidential Difficulties*, Belfast: Healing Through Remembering.

Boyle, K., Hadden, T. and Hillyard, P. (1980) *Ten Years on in Northern Ireland: The Legal Control of Political Violence*, London: Cobden Trust.

Bradfield, P. (2008) 'Victims hit out over talks on amnesty', *News Letter*, 17 January 2008.

Branche, R. and House, J. (2010) 'Silences on state violence during the Algerian War of Independence: France and Algeria, 1962–2007', in E. Ben-Ze'ev, R. Ginio and J. Winter (eds.) *Shadows of War: A Social History of Silence in the Twentieth Century*, Cambridge: Cambridge University Press.

Brett, R. (1998) 'Non-governmental human rights organisations and international humanitarian law', *International Review of the Red Cross*, 324: 531–6.

Brewer, J. (2006) 'Memory, truth and victimhood in post-trauma societies', in G. Delanty and K. Kumar (eds.) *The Sage Handbook of Nations and Nationalisms*, London: Sage.

Brewer, J. (2010) *Peace Processes: A Sociological Approach*, Cambridge: Polity.

Brewer, J. (2011) 'Dealing with Emotions in Peacemaking', in S. Karstedt, I. Loader and H. Strang (eds.) *Emotions, Crime and Justice*, Oxford: Hart Publishing Ltd.

Brewer, J. and Hayes, B. (2011) 'Victims as moral beacons: victims and perpetrators in Northern Ireland', *Contemporary Social Science*, (6)1: 73–88.

Brewer, J., Mitchell, D. and Leavey, G. (2013) *Ex-Combatants, Religion and Peace in Northern Ireland*, Basingstoke: Palgrave Macmillan.

Brewer, J., Guelke, A., Hume, I., Moxon-Browne, E. and Wilford, R. (1988) *The Police, Public Order and the State: Policing in Great Britain, Northern Ireland, the Irish Republic, the USA, Israel, South Africa and China*, Basingstoke: Macmillan.

Brogden, M. and Shearing, C. (1993) *Policing for a new South Africa*, London: Routledge.

Brooks, R. (1999) *When Sorry isn't Enough: The Controversy over Apologies and Reparations for Human Injustice*, New York: New York University Press.

Brown, J. (2005) *Into the Dark: 30 years in the RUC*, Dublin: Gill and Macmillan.

Brown, K. (2011) 'Rights and victims, martyrs and memories: the European Court of Human Rights and political transition in Northern Ireland', in M. Hamilton and A. Buyse (eds.) *Transitional Jurisprudence and the ECHR. Justice, Politics and Rights*, Cambridge: Cambridge University Press.

Brown, K. (2012) '"What it was Like to Live through a Day": Transitional Justice and the Memory of the Everyday in a Divided Society', *International Journal of Transitional Justice*, (6)3: 444–66.

Bruce, S. (1986) *God Save Ulster. The religion and politics of Paisleyism*, Oxford: Clarendon.

Bruce, S. (1992a) *The Red Hand: Protestant Paramilitaries in Northern Ireland*, Oxford: Oxford University Press.

Bruce, S. (1992b) 'The Problems of "Pro-State" Terrorism: Loyalist Paramilitaries in Northern Ireland', *Terrorism and Political Violence*, 4(1): 67–88.

Bruce, S. (1994) *The Edge of the Union*, Oxford: Oxford University Press.

Bruce, S. (2003) *Politics and Religion*, Cambridge: Polity.

Bruce, S. (2004) 'Turf War and Peace: Loyalist Paramilitaries Since 1994', *Terrorism and Political Violence*, (16)3: 501–21.

Bruce, S. (2007) *Paisley: Religion and Politics in Northern Ireland*, Oxford: Oxford University Press.

Bryman, A. (2004) *Social Research Methods*, 2nd ed, Oxford: Oxford University Press.

Buckland, P. (1979) *A Factory of Grievances: Devolved Government in Northern Ireland 1921–39*, Dublin: Gill and Macmillan.

Butalia, U. (2000) *The Other Side of Silence*, London: Hurst.

Butler, J. (2006) *Precarious Life: The Power of Mourning and Violence*, London: Verso.

Cairns, E., Van Til, J. and Williamson, A. (2003) *Social Capital, Collectivism – Individualism and Community Background in Northern Ireland.* Report for the Office of the First Minister and Deputy First Minister and the Head of the Voluntary and Community Unit of the Department for Social Development. Online. Available at: www.ofmdfmni.gov.uk/socialcapital.pdf (accessed on 10 October 2013).

Campbell, C. (1994) *Emergency Law in Ireland, 1918–1925*, Oxford: Clarendon Press.

Campbell, C. (2010) 'The Spectre Returns: Conflicted Democracies, Truth Commissions and the Law', *Web Journal of Current Legal Issues*, 1. Online. Available at: http://webjcli.ncl.ac.uk/2010/issue1/campbell1.html (accessed 14 January 2011).

Campbell, C. and Connolly, I. (2006) 'Making 'Wars on Terror'? Global Lessons from Northern Ireland', *Modern Law Review*, (69)6: 935–57.

Campbell, C. and Connolly, I. (2012) 'The Sharp End: Armed Opposition Movements, Transitional Truth Processes and the Rechtsstaat', *International Journal of Transitional Justice*, (6)1: 11–39.

Campbell, C. and Ni Aolain, F. (2003) 'Local Meets Global – Transitional Justice in Northern Ireland', *Fordham International Law Journal*, (26)4: 871–92.

Campbell, C. and Turner, C. (2008) 'Utopia and the doubters: truth, transition and the law', *Legal Studies*, (28)3: 374–95.

Campbell, G. (2010) 'Saville Report: Lesson on how not to examine the past', *News Letter*, 15 June 2010.

Cassidy, K. (2008) 'Organic Intellectuals and the New Loyalism: Re-Inventing Protestant Working-Class Politics in Northern Ireland', *Irish Political Studies*, (23)3: 411–30.

Cherry, J. (2000) 'Historical truth: something to fight for', in C. Villa-Vicencio and W. Verwoerd (eds.) *Looking Back, Reaching Forward: Reflections on the Truth and Reconciliation Commission of South Africa*, London: Zed Books Ltd.

Christie, N. (1977) 'Conflicts as Property', *British Journal of Criminology*, (17)1: 1–15.

Christie, N. (1986) 'The Ideal Victim', in E. Fattah (ed.) *From Crime Policy to Victim Policy: Reorienting the Justice System*, London: The Macmillan Press Ltd.

Clarke, L. (2009) 'Troubles' toxic debt needs a 'bad bank' ', *The Sunday Times*, 25 January 2009.

Clarke, L. (2011a) 'Al Hutchinson must spell out the problems of cold cases', *Belfast Telegraph*, 5 September 2011.

Clarke, L. (2011b) 'Toxic residue of troubles still claiming victims', *The Sunday Times*, 12 September 2011.

Cobban, H. (2006) *Amnesty after Atrocity?* Boulder: Paradigm.

Cochrane, C. (1997) *Unionist Politics and the Politics of Unionism since the Anglo-Irish Agreement*, Cork: Cork University Press.

Cochrane, F. (1999) 'The Past in the Present', in P. Mitchell and R. Wilford (eds.) *Politics in Northern Ireland*, Oxford: Westview Press.

Cochrane, F. (2013) *Northern Ireland: The Reluctant Peace*, New York: Yale University Press.

Cohen, S. (1995) 'State Crimes of Previous Regimes: Knowledge, Accountability, and the Policing of the Past', *Law and Social Inquiry*, (20)1: 7–50.

Cohen, S. (2001) *States of Denial*, Cambridge: Polity Press.

Collins, C. (2010a) *Post-Transitional Justice: Human Rights Trials in Chile and El Salvador*, Pennsylvania: The Pennsylvania State University Press.

Collins, C. (2010b) 'Human Rights Trials in Chile during and after the "Pinochet Years"', *International Journal of Transitional Justice*, (4)1: 67–86.

Combined Loyalist Military Command (1994) *Ceasefire Statement*, 13 October 1994. Online. Available at: http://cain.ulst.ac.uk/events/peace/docs/clmc131094.htm (accessed 12 October 2008).

Commission for Victims and Survivors Northern Ireland (2010a) *Comprehensive Needs Assessment – First Interim Report*, Belfast: Commission for Victims and Survivors Northern Ireland.

Commission for Victims and Survivors Northern Ireland (2010b) *Advice to Government: Dealing with the Past*, Belfast: Commission for Victims and Survivors Northern Ireland.

Commission for Victims and Survivors Northern Ireland (2012) *Comprehensive Needs Assessment*, Belfast: Commission for Victims and Survivors Northern Ireland.

Committee on the Administration of Justice (2011a) *Human Rights and Dealing with Historic Cases – A Review of the Office of the Police Ombudsman for Northern Ireland*, Belfast: Committee on the Administration of Justice.

Committee on the Administration of Justice (2011b) 'CAJ's initial comments on Rosemary Nelson Inquiry Report', Press Release, 23 May 2011.

Connerton, P. (1989) *How Societies Remember*, Cambridge: Cambridge University Press.

Connerton, P. (2008) 'Seven types of forgetting', *Memory Studies*, (1)1: 59–71.

Connor, J. (2007) *The Sociology of Loyalty*, New York: Springer.

Consultative Group on the Past (2009) *Report of the Consultative Group on the Past*, Belfast: Consultative Group on the Past.

Coogan, T.P. (1998) *The Irish Civil War*, London: Weidenfeld and Nicholson.

Coogan, T.P. (2002) *The IRA*, New York: Palgrave for St Martin's Press.

Corbetta, P. (2003) *Social Research. Theory, Methods and Techniques*, London: Sage.

Cory, P. (2003) *Cory Collusion Inquiry Report: Chief Superintendent Breen and Superintendent Buchanan*, London: The Stationery Office.

Cory, P. (2004a) *Cory Collusion Inquiry Report: Rosemary Nelson*, London: The Stationery Office.

Cory, P. (2004b) *Cory Collusion Inquiry Report: Billy Wright*, London: The Stationery Office.

Cory, P. (2004c) *Cory Collusion Inquiry Report: Robert Hamill*, London: The Stationery Office.

Cory, P. (2004d) *Cory Collusion Inquiry Report: Patrick Finucane*, London: The Stationery Office.

Coulter, C. (1994) 'The Character of Unionism', *Irish Political Studies*, (9)1: 1–24.

Criminal Justice Inspection Northern Ireland (2011) *An Inspection into the Independence of the Office of the Police Ombudsman for Northern Ireland*, Belfast: Criminal Justice Inspection Northern Ireland.

Criminal Justice Inspection Northern Ireland (2013) *The independence of the Office of the Police Ombudsman for Northern Ireland*, Belfast: Criminal Justice Inspection Northern Ireland.

Curtis, L. (1984) *Ireland: The Propaganda War. The British media and the battle for hearts and minds*, London: Pluto Press.

Daly, E. (2008) 'Truth Skepticism: An Inquiry into the Value of Truth in Times of Transition', *International Journal of Transitional Justice*, (2)1: 23–41.

David, R. and Choi, S. (2009) 'Getting Even or Getting Equal? Retributive Desires and Transitional Justice', *Political Psychology*, (30)2: 161–92.

Davies, M. (2005) 'Is Spain Recovering its Memory? Breaking the Pacto del Olvido', *Human Rights Quarterly*, (27)3: 858–80.

Dawson, G. (2003) 'Mobilising Memories: Protestant and Unionist Victims Groups and the Politics of Victimhood in the Irish Peace Process', in P. Gready (ed.) *Political Transition: Politics and Cultures*, London: Pluto.

Dawson, G. (2007) *Making Peace with the Past? Memory, trauma and the Irish Troubles*, Manchester: Manchester University Press.

De Brito, A., Gonzalez Enriquez, C. and Aguilar, P. (2001) *The Politics of Memory: Transitional Justice in Democratizing Societies*, Oxford: Oxford University Press.

De Greiff, P. (2006) *The Handbook on Reparations*, Oxford: Oxford University Press.

De Soucey, M., Pozner, J., Fields, C., Dobronsky, K. and Fine, G. (2008) 'Memory and Sacrifice: An Embodied Theory of Martyrdom', *Cultural Sociology*, (2)1: 99–121.

Democratic Unionist Party (2003) *A Voice for Victims: The Democratic Unionist Party's policy on innocent victims of terrorism*, Belfast: Democratic Unionist Party.

Democratic Unionist Party (2007) 'Distinction Between the Innocent and Guilty Must be Maintained', Press Release, 22 June 2007.

Democratic Unionist Party (2008) 'An amnesty utterly ruled out says Dodds', Press Release, 10 January 2008.

Democratic Unionist Party (2009a) *Dealing with the Past in Northern Ireland*, Belfast: Democratic Unionist Party.

Democratic Unionist Party (2009b) 'Saville costs £35million without hearing a witness', Press Release, 20 November 2009.

Democratic Unionist Party (2009c) 'DUP response to Eames-Bradley unveiled', Press Release, 20 November 2009.

Democratic Unionist Party (2009d) 'Dodds lashes Eames-Bradley at Prime Minister's Question Time', Press Release, 29 January 2009.

Democratic Unionist Party (2010a) 'Bell – Some victims more equal than others', Press Release, 16 June 2010.

Democratic Unionist Party (2010b) 'Gregory Campbell Responds to Saville Report', Press Release, 16 June 2010.

Democratic Unionist Party (2010c) 'Inquiries have created hierarchy of victims – Campbell', Press Release, 15 June 2010.

Democratic Unionist Party (2011) *Moving Forward. Manifesto 2011*, Belfast: Democratic Unionist Party.

Democratic Unionist Party (2012) 'Arlene Foster: Talks on the Past Must Focus on Victims', Press Release, 9 January 2012.

Dexter, L. (2006) *Elites and Specialised Interviewing*, Colchester: ECPR Press.

Dillenburger, K., Fargas, M. and Akhonzada, R. (2005) 'Victims or survivors? Debate about victimhood in Northern Ireland', *International Journal of Humanities*, (3)5: 222–31.

Dimitrijevic, N. (2006) 'Justice beyond Blame. Moral Justification of (the idea of) a Truth Commission', *Journal of Conflict Resolution*, (50)3: 368–82.

Dixon, J. (2010) 'Defending the Nation? Maintaining Turkey's Narrative of the Armenian Genocide', *South European Society and Politics*, (15)3: 467–85.

Dixon, P. (2001) *Northern Ireland: The Politics of War and Peace*, Basingstoke: Palgrave.

Dixon, P. (2002) 'Political Skills or Lying and Manipulation? The Choreography of the Peace Process', *Political Studies*, (50)4: 725–41.

Dolan, A. (2003) *Commemorating the Irish Civil War: History and Memory*, Cambridge: Cambridge University Press.

Donnan, H. and Simpson, K. (2007) 'Silence and Violence among Northern Ireland Border Protestants', *Ethnos*, (72)1: 5–28.

Druba, V. (2002) 'The Problem of Child Soldiers', *International Review of Education*, (48)3–4: 271–7.

Dudai, R. and Cohen, H. (2007) 'Triangle of Betrayal: Collaborators and Transitional Justice in the Israeli-Palestinian Conflict', *Journal of Human Rights*, (6)1: 37–58.

Duffy, A. (2010) 'A Truth Commission for Northern Ireland?', *International Journal of Transitional Justice*, (4)1: 26–46.

Duthie, R. (2005) 'Transitional Justice and Social Reintegration', Paper prepared for the Stockholm Initiative on Disarmament, Demobilisation and Reintegration (SIDDR), Working Group 3: Reintegration and Peace Building meeting, 4–5 April. Online. Available at: www.government.se/content/1/c6/06/54/02/7545e870.pdf (accessed on 9 May 2010).

Dwyer, C. (2007) 'Risk, Politics and the 'Scientification' of Political Judgment: Prisoner Release and Conflict Transformation in Northern Ireland', *British Journal of Criminology*, (47)5: 779–97.

Dyzenhaus, D. (1998) *Judging the Judges: Judging Ourselves*, Oxford: Hart.

Eames, R. and Bradley, D. (2008) 'Eames: The speech in full', *Belfast Telegraph*, 29 May 2008.

Edkins, J. (2011) *Missing: Persons and Politics*, Cornell: Cornell University Press.

Elias, R. (1986) *The Politics of Victimisation: Victims, Victimology and Human Rights*, Oxford: Oxford University Press.

Ellison, G. (2007) 'A Blueprint for Democratic Policing Anywhere in the World?: Police Reform, Political Transition and Conflict Resolution in Northern Ireland', *Police Quarterly*, (10)3: 243–69.

Ellison, G. and Martin, G. (2000) 'Policing, collective action and social movement theory: The case of the Northern Ireland civil rights campaign', *British Journal of Sociology*, (51)4: 681–99.

Ellison, G. and Mulcahy, A. (2001) 'The Language of Policing and the Struggle for Legitimacy in Northern Ireland', *Policing and Society*, (11)3–4: 383–404.

Ellison, G. and Smyth, J. (2000) *The Crowned Harp: Policing Northern Ireland*, London: Pluto.

Encarnacion, O. (2001) 'Civil society and the consolidation of democracy in Spain', *Political Science Quarterly*, (116)1: 53–79.

Eng, D. (2002) 'The Value of Silence', *Theatre Journal*, (54)1: 85–94.

English, R. (2003) *Armed Struggle. The History of the IRA*, Oxford: Macmillan.

Enns, D. (2012) *The Violence of Victimhood*, Pennsylvania: Penn State University Press.

Ensalaco, M. (1994) 'Truth Commissions for Chile and El Salvador: A Report and Assessment', *Human Rights Quarterly*, (16)4: 656–75.

Eolas Project/Relatives for Justice (2003) *Consultation Paper on Truth and Justice: A Discussion Document*, Belfast: Relatives for Justice.

Erwin, R. (1992) 'Loyalty and the Virtues', *The Philosophical Quarterly*, (42)169: 403–19.

Ex-Prisoners Interpretive Centre (2004) *Truth Recovery: A Contribution from within Loyalism*, Belfast: Ex-Prisoners Interpretive Centre.

Farran, C. and Amago, S. (2010) *Unearthing Franco's Legacy: Mass Graves and the Recovery of Historical Memory in Spain*, Notre Dame: University of Notre Dame Press.

Farrington, C. (2006) *Ulster Unionism and the Peace Process in Northern Ireland*, Hampshire: Palgrave Macmillan.

Farrington, C. (2008) 'Mobilization, State Crisis and Counter-Mobilization: Ulster Unionist Politics and the Outbreak of the Troubles', *Irish Political Studies*, (23)4: 513–32.

Fealty, M. (2005) *What is Whataboutery?* Online. Available at: http://sluggerotoole.com/2005/02/09/glossary_what_is_whataboutery/ (accessed 12 October 2013).

Ferguson, N., Burgess, M. and Hollywood, I. (2010) 'Who are the Victims? Victimhood Experiences in Post-agreement Northern Ireland', *Political Psychology*, (31)6: 857–86.

Ferran, O. (2007) *Working Through Memory: Writing and Remembrance in Contemporary Spanish Narrative*, Lewisburg, Pennsylvania: Bucknell University Press.

Fierke, K. (2009) 'Terrorism and Trust in Northern Ireland', *Critical Studies on Terrorism*, (2)3: 497–511.

Finlay, A. (2001) 'Reflexivity and the Dilemmas of Identification: An Ethnographic Encounter in Northern Ireland', in M. Smyth and G. Robinson (eds.) *Researching Violently Divided Societies: Ethical and Methodological Issues*, London: Pluto.

Finucane, G. (2011) Statement by Geraldine Finucane on behalf of the Finucane Family, 14 October 2011. Online. Available at: www.patfinucanecentre.org/ (accessed on 14 October 2011).

Fletcher, G. (1993) *Loyalty: An Essay on the Morality of Relationships*, New York: Oxford University Press.

Fletcher, L., Weinstein, H. and Rowan, J. (2009) 'Context, Timing and the Dynamics of Transitional Justice: A Historical Perspective', *Human Rights Quarterly*, (31)1: 163–220.

Forsberg, T. and Teivainen, T. (2004) *Past Injustice in World Politics: Prospects of Truth Commission Like Global Institutions*. Online. Available at: www.helsinki.fi/globalgovernance/research/muut%20dokumentit/Past_Injustice_in_World_Politics_forsberg_teivainen.pdf (accessed on 11 October 2013).

Foster, A. (2003) 'Protestants Need Rights Explained to Them', *Fortnight*, 411: 12–13.

Foucault, M. (1995) *Power/knowledge: selected interviews and other writings, 1972–1977*, Harlow: Pearson Education.

Frijda, N.H. (1997) 'Commemorating', in J.W. Pennebaker, D. Paez and B. Rime (eds.) *Collective Memory of Political Events*, Mahwah, New Jersey: Lawrence Erlbaum.

Gallaher, C. (2007) *After the Peace: Loyalist Paramilitaries in Post-Accord Northern Ireland*, Cornell: Cornell University Press.

Ganiel, G. (2007) '"Preaching to the Choir?" An Analysis of DUP Discourses about the Northern Ireland Peace Process', *Irish Political Studies*, (22)3: 303–20.

Garland, D. (1990) *Punishment and Modern Society*, Oxford: Clarendon.

Gear, S. (2002) 'Wishing Us Away: Challenges Facing Ex-Combatants in the "New" South Africa', *Violence and Transition Series*, 8, Johannesburg: Centre for the Study of Violence and Reconciliation.

Geertz, C. (1983) *Local Knowledge: Further Essays in Interpretive Sociology*, London: Fontana Press.

Gibson, J. (2004) 'Does Truth Lead to Reconciliation? Testing the Causal Assumptions of the South African Truth and Reconciliation Commission', *American Journal of Political Science*, (48)2: 201–17.

Gibson, J. (2006) 'The Contributions of Truth to Reconciliation: Lessons from South Africa', *The Journal of Conflict Resolution*, (50)3: 409–32.

Gilligan, C. (2003) 'Constant Crisis/Permanent Process: Diminished Agency and Weak Structures in the Northern Ireland Peace Process', *The Global Review of Ethnopolitics*, (3)1: 22–37.

Glaspy, P. (2008) 'Justice Delayed? Recent Developments at the Extraordinary Chambers in the Courts of Cambodia', *Harvard Human Rights Journal*, (21)1: 143–54.

Goldstein, K. (2002) 'Getting in the Door: Sampling and Completing Elite Interviews', *Political Science and Politics*, (35)4: 669–72.

Gormally, B. (2006) *Acknowledgement and its Role in Preventing Future Violence: Discussion Paper and Proposal*, Belfast: Healing Through Remembering.

Govier, T. and Verwoerd, W. (2004) 'How not to polarize "Victims" and "Perpetrators"', *Peace Review: A Journal of Social Justice*, (16)3: 371–7.

Graff-McRae, R. (2010) *Remembering and Forgetting 1916: Commemoration and Conflict in Post-Peace Process Ireland*, Dublin: Irish Academic Press.

Graham, B. (1998) 'Contested images of place among Protestants in Northern Ireland', *Political Geography*, (17)2: 129–44.

Graham, B. and Shirlow, P. (2002) 'The Battle of the Somme in Ulster memory and identity', *Political Geography*, (21)7: 881–904.

Grand Orange Lodge of Ireland (1999) 'Initial Reaction to the Patten Report', Press Release, 9 September 1999.

Graybill, L. and Lanegran, K. (2004) 'Truth, Justice and Reconciliation in Africa: Issues and Cases', *African Studies Quarterly*, (8)1: 1–18.

Gready, P. (2011) *The Era of Transitional Justice. The Aftermath of the Truth and Reconciliation Commission in South Africa and Beyond*, Abingdon: Routledge.

Green, E. and Honwana, A. (1999) 'Indigenous Healing of War-affected Children in Africa', World Bank, *IK Notes*, No. 10, July, New York: World Bank.

Gribbin, V., Kelly, R. and Mitchell, C. (2005) *Loyalist Conflict Transformation Initiatives*. Report for the Office of the First Minister and Deputy First Minister. Available at: www.ofmdfmni.gov.uk/conflict.pdf (accessed on 12 October 2013).

Guatemalan Commission for Historical Clarification (1999) *Memory of Silence: Report of the Guatemalan Commission of Historical Clarification*, Guatemala: Guatemalan Commission for Historical Clarification. Online. Available at: http://shr.aaas.org/projects/human_rights/guatemala/ceh/mos_en.pdf (accessed 12 October 2013).

Guelke, A. (2008) 'The Lure of the Miracle? The South African Connection and the Northern Ireland Peace Process', in C. Farrington (ed.) *Global Change, Civil Society and the Northern Ireland Peace Process: Implementing the Political Settlement*, Basingstoke: Palgrave Macmillan.

Guembe, M. (2006) 'Economic Reparations for Grave Human Rights Violations: The Argentinean Experience' in P. De Greiff (ed.) *The Handbook on Reparations*, Oxford: Oxford University Press.

Halbwachs, M. (1992) *On Collective Memory*, Edited and Translated by L. Coser, London: University of Chicago Press.

Hamber, B. (1998) 'Remembering to forget: issues to consider when establishing structures for dealing with the past', in B. Hamber (ed.) *Past Imperfect: Dealing with the Past in Northern Ireland and South Africa,* Londonderry: INCORE/ University of Ulster.

Hamber, B. (2003) 'Rights and Reasons: Challenges for Truth Recovery in South Africa and Northern Ireland', *Fordham International Law Journal*, (26)4: 1074–94.

Hamber, B. (2009) *Transforming Societies after Political Violence. Truth, Reconciliation and Mental Health*, New York: Springer.

Hamber, B. and Wilson, R. (2002) 'Symbolic Closure through Memory, Reparation and Revenge in Post-Conflict Societies', *Journal of Human Rights*, (1)1: 35–53.

Happold, M. (2008) 'Child Soldiers: Victims or Perpetrators?', *University La Verne Law Review*, 29: 56–87.

Hayes, G. (1998) 'We Suffer Our Memories: Thinking about the Past, Healing and Reconciliation', *American Imago*, (55)1: 29–50.

Hayes, M. (1997) *A Police Ombudsman for Northern Ireland?: a review of the police complaints system in Northern Ireland,* Belfast: The Stationery Office.

Hayes, B. and McAllister, I. (2004) 'Protestant Disillusionment with the Northern Ireland Peace Agreement', *Irish Journal of Sociology*, (13)1: 109–25.

Hayes, B., McAllister, I. and Dowds, L. (2005) 'The Erosion of Consent: Protestant Disillusionment with the 1998 Northern Ireland Agreement', *Journal of Elections, Public Opinion and Parties*, (15)2: 147–67.

Hayner, P. (2011) *Unspeakable Truths: Transitional Justice and the Challenge of Truth Commissions*, London: Routledge.

Hayward, K. and Mitchell, C. (2003) 'Discourses of equality in post-Agreement Northern Ireland', *Contemporary Politics,* (9)3: 293–312.

Healing Through Remembering (2013) *Dealing with the Past? An Overview of the Legal and Political Approaches*, Belfast: Healing Through Remembering.

Hegarty, A. (2003) 'The Government of Memory: Public Inquiries and the Limits of Justice in Northern Ireland', *Fordham International Law Journal*, (26)4: 1148–92.

Hegarty, A. (2004) 'Truth, Law and Official Denial: The Case of Bloody Sunday', *Criminal Law Forum*, (15)1–2: 199–246.

Helin, K. and Lindstrom, U. (2003) 'Sacrifice: an ethical dimension of caring that makes suffering meaningful', *Nursing Ethics*, (10)4: 414–27.

Henry, L. (2008) 'Victims left outraged at amnesty plan for killers', *Belfast Telegraph*, 9 January 2008.

Her Majesty's Inspectorate of Constabulary (2013) *Inspection of the Police Service of Northern Ireland Historical Enquiries Team*, London: Her Majesty's Inspectorate of Constabulary.

Hetherington, M.J. (1998) 'The Political Relevance of Political Trust', *American Political Science Review*, (92)4: 791–808.

Hickey, J. (1984) *Religion and the Northern Ireland Problem*, Dublin: Gill and Macmillan.

Hirschman, A. (1970) *Exit, Voice and Loyalty: Responses to Decline in Firms, Organisations and States*, Cambridge: Harvard University Press.

Historical Enquiries Team (undated) *Policing the Past. Introducing the work of the Historical Enquiries Team*, Belfast: Police Service of Northern Ireland.

Hogan, G. and Walker, C. (1989) *Political violence and the law in Ireland*, Manchester: Manchester University Press.

Holland, J. and Phoenix, S. (1996) *Phoenix: Policing the Shadows*, London: Hodder and Stoughton.

Honwana, A. (1998) 'Sealing the past, facing the future: trauma healing in rural Mozambique', *Conciliation Resources*. Online. Available at: www.c-r.org/our-work/accord/mozambique/past-future.php (accessed on 21 February 2008).

Honwana, A. (1999) 'The collective body: challenging western concepts of trauma and healing', *Track Two*, 18, 1: July.

Honwana, A. (2006) *Child Soldiers in Africa*, Philadelphia, Pennsylvania: University of Pennsylvania Press.

Horne, C. (2012) 'Trust and Transitional Justice', in L. Stan and N. Nedelsky (eds.) *Encyclopedia of Transitional Justice*, New York: Cambridge University Press.

Hosmer, L. (1995) 'Trust: The Connecting Link between Organisational Theory and Philosophical Ethics', *Academy of Management Review*, (20)2: 379–403.

Hovannisian, R. (1999) *Remembrance and Denial: The Case of the Armenian Genocide*, Detroit: Wayne State University Press.

Hughes, J. and Donnelly, C. (2003) 'Attitudes to Community Relations in Northern Ireland: Signs of Optimism in the Post Cease-Fire Period?', *Terrorism and Political Violence*, (16)3: 567–92.

Humphrey, M. (2003) 'From Victim to Victimhood: Truth Commissions and Trials as Rituals of Political Transition and Individual Healing', *The Australian Journal of Anthropology*, (14)2: 171–87.

Humphrey, M. and Valverde, E. (2008) 'Human Rights and Injustice: Transitional Justice in Argentina and South Africa', *International Journal of Transitional Justice*, (2)1: 1–23.

Hunt, T. (2004) 'Whose Truth? Objective Truth and a Challenge for History', *Criminal Law Forum*, (15)1–2: 193–8.

Hutchinson, B. (2012) 'Why loyalism feels cut drift – Billy Hutchinson explains', EamonnMallie.com, 15 October 2012. Online. Available at: http://eamonnmallie.com/2012/10/why-loyalism-feel-cut-adrift-billy-hutchinson-explains/ (accessed on 17 October 2012).

Huntington, S. (1991) *The Third Wave: Democratization in the late Twentieth Century*, Norman, Oklahoma: University of Oklahoma Press.

Huyse, L. (2003) 'Victims', in D. Bloomfield, T. Barnes and L. Huyse (eds.) *Reconciliation After Violent Conflict: A Handbook*, Stockholm: International Institute for Democracy and Electoral Assistance.

Huyse, L. (2013) *Transitional Justice after War and Dictatorship. Learning from European Experiences (1945–2010)*, Brussels: Centre for Historical Research and Documentation on War and Contemporary Society.

Ignatieff, M. (1994) *Blood and Belonging: Journeys into the new Nationalism*, London: Vintage.

Ignatieff, M. (1996) 'Articles of Faith', *Index on Censorship*, (25)5: 110–22.

Ignatieff, M. (1998) *The Warrior's Honour: Ethnic War and the Modern Conscience*, New York: Henry Holt & Co.

Independent Commission on Policing (1999) *A New Beginning: Policing in Northern Ireland. The Report of the Independent Commission on Policing in Northern Ireland*, Belfast: The Stationery Office.

Innes, M. (2004) 'Signal crimes and signal disorders: notes on deviance as communicative action', *British Journal of Sociology*, (55)3: 335–55.

International Centre for Transitional Justice (2011) *A Year of Change: A Decade of Hope. Annual Report*, New York: International Centre for Transitional Justice.

International Centre for Transitional Justice (2013a) *Truth Seeking: Elements of Creating an Effective Truth Commission*, New York: International Centre for Transitional Justice.

International Centre for Transitional Justice (2013b) *Drafting a Truth Commission Mandate: A Practical Tool*, New York: International Centre for Transitional Justice.

Irish Independent (2007) 'The O'Loan Report: RUC probe hit 'wall of silence' by former Officers', *Irish Independent*, 23 January 2007.

Irish News (2007) 'Strong case for a truth commission', *Irish News*, 22 February 2007.

Isaacs, A. (2010) 'At War with the Past? The Politics of Truth Seeking in Guatemala', *International Journal of Transitional Justice*, (4)2: 251–74.

James, M. (2012) 'A Carnival of Truth? Knowledge, Ignorance and the Canadian Truth and Reconciliation Commission', *International Journal of Transitional Justice*, (6)2: 182–204.

Jamieson, R. and McEvoy, K. (2005) 'State Crime by Proxy and Juridical Othering', *British Journal of Criminology*, (45)4: 504–27.

Jamieson, R., Shirlow, P. and Grounds, A. (2010) *Aging and Social Exclusion among former politically motivated prisonsers in Northern Ireland and the border region of Ireland*, Belfast: The Community Foundation for Northern Ireland.

Jeffrey, R. (2011) 'Forgiveness, amnesty and justice: The case of the Lords Resistance Army in northern Uganda', *Cooperation and Conflict*, (16)1: 78–95.

Jelin, E. (2007) 'Public Memorialization in Perspective: Truth, Justice and Memory of Past Repression in the Southern Cone of South America', *International Journal of Transitional Justice*, (1)1: 138–56.

Jollimore, T. (2012) *On Loyalty*, London: Routledge.

Jupp, V., Davies, P. and Francis, P. (2000) *Doing Criminological Research*, London: Sage Publications Ltd.

Kane, A. (2009) 'Terrorists are not and never will be "victims"', *News Letter*, 26 January 2009.

Keenan, D. (2008) 'DUP says Maze film was platform for republican boasting', *Irish Times*, 24 September 2008.

Keenan, D. and Hennessy, M. (2010) 'Wright's father rejects finding as "firm proof of collusion"', *Irish Times*, 14 September 2010.

Kent, L. (2011) 'Local Memory Practices in East Timor: Disrupting Transitional Justice Narratives', *International Journal of Transitional Justice*, (5)3: 434–55.

Kingma, K. (2001) *Demobilization and Reintegration of Ex-Combatants in Post-War and Transition Countries: Trends and Challenges of External Support*, Deutsche GTZ: Eschborn.

Klosterman, T. (1998) 'The Feasibility and Propriety of a Truth Commission in Cambodia: Too Little? Too Late?' *Arizona Journal of International and Comparative Law*, (15)3: 833–70.

Koehler, J. and Gershoff, A. (2003) 'Betrayal Aversion: When agents of protection become agents of harm', *Organizational Behaviour and Human Decision Making Processes*, (90)2: 244–61.

Kovras, I. (2013) 'Explaining Prolonged Silences in Transitional Justice: The

Disappeared in Cyprus and Spain', *Comparative Political Studies*, (46)6: 730–56.

Lamb, M. (2010) 'Loyalty and human rights: liminality and social action in a divided society', *International Journal of Human Rights*, (14)6: 994–1012.

Lambourne, W. (2009) 'Transitional Justice and Peace building after Mass Violence', *International Journal of Transitional Justice*, (3)1: 28–48.

Laplante, L. (2008) 'Transitional Justice and Peace Building: Diagnosing and Addressing the Socioeconomic Roots of Violence through a Human Rights Framework', *International Journal of Transitional Justice*, (2)3: 331–55.

Laplante, L. and Theidon, K. (2007) 'Truth with Consequences: Justice and Reparations in Post Truth Commission Peru', *Human Rights Quarterly*, (29)1: 228–50.

Lashmar, P. (2003) *The Stalker Affair. Violations of Rights in Britain*, London: Charter 88. Online. Available at: www.charter88.org.uk/publications/violations/lashmar2.html (accessed on 23 October 2007).

Lawther, C. (2010) '"Securing" the Past: Policing and the Contest over Truth in Northern Ireland', *British Journal of Criminology*, (50)3: 455–73.

Lawther, C. (2011) 'Unionism, Truth Recovery and the Fearful Past', *Irish Political Studies*, (26)3: 361–82.

Lawther, C. (2013) 'Denial, Silence and the Politics of the Past: Unpicking the Opposition to Truth Recovery in Northern Ireland', *International Journal of Transitional Justice*, (7)1: 157–77.

Leebaw, B. (2008) 'The Irreconcilable Goals of Transitional Justice', *Human Rights Quarterly*, (30)1: 95–118.

Leebaw, B. (2011) *Judging State-Sponsored Violence, Imagining Political Change*, New York: Cambridge University Press.

Leebaw, B. (2012) 'Transitional Justice and the Challenge of Grey Zones', paper presented at the 'What Next? Dealing with the Past in Northern Ireland' conference, organised by the Transitional Justice Institute, University of Ulster, Belfast, 25 May 2012. Podcast available at: www.transitionaljustice.ulster.ac.uk/DWPVideos.htm (accessed on 30 May 2012).

Levi, P. (1989) *The Drowned and the Saved*, London: Abacus.

Lilleker, D. (2003) 'Interviewing the Political Elite: Navigating a Potential Minefield', *Politics*, (23)3: 207–14.

Lister, S. (2010) 'Tearful McCrea names 'forgotten victims' of Provo's', *Belfast Telegraph*, 7 July 2010.

Little, A. (2012) 'Disjunctured narratives: rethinking reconciliation and conflict transformation', *International Political Science Review*, (33)1: 82–98.

Livingstone, S. and Murray, R. (2005) *Evaluating the Effectiveness of National Human Rights Institutions: The Northern Ireland Human Rights Commission with Comparisons from South Africa*, Belfast: Queen's University Belfast.

Loader, I. and Mulcahy, A. (2003) *Policing and the Condition of England: Memory, Politics and Culture*, Oxford: Oxford University Press.

Loader, I. and Walker, N. (2001) 'Policing as a Public Good: Reconstituting the Connections between Policing and the State', *Theoretical Criminology*, (5)1: 9–35.

Loughlin, J. (1995) *Ulster unionism and British national identity since 1885*, London: Pinter.

Loytomaki, S. (2013) 'The Law and Collective Memory of Colonialism: France and the Case of 'Belated' Transitional Justice', *International Journal of Transitional Justice*, (7)2: 205–23.

Lu, C. (2002) 'Human Wrongs and the Tragedy of Victimhood', *Ethics and International Affairs*, (16)2: 109–17.

Lundy, P. (2009a) 'Can the Past be Policed? Lessons form the Historical Enquiries Team Northern Ireland', *Law and Social Challenges*, (11)Spring/Summer: 109–171.

Lundy, P. (2009b) 'Exploring Home-Grown Transitional Justice and Its Dilemmas: A Case Study of the Historical Enquiries Team, Northern Ireland', *International Journal of Transitional Justice*, (3)3: 321–40.

Lundy, P. (2010) 'Commissioning the Past in Northern Ireland', *Review of International Affairs*, (LX)1138–1139: 101–133.

Lundy, P. (2012) *Research Brief: Assessment of the Historical Enquiries Team (HET) Review Processes and Procedures in Royal Military Police (RMP) Investigation Cases.* Online. Available at: www.socsci.ulst.ac.uk/sociology/profiles/p.lundy/research.phtml (accessed on 14 May 2013).

Lundy, P. and McGovern, M. (2005) *Community, 'Truth-telling' and Conflict Resolution: A Critical Evaluation of the Role of Community-based 'Truth-telling' Processes for Post-Conflict Transition. A Case Study of the Ardoyne Commemoration Project.* Online. Available at: http://cain.ulst.ac.uk/issues/victims/ardoyne/lundymcgovern05.pdf (accessed on 12 November 2007).

Lundy, P. and McGovern, M. (2006) 'Participation, Truth and Partiality: Participatory Action Research, Community-based Truth-telling and Post-conflict Transition in Northern Ireland', *Sociology*, (40)1: 71–88.

Lundy, P. and McGovern, M. (2007) 'Attitudes Towards a Truth Commission for Northern Ireland in Relation to Party Political Affiliation', *Irish Political Studies*, (22)3: 321–38.

Lundy, P. and McGovern, M. (2008a) 'Truth, Justice and Dealing with the Legacy of the Past in Northern Ireland', *Ethnopolitics*, (7)1: 117–33.

Lundy, P. and McGovern, M. (2008b) 'A Trojan Horse? Unionism, Trust and Truth Telling in Northern Ireland', *International Journal of Transitional Justice*, (2)1: 42–62.

MacBride, P. (2011) *Reparations in Northern Ireland – A duty to victims?* Belfast: Commission for Victims and Survivors Northern Ireland. Talk at Transitional Justice Institute, University of Ulster, 16 November 2011. Online. Available at: www.transitionaljustice.ulster.ac.uk/documents/ReparationsinNorthernIrelandPMBNovember2011.pdf (accessed on 5 December 2011).

MacDonald, R. and Bernardo, M. (2006) 'The Politics of Victimhood: Historical Memory and Peace in Spain and the Basque Region', *Journal of International Affairs*, (60)1: 173–96.

MacGinty, R. (2004) 'Unionist political attitudes after the Belfast Agreement', *Irish Political Studies*, (19)1: 87–99.

MacLean, R., Coyle, A. and Oliver, J. (2010) *The Billy Wright Inquiry Report*, London: The Stationery Office.

MacMaster, N. (2002) 'The torture controversy (1998–2002): Towards a 'new history' of the Algerian war?', *Modern and Contemporary France*, (10)4: 449–59.

McAdam, N. (2012) 'Troubles amnesty and Truth Commission are ruled out by Robinson', *Belfast Telegraph*, 27 February 2012.

McAlinden, A. (2013) 'An inconvenient truth: barriers to truth recovery in the aftermath of institutional child abuse in Ireland', *Legal Studies*, (33)2: 189–214.

McAuley, J. (2004) ' 'Just Fighting to Survive': Loyalist Paramilitary Politics and the Progressive Unionist Party', *Terrorism and Political Violence*, (16)3: 522–43.

McAuley, J. (2005) 'Whither New Loyalism? Changing Loyalist Politics after the Belfast Agreement', *Irish Political Studies*, (20)3: 323–40.

McAuley, J. (2010) *Ulster's last stand? Reconstructing unionism after the peace process*, Dublin: Irish Academic Press.

McAuley, J. and Tonge, J. (2007) ' 'For God and for the Crown': Contemporary Political and Social Attitudes among Orange Order members in Northern Ireland', *Political Psychology*, (28)1: 33–52.

McAuley, J., Tonge, J. and Shirlow, P. (2009) 'Conflict, Transformation, and Former Loyalist Paramilitary Prisoners in Northern Ireland', *Terrorism and Political Violence*, (22)1: 22–40.

McBride, I. (2001) *History and Memory in Modern Ireland*, Cambridge: Cambridge University Press.

McDonald, H. (2011a) 'Pat Finucane's family's anger over inquiry decision', *The Guardian*, 11 October 2011.

McDonald, H. (2011b) 'Full excavation of past could dig up more controversy for our politicians', *Belfast Telegraph*, 10 December 2011.

McDonald, H. (2012) 'Belfast 'supergrass' trial judge clears a dozen loyalists of terror charges', *The Guardian*, 22 February 2012.

McDonald, H. and Bowcott, O. (2012) 'David Cameron admits 'shocking levels of collusion' in Pat Finucane murder', *The Guardian*, 12 December 2012.

McDowell, L. (2008) 'Why unionism fails to star on the big screen', *Belfast Telegraph*, 5 November 2008.

McDowell, S. (2007) 'Victims' needs in post-conflict Northern Ireland: an analysis of government policy between 1997 and 2007'. Online. Available at: http://cain.ulst.ac.uk/victims/policy/smcd07victimsneeds.html (accessed on 14 January 2011).

McEldowney, J. (2003) 'Public management reform and administrative law in local public service in the UK', *International Review of Administrative Sciences*, (69)1: 69–82.

McEvoy, J. (2006) 'Elite Interviewing in a Divided Society: Lessons from Northern Ireland', *Politics*, (26)3: 184–91.

McEvoy, K. (2001) *Paramilitary imprisonment in Northern Ireland: resistance, management and release*, Oxford: Oxford University Press.

McEvoy, K. (2003) 'Beyond the Metaphor: Political Violence, Human Rights and 'new' Peacemaking Criminology', *Theoretical Criminology*, (7)3: 319–46.

McEvoy, K. (2006) *Making Peace with the Past: Options for truth recovery regarding the conflict in and about Northern Ireland*, Belfast: Healing Through Remembering.

McEvoy, K. (2007) 'Beyond Legalism: Towards a Thicker Understanding of Transitional Justice', *Journal of Law and Society*, (34)4: 411–40.

McEvoy, K. (2014) *The Trouble with Truth: Transition, Reconciliation and Struggling with the Past in Northern Ireland*, London: Routledge. Forthcoming.

McEvoy, K. and Conway, H. (2004) 'The Dead, the Law and the Politics of the Past', *Journal of Law and Society*, (31)4: 539–62.

McEvoy, K. and Eriksson, A. (2006) 'Restorative Justice in Transition: Ownership,

Leadership and 'Bottom Up' Human Rights', in D. Sullivan and L. Tift (eds.) *Handbook of Restorative Justice: A Global Perspective*, London: Routledge.
McEvoy, K. and McConnachie, K. (2012) 'Victimology in transitional justice: Victimhood, innocence and hierarchy', *European Journal of Criminology*, (9)5: 527–38.
McEvoy, K. and McConnachie, K. (2013) 'Victims and Transitional Justice: Voice, Agency and Blame', *Social and Legal Studies*, (22)4: 489–513, 11 September 2013. DOI: 10.1177/0964663913499062.
McEvoy, K. and Mallinder, L. (2008) *Article Two Compliant Truth Recovery and Guarantees of Non-Prosecution*, Submission to the Consultative Group on the Past. Online. Available at: www.law.qub.ac.uk/schools/SchoolofLaw/Research/InstituteofCriminologyandCriminalJustice/Research/BeyondLegalism/Publications/ (accessed on 9 January 2009).
McEvoy, K. and Shirlow, P. (2009) 'Reimaging DDR: Ex-combatants, leadership and moral agency in Conflict Transformation', *Theoretical Criminology*, (13)1: 31–59.
McEvoy, K., Shirlow, P. and McElrath, K. (2004) 'Resistance, Transition and Exclusion: Politically Motivated Ex-Prisoners and Conflict Transformation in Northern Ireland', *Terrorism and Political Violence*, (16)3: 646–70.
McGarry, J. (2000) 'Police reform in Northern Ireland', *Irish Political Studies*, (15)1: 173–82.
McGarry, J. (2001) 'Introduction: The Comparable Northern Ireland', in J. McGarry (ed.) *Northern Ireland and the Divided World: Post Agreement Northern Ireland in Comparative Perspective*, Oxford: Oxford University Press.
McGarry, J. and O'Leary, B. (1995) *Explaining Northern Ireland: Broken Images*, Oxford: Blackwell.
McGladdery, G. (2002) 'Perceptions of 'Siege Mentality': Northern Irish Protestants and White South Africans in the New Political Dispensation', *Irish Studies in International Affairs*, 13: 87–103.
McKittrick, D. (2002) 'Paisley denounces inquiry "witch hunt"', *The Independent*, 9 May 2002.
McKittrick, D., Kelters, S., Feeney, B., Thornton, C. and McVea, D. (2007) *Lost Lives: The Stories of the Men, Women and Children who Died as a Result of the Northern Ireland Troubles*, Edinburgh: Mainstream.
McKittrick, D. and McVea, D. (2012) *Making Sense of the Troubles: A History of the Northern Ireland Conflict*, London: Penguin Books.
McLaughlin, E., Muncie, J. and Hughes, G. (2001) 'The Permanent Revolution: New Labour, New Public Management and the Modernisation of Criminal Justice', *Criminology and Criminal Justice*, (1)3: 301–18.
McVeigh, R. and Rolston, B. (2007) 'From Good Friday to Good Relations: sectarianism, racism and the Northern Ireland state', *Race and Class*, (48)4: 1–23.
Mailhes, C. (2005) 'Northern Ireland in Transition: The Role of Justice', *Estudios Irlandeses*, 0: 77–90.
Mallinder, L. (2008) *Amnesty, Human Rights and Political Transitions. Bridging the Peace and Justice Divide*, Oxford: Hart Publishing.
Mallinder, L. and McEvoy, K. (2011) 'Rethinking amnesties: atrocity, accountability and impunity in post-conflict societies', *Contemporary Social Science*, (6)1: 107–28.
Marks, S. (1994) 'Forgetting 'The Policies and Practices of the Past': Impunity in Cambodia', *Fletcher Forum of World Affairs*, (18)2: 17–44.

Marshall, C. and Rossman, B. (1999) *Designing Qualitative Research*, 3rd ed, London: Thousand Oaks.

May, T. (2001) *Social Research. Issues, methods and process*, 3rd ed, Berkshire: Open University Press.

Memmi, A. (1990) *The Colonizer and the Colonized*, London: Earthscan.

Mendeloff, D. (2004) 'Truth-Seeking, Truth-Telling and Postconflict Peacebuilding: Curb the Enthusiasm', *International Studies Review*, (6)3: 355–80.

Mendeloff, D. (2009) 'Trauma and Vengeance: Assessing the Psychological and Emotional Effects of Post-Conflict Justice', *Human Rights Quarterly*, (31)3: 592–623.

Michael, M. (2011) 'Egypt after Mubarak: finding truth in transition', *Open Democracy*. Online. Available at: www.opendemocracy.net/opensecurity/marc-michael/egypt-after-mubarak-finding-truth-in-transition (accessed on 11 July 2013).

Mihr, A. (2012) 'Transitional Justice and the Quality of Democracy – From Democratic Institution Building to Reconciliation', in A. Mihr (ed.) *Transitional Justice: Between Criminal Justice, Atonement and Democracy*, Utrecht: Sim.

Miller, D. (1994) *Don't Mention the War. Northern Ireland, Propaganda and the Media*, London: Pluto Press.

Minow, M. (1998) *Between Vengeance and Forgiveness*, Massachusetts: Beacon Press.

Mishler, W. and Rose, R. (2001) 'What are the Origins of Political Trust? Testing Institutions and Cultural Theories in Post-Communist Societies', *Comparative Political Studies*, (34)1: 30–62.

Misztal, B. (2003) *Theories of Social Remembering*, Open University Press: Maidenhead.

Misztal, B. (2011) 'Forgiveness and the construction of new conditions for a common life', *Contemporary Social Science*, (6)1: 39–53.

Mitchell, C. (2003) 'Protestant identification and political change in Northern Ireland', *Ethnic and Racial Studies*, (26)4: 612–31.

Mitchell, C. (2008) 'The Limits of Legitimacy: Former Loyalist Combatants and Peace-Building in Northern Ireland', *Irish Political Studies*, (23)1: 1–19.

Mitchell, G. (1996) *George Mitchell: in search of peace*, Farmington: Heritage Publications.

Moeller, S. (1999) *Compassion Fatigue: How the Media Sell Disease, Famine, War and Death*, London: Routledge.

Moloney, E. (2002) *A Secret History of the IRA*, London: Allen Lane.

Moon, C. (2007) 'States of acknowledgement: the politics of memory, apology and therapy', in D. Downes, P. Rock, C. Chinkin and C. Gearty (eds.) *Crime, Social Control and Human Rights: From Moral Panics to States of Denial. Essays in honour of Stan Cohen*, Cullompton: Willan Publishing.

Moon, C. (2008) *Narrating Political Reconciliation. South Africa's Truth and Reconciliation Commission*, Plymouth: Lexington Books.

Moon, C. (2009) 'Healing past violence: traumatic assumptions and therapeutic interventions in war and reconciliation', *Journal of Human Rights*, (8)1: 71–91.

Moon, C. (2012) 'Who'll pay reparations on my soul? Compensation, social control and social suffering', *Social and Legal Studies*, (21)2: 187–99.

Morgan, A. (2002) 'The Northern Ireland (Location of Victims' Remains) Act 1999: amnesty, immunity or what?', *Irish Jurist*, (37)306: np.

Morland, M., Strachan, V. and Burden, A. (2011) *The Rosemary Nelson Inquiry Report*, London: The Stationery Office.

Morris, M. (2008) *Routledge philosophy guidebook to Wittgenstein and the Tractatus*, London: Routledge.

Muddell, K. (2003) *Transitional Justice in Cambodia: Challenges and Opportunities. Symposium Report*, New York: International Centre for Transitional Justice.

Mulcahy, A. (2000) 'Policing history: the official discourse and organisational memory of the Royal Ulster Constabulary', *British Journal of Criminology*, (40)1: 68–87.

Mulcahy, A. (2006) *Policing Northern Ireland. Conflict, legitimacy and reform*, Cullompton: Willan Publishing.

Mulcahy, A. and Ellison, G. (2001) 'The Language of Policing and The Struggle for Legitimacy in Northern Ireland', *Policing and Society*, (11)3–4: 383–404.

Mullan, D. (2003) *New Lodge Six Report of the Community Inquiry into The Killings Of Jim McCann, Jim Sloan, Tony Campbell, Brendan Maguire, John Loughran, Ambrose Hardy*. Online. Available at: www.thebarrack.com (accessed on 12 November 2007).

Munce, P. (2012) 'Unionism and the Northern Ireland Human Rights Commission 1999–2005: Hostility, Hubris and Hesitancy', *Irish Political Studies*. DOI: 10.1080/07907184.2012.708656.

Munce, P. (2013) 'Unionists as 'Court Sceptics': Exploring Elite-Level Unionist Discourses about a Northern Ireland Bill of Rights', *The British Journal of Politics and International Relations*, (15)4: 647–67.

Neumann, P. (2003) 'The Myth of Ulsterization in British Security Policy in Northern Ireland', *Studies in Conflict and Terrorism*, (26)5: 365–77.

News Letter (2007) 'Ombudsman "pursued a witch-hunt against the RUC"', *News Letter*, 6 November 2007.

News Letter (2008a) 'IRA refuses to meet Eames-Bradley body', *News Letter*, 26 February 2008.

News Letter (2008b) 'Victims' anger at "amnesty for terrorists"', *News Letter*, 9 January 2008.

News Letter (2008c) 'Hunger film "ignores Protestants"', *News Letter*, 18 October 2008.

News Letter (2009) 'Anger continues over proposed £12k for all victims of Troubles', *News Letter*, 25 January 2009.

News Letter (2012a) 'Paisley's growing support struck terror in ministers', *News Letter*, 6 January 2012.

News Letter (2012b) 'No history re-write, pledges Robinson', *News Letter*, 27 February 2012.

Newton, K. (2001) 'Trust, social capital, civil society and democracy', *International Political Science Review*, (22)2: 201–14.

Ni Aolain, F. (2000) *The politics of force: conflict management and state violence in Northern Ireland*, Belfast: Blackstaff.

Ni Aolain, F. (2002) 'Truth Telling, Accountability and The Right to Life in Northern Ireland', *European Human Rights Law Review*, (5): 572–90.

Ni Aolain, F. and Campbell, C. (2005) 'The Paradox of Transition in Conflicted Societies', *Human Rights Quarterly*, (27)1: 172–213.

Ni Aolain, F., Hayes, D. and Cahn, N. (2011) *On the Frontlines: Gender, War and the Post-Conflict Process*, Oxford: Oxford University Press.

Noaks, L. and Wincup, E. (2004) *Criminological Research: Understanding Qualitative Methods*, London: Sage.

Nolan, P. (2013) *The Northern Ireland Peace Monitoring Report, Number Two*, Belfast: Community Relations Council.

Nora, P. (1996) *Realms of Memory: Rethinking the French Past. Vol.1. Conflicts and Divisions*, New York: Columbia University Press.

Nordstrom, C. (2005) *A Different Kind of War Story*, Philadelphia: University of Pennsylvania Press.

Northern Ireland Affairs Committee (2005a) *Ways of Dealing with Northern Ireland's Past: Interim Report – Victims and Survivors*, London: The Stationery Office.

Northern Ireland Affairs Committee (2005b) *The Functions of the Office of the Police Ombudsman for Northern Ireland*, London: The Stationery Office.

Northern Ireland Affairs Committee (2008) *Policing and Criminal Justice: the Cost of Policing the Past*, London: The Stationery Office.

Northern Ireland Affairs Committee (2009) *The Report of the Consultative Group on the Past*, London: The Stationery Office.

Northern Ireland Affairs Committee (2013) *Current Issues facing the PSNI*, London: The Stationery Office.

Northern Ireland Human Rights Commission (2003) *Human Rights and Victims of Violence*, Belfast: Northern Ireland Human Rights Commission.

Northern Ireland Life and Times Survey (2003) *Northern Ireland Life and Times Survey 2003*. Available at: www.ark.ac.uk/nilt (accessed on 17 October 2007).

Northern Ireland Office (1998) *The Belfast Agreement: An agreement reached at the multi-party talks on Northern Ireland*, London: The Stationery Office.

Northern Ireland Office (2007) 'Hain announces group to look at the past', Press Release, 22 June 2007.

Northern Ireland Office (2009) *Consultation Paper. Dealing with the Past in Northern Ireland: The Recommendations of the Consultative Group on the Past*, London: Northern Ireland Office.

Northern Ireland Office (2010) *Summary of Responses to Consultation. Dealing with the Past in Northern Ireland: The Recommendations of the Consultative Group on the Past*, London: Northern Ireland Office.

Northern Ireland Office (2013) 'Dr Richard Haass to Chair All-Party Talks', Press Release, 9 July 2013.

Northern Ireland Policing Board (2013) 'HMIC Report on the Inspection of the PSNI HET', Press Release, 4 July 2013.

Northern Ireland Retired Police Officers Association (2008) *Submission to the Consultative Group on the Past*, Belfast: Northern Ireland Retired Police Officers Association.

Northern Ireland Retired Police Officers Association (2009) *Response to the Northern Ireland Office Consultation Paper on the Report of the Consultative Group on the Past (Eames-Bradley)*, Belfast: Northern Ireland Retired Police Officers Association.

Novick, P. (1999) *The Holocaust in American Life*, Boston, MA: Houghton Mifflin.

O'Callaghan, M. and O'Donnell, C. (2006) 'The Northern Ireland Government, the

'Paisleyite Movement' and Ulster Unionism in 1966', *Irish Political Studies*, (21)2: 203–22.

O'Leary, B. and McGarry, J. (1996) *The Politics of Antagonism: Understanding Northern Ireland*, 2nd ed, London: Atlantic Highlands.

O'Loan, N. (2010) 'The Police Ombudsman for Northern Ireland: some reflections', in J. Doyle (ed.) *Policing the Narrow Ground: Lessons from the transformation of policing in Northern Ireland*, Dublin: Royal Irish Academy.

O'Rawe, M. (2003) 'Transitional Policing Arrangements in Northern Ireland: The Can't and The Won't of the Change Dialectic', *Fordham International Law Journal*, (26)3: 1015–73.

O'Rourke, C. (2013) *Gender Politics in Transitional Justice*, London: Routledge.

Oakeshott, M. (1983) *On History*, Cambridge: Blackwell.

Office of the Police Ombudsman for Northern Ireland (2005) *Statement under Section 62 of the Police (NI) Act 1998 on the Investigation by Police of the Murder of Eoin David Morley on 15 April 1990*, Belfast: Office of the Police Ombudsman for Northern Ireland.

Office of the Police Ombudsman for Northern Ireland (2007) *Statement by the Police Ombudsman for Northern Ireland on her investigation into the circumstances surrounding the death of Raymond McCord Junior and related matters*, Belfast: Office of the Police Ombudsman for Northern Ireland.

Office of the Police Ombudsman for Northern Ireland (2011a) *Annual Report and Accounts*, Belfast: Office of the Police Ombudsman for Northern Ireland.

Office of the Police Ombudsman for Northern Ireland (2011b) *Police Ombudsman Response to Recommendations made in the Criminal Justice Inspection Report*, Belfast: Office of the Police Ombudsman for Northern Ireland.

Office of the Police Ombudsman for Northern Ireland (2013) *Public Statement by the Police Ombudsman under Section 62 of the Police (Northern Ireland) Act 1998 relating to the complaints by the relatives of a victim in respect of the Events Surrounding the Bombing and Murders at 38 Kildrum Gardens on 31 August 1988*, Belfast: Office of the Police Ombudsman for Northern Ireland.

Olsen, T., Payne, L. and Reiter, A. (2010) 'The Justice Balance: When Transitional Justice Improves Human Rights and Democracy', *Human Rights Quarterly*, (32)4: 980–1007.

Orde, H. (2005) 'War is easy to declare, peace is an elusive prize', paper presented at the Telling the Truth in Ireland Conference, Dublin: Trinity College Dublin.

Organisation for Economic Co-operation and Development (1998) 'Social Capital: the Missing Link?', Social Capital Initiative, Working Paper No. 3, World Bank. Online. Available at: http://stats.oecd.org/glossary/detail.asp?ID=3560.

Osiel, M. (2000) *Mass Atrocity, Collective Memory and the Law*, London: Transaction Publishers.

Paez, D., Basabe, N. and Gonzales, J.L. (1997) 'A cross-cultural approach to remembering', in J.W. Pennebaker, D. Paez and B. Rime (eds.) *Collective Memory of Political Events*, Mahwah, New Jersey: Lawrence Erlbaum.

Paisley, I. (1991) *Reasonable doubt: the case for the UDR Four*, Cork: Mercier.

Parkinson, A. (1998) *Ulster Loyalism and the British Media*, Dublin: Four Courts Press.

Paterson, O. (2010) 'Building the Future - Dealing with the Past', Leonard Steinberg Memorial Lecture, London, 16 November 2010. Online. Available at:

http://cain.ulst.ac.uk/issues/politics/docs/nio/op161110.htm (accessed on 11 July 2013).

Paterson, O. (2011) 'Statement to Parliament on the murder of Pat Finucane – Oral statement to Parliament', 12 October 2011. Online. Available at: https://www.gov.uk/government/speeches/statement-to-parliament-on-the-murder-of-patrick-finucane (accessed on 11 July 2013).

Patterson, H. (2004) 'The Limits of "New Unionism": David Trimble and the Ulster Unionist Party', *Eire-Ireland,* (39)1&2: 163–88.

Patterson, H. (2008) 'Victims who must wait for the truth', *Parliamentary Brief,* 10 April 2008.

Patterson, H. (2009) 'Truth and Reconciliation in NI? Not much hope of either', *Parliamentary Brief,* 9 February 2009.

Patterson, H. (2011) 'People who risk being written out of history', *Belfast Telegraph,* 28 July 2011.

Patterson, H. (2013) *Ireland's Violent Frontier: The Border and Anglo-Irish Relations During the Troubles,* Basingstoke: Palgrave Macmillan.

Payne, L. (2008) *Unsettling Accounts: Neither Truth nor Reconciliation in Confessions of State Violence,* Durham: Duke University Press.

Peabody, R., Hammond, S., Torcom, J., Brown, L., Thompson, C. and Kolodny, R. (1990) 'Interviewing Political Elites', *Political Science and Politics,* (23)3: 451–5.

Peatling, G. (2004) 'Unionist Identity, External Perceptions of Northern Ireland and the Problem of Unionist Legitimacy', *Eire-Ireland,* (39)1&2: 215–36.

Penal Reform International (2004) *Gacaca Research Report No.6: From camp to hill, the reintegration of released prisoners.* Online. Available at: www.penalreform.org/wp-content/uploads/2013/06/rep-ga6-2004-released-prisoners-en_0.pdf (accessed on 12 October 2013).

Phelps, T. (2006) *Shattered Voices: Language, Violence and the Work of Truth Commissions,* Pennsylvania: University of Pennsylvania Press.

Pine, E. (2011) *The Politics of Irish Memory: Performing Remembrance in Contemporary Irish Culture,* Basingstoke: Palgrave Macmillan.

Pockrass, R. (1986) 'The police response to terrorism: the Royal Ulster Constabulary', *Police Journal,* (59)2: 143–57.

Police Federation for Northern Ireland (1999) *Police Beat,* July, Belfast: Police Federation for Northern Ireland.

Police Federation for Northern Ireland (2003) 'Federation Dismisses Idea of Truth and Reconciliation Commission', Press Release, 20 June 2003.

Police Federation for Northern Ireland (2008a) *Submission by the Police Federation for Northern Ireland to the Consultative Group on the Past,* Belfast: Police Federation for Northern Ireland.

Police Federation for Northern Ireland (2008b) 'Comment by Police Federation on Belfast meeting of the Eames Bradley Consultative Group', Press Release, 8 January 2008.

Police Federation for Northern Ireland (2009) 'Eames-Bradley: A view by Terry Spence Chairman of Police Federation for Northern Ireland', Press Release, 2 February 2009.

Police Federation for Northern Ireland (2012) 'Bloody Sunday Murder Investigation', Press Release, 6 July 2012.

Porter, N. (1996) *Rethinking Unionism: an alternative vision for Northern Ireland*, Belfast: Blackstaff.

Posel, D. (2002) 'The TRC Report: What Kind of History? What Kind of Truth?', in D. Posel and G. Simpson (eds.) *Commissioning the Past. Understanding South Africa's Truth and Reconciliation Commission*, Johannesburg: Witwatersrand University Press.

Posel, D. and Simpson, G. (2002) *Commissioning the Past. Understanding South Africa's Truth and Reconciliation Commission*, Johannesburg: Witwatersrand University Press.

Prenzler, T. and Ronkin, C. (2001) 'Models of police oversight: A critique', *Policing and Society*, 11(2): 151–80.

Preston, R. (2012) *The Spanish Holocaust: Inquisition and Extermination in Twentieth-Century Spain*, London: Harper Press.

Pride (2002) *Ex-Combatant Views of the Truth and Reconciliation Commission and the Special Court in Sierra Leone*, Freetown: Pride/International Centre for Transitional Justice.

Progressive Unionist Party (2013) 'Transforming the Legacy', Press Release, 23 April 2013.

Puwar, N. (1997) 'Reflections on Interviewing Women MPs', *Sociological Research Online*, (2)1. Online. Available at: www.socresonline.org.uk/2/1/4.html (accessed on 1 July 2010).

Rankin, A. and Ganiel, G. (2008) 'DUP Discourses on Violence and their Impact on the Northern Ireland Peace Process', *Peace and Conflict Studies*, (15)1: 116–35.

Rayner, G. (2012) 'Bloody Sunday soldiers could face murder charges as police announce criminal investigations', *The Telegraph*, 5 July 2012.

Reed, R. (2012) 'Researching Ulster Loyalism: The Methodological Challenges of the Divisive and Sensitive Subject', *Politics*, (32)3: 207–19.

Renshaw, L. (2011) *Exhuming Loss: Memory, Materiality and Mass Graves of the Spanish Civil War*, California: Left Coast Press Inc.

Requa, M. (2007) 'Truth, Transition and the Inquiries Act 2005', *European Human Rights Law Review*, 4: 404–26.

Restubog, S. and Bordia, P. (2006) 'Workplace Familism and Psychological Contract Breach in the Philippines', *Applied Psychology*, (55)4: 563–85.

Retzinger, S. and Scheff, T. (2000) 'Emotion, alienation and narratives: Resolving Intractable Conflict', *Conflict Resolution Quarterly*, (18)1: 71–85.

Reuss-Ianni, E. and Ianni, F. (2005) 'Street cops and management cops: the two cultures of policing', in T. Newburn (ed.) *Policing: Key Readings*, Cullompton: Willan.

Ricoeur, R. (1999) 'Memory and Forgetting', in R. Kearney and M. Dooley (eds.) *Questioning Ethics: Contemporary Debates in Continental Philosophy*, London: Routledge.

Ricoeur, R. (2004) *Memory, History, Forgetting*, Chicago: University of Chicago Press.

Robins, S. (2013) *Families of the Missing: A Test for Contemporary Approaches to Transitional Justice*, London: Routledge.

Robinson, P. (2013) 'Leaders Letter on Maze Development', DUP Press Release, 14 August 2013.

Roche, D. (2005) 'Truth Commissions, Amnesties and the International Criminal Court', *British Journal of Criminology*, (45)4: 465–81.

Rolston, B. (2000) *Unfinished Business: State Killings and the Quest for Truth*, Belfast: Beyond the Pale Publications Ltd.

Rolston, B. (2002) 'Assembling The Jigsaw: Truth, Justice and Transition in The North of Ireland', *Race and Class*, (44)1: 87–106.

Rolston, B. (2005) '"An effective mask for terror": Democracy, death squads and Northern Ireland', *Crime, Law and Social Change*, (44)2: 181–203.

Rolston, B. (2006) 'Dealing with the Past: Pro-State Paramilitaries, Truth and Transition in Northern Ireland', *Human Rights Quarterly*, (28)3: 652–75.

Rolston, B. and Scraton, P. (2005) 'In the full glare of English politics: Ireland, Inquiries and the British state', *British Journal of Criminology*, (45)4: 547–64.

Rosen, D. (2005) *Armies of the Young: Child Soldiers in War and Terrorism*, New Jersey: Rutgers University Press.

Rosland, S. (2009) 'Victimhood, Identity, and Agency in the Early Phase of the Troubles in Northern Ireland', *Identities: Global Studies in Culture and Power*, (16)3: 294–320.

Ross, F. (2003) 'On Having Voice and Being Heard', *Anthropological Theory*, (3)3: 325–41.

Rothstein, J. (2001) 'Family Loyalty: Implications for Planners', *Journal of Financial Planning*, 14(3): 50–4.

Rousso, H. (1991) *The Vichy Syndrome: History and Memory in France since 1944*, London: Harvard University Press.

Rowan, B. (2005) *Paisley and the Provos*, Belfast: The Brehon Press.

Rowan, B. (2008) 'Purvis dismisses Truth Commission', *Belfast Telegraph*, 27 September 2008.

Rowan, B. (2011) 'Why the Government is so keen to let sleeping dogs lie', *Belfast Telegraph*, 14 October 2011.

Rowan, B. (2012a) 'Loyalist Billy Hutchinson on the play for the past', Eamonn Mallie.com, 28 October 2012. Online. Available at: http://eamonnmallie.com/2012/10/loyalist-billy-hutchinson-on-the-play-for-the-past/ (accessed on 1 February 2013).

Rowan, B. (2012b) 'Unionists must realize it would do them good to talk', *Belfast Telegraph*, 30 May 2012.

Rowan, B. (2012c) 'Delay, Dithering and Deadlock on the Past', Eamonnmaille.com, 12 November 2012. Online. Available at: http://eamonnmallie.com/2012/11/delay-dithering-and-deadlock-on-the-past/ (accessed on 1 August 2013).

Royal Ulster Constabulary George Cross Foundation (2011) 'RUC GC Foundation Reaction to Rosemary Nelson Inquiry Report', Press Release, 24 May 2011.

Ruane, J. and Todd, J. (2003) 'The roots of intense ethnic conflict may not in fact be ethnic: categories, communities and path dependence', University College Dublin: Institute for the Study of Social Change.

Rutherford, A. (2011) 'Supergrass Trial: Two brothers, a bloody feud and an unprecedented trial in court 12', *Belfast Telegraph*, 3 September 2011.

Ryder, C. (2000) *The RUC 1922–2000: a force under fire*, London: Arrow.

Said, E. (2003) *Orientalism*, London: Penguin.

Sarkin, J. (1999) 'The Necessity and Challenges of Establishing a Truth and Reconciliation Commission in Rwanda', *Human Rights Quarterly*, (21)3: 767–823.

Sarkin, J. (2004) *Carrots and Sticks: The TRC and the South African Amnesty Process*, Belgium: Intersentia.

Saville, M., Hoyt, W. and Toohey, J. (2010) *Report of the Bloody Sunday Inquiry*. Vol. 1: Principle Conclusions and Overall Assessment of the Bloody Sunday Inquiry, London: The Stationery Office.

Schabas, W. (2003) 'The Relationship between Truth Commissions and International Courts: The Case of Sierra Leone', *Human Rights Quarterly*, (25)4: 1035–66.

Schapp, A. (2005) *Political Reconciliation*, London: Routledge.

Scheff, T. (1994) *Bloody Revenge*, Boulder: Westview.

Scheff, T. (2011) 'Dealing with Emotions in Peacemaking', in S. Karstedt, I. Loader and H. Strang (eds.) *Emotions, Crime and Justice*, Oxford: Hart Publishing Ltd.

Scott, J.C. (1992) *Domination and the Arts of Resistance: Hidden Transcripts*, London: Yale University Press.

Shackleford, T. and Buss, D. (1996) 'Betrayal in mateships, friendships and coalitions', *Personality and Social Psychology Bulletin*, (22)11: 1151–64.

Shaw, R. (2005) 'Rethinking Truth and Reconciliation Commissions. Lessons from Sierra Leone', *USIP Special Report*, 130: 1–12.

Shaw, R. (2007) 'Memory Frictions: Localizing the Truth and Reconciliation Commission in Sierra Leone', *International Journal of Transitional Justice*, (1)2: 183–207.

Sheahan, F. (2013) 'IRA members refuse to testify at ambush tribunal', *Irish Independent*, 1 February 2013.

Shirlow, P. (2012) *The End of Ulster Loyalism?* Manchester: Manchester University Press.

Shirlow, P. and McEvoy, K. (2008) *Beyond the Wire. Former Prisoners and Conflict Transformation in Northern Ireland*, London: Pluto Press.

Shirlow, P., Tonge, J., McAuley, J. and McGlynn, C. (2010) *Abandoning Historical Conflict? Former paramilitary prisoners and political reconciliation in Northern Ireland*, Manchester: Manchester University Press.

Shirlow, P., Graham, B., McEvoy, K., O' hAdhmaill, F. and Purvis, D. (2005) *Politically Motivated Former Prisoner Groups: Community Activism and Conflict Transformation*, Belfast: Northern Ireland Community Relations Council.

Sider, G. and Smith, G. (1997) *Between history and histories: The making of silences and commemorations*, London: University of Toronto Press.

Sikkink, K. (2011) *The Justice Cascade: How Human Rights Prosecutions are Changing World Politics*, New York: N.W. Norton and Company, Inc.

de Silva, D. (2012) *The Report of the Patrick Finucane Review*, London: The Stationery Office.

Simmel, G. (2004) *The Philosophy of Money*, London: Routledge.

Simpson, K. (2007) 'Victims of Political Violence: A Habermasian Model of Truth Recovery', *Journal of Human Rights*, (6)3: 325–43.

Simpson, K. (2008) 'Untold Stories: Unionist Remembrance of Political Violence and Suffering in Northern Ireland', *British Politics*, (3)4: 465–89.

Simpson, K. (2009) *Unionist Voices and the Politics of Remembering the Past in Northern Ireland*, Hampshire: Palgrave Macmillan.

Sinn Fein (2003) *Truth: A Sinn Fein Discussion Document*, Belfast: Sinn Fein.

Sinn Fein (2008) 'Sinn Fein backs Independent International Truth Commission', Press Release, 28 September 2008.

Sinn Fein (2011) 'Independent International Truth Commission', Press Release, 12 June 2011.

Sinn Fein (2012) 'British Government cannot rule out Truth Commission – SF MP tells Paterson', Press Release, 28 February 2012.

Sinn Fein (2013) 'Adams calls for Truth Commission', Press Release, 31 March 2013.

Slye, R. (2000) 'Justice and amnesty', in C. Villa-Vicencio and W. Verwoerd (eds) *Looking Back, Reaching Forward. Reflections on the Truth and Reconciliation Commission of South Africa*, Cape Town: University of Cape Town Press.

Smyth, M. (1998) 'Remembering in Northern Ireland: Victims, Perpetrators and Hierarchies of Pain and Responsibility', in B. Hamber (ed.) *Past Imperfect: Dealing with the Past in Northern Ireland and Societies in Transition*, Londonderry: INCORE/University of Ulster.

Smyth, M. (2003) 'Truth, Partial Truth and Irreconcilable Truths: Reflections on the Prospects for Truth Recovery in Northern Ireland', *Smith Studies in Social Work*, (73)2: 205–25.

Smyth, M. (2007) *Truth Recovery and Justice After Conflict. Managing Violent Pasts*, London: Routledge.

Smyth, M. (2009) 'Hierarchies of Pain and Responsibility: 'Terrorists', Victims, War by Other Means and Prospects for Reconciliation in Northern Ireland', *Tripodos* (Spain), 25: 27–40.

Smyth, L. and Rowan, B. (2009) 'Troubles compensation an insult to victims, says First Minister', *Belfast Telegraph*, 24 January 2009.

Social Democratic and Labour Party (2009) 'Attwood: Many concerns on Eames Bradley proposals', Press Release, 28 January 2009.

Social Democratic and Labour Party (2010) 'Durkan: Eames-Bradley should be revisited', Press Release, 18 June 2010.

Social Democratic and Labour Party (2012a) 'McDonnell: Comprehensive look at our past holds key to meaningful reconciliation', Press Release, 23 April 2012.

Social Democratic and Labour Party (2012b) *Addressing the Past: A comprehensive truth process and the ethical way forward*, Belfast: Social Democratic and Labour Party.

Southern, N. (2005) 'Ian Paisley and Evangelical Democratic Unionists: an Analysis of the Role of Evangelical Protestantism within the Democratic Unionist Party,' *Irish Political Studies*, (20)2: 127–45.

Southern, N. (2007) 'Protestant Alienation in Northern Ireland: A Political, Cultural and Geographical Examination', *Journal of Ethic and Migration Studies*, (33)1: 159–80.

South African Truth and Reconciliation Commission (1998) *Truth and Reconciliation Commission of South Africa Report*, Vols 1–6, Cape Town: Juta.

Spencer, G. (2008) *The State of Loyalism in Northern Ireland*, Hampshire: Palgrave Macmillan.

Sriram, C., Garcia-Godos, J., Herman, J. and Martin-Ortega, O. (2012) *Transitional Justice and Peacebuilding on the Ground. Victims and Ex-Combatants*, London: Routledge.

Stack, S. (2013) 'Smithwick Tribunal: "colourful" evidence amid tedium', *News Letter*, 22 June 2013.

Stalker, J. (1988) *Stalker*, London: Harrap.

Stanley, E. (2002) 'What next? The aftermath of organised truth telling', *Race and Class*, (44)1: 1–15.

Stanley, E. (2005) 'Truth Commissions and the Recognition of State Crime', *British Journal of Criminology*, (45)4: 582–97.

Stevens, J. (2003) *Stevens Three: Overview and Recommendations*. Online. Available at: http://cain.ulst.ac.uk/issues/collusion/stevens3/stevens3summary.htm (accessed on 29 November 2007).

Stevenson, C., Condor, S. and Abell, J. (2007) 'The Minority-Majority Conundrum in Northern Ireland: An Orange Order Perspective', *Political Psychology*, (28)1: 105–25.

Suarez-Orozco, M. (1991) 'The Heritage of Enduring a Dirty War: Psychological Aspects of Terror in Argentina', *The Journal of Psychohistory*, (18)4: 469–505.

Switzer, C. and Graham, B. (2009) ' 'From thorn to thorn': commemorating the Royal Ulster Constabulary in Northern Ireland', *Social and Cultural Geography*, (10)2: 153–71.

Taylor, P. (1987) *Stalker: The Search for the Truth*, London: Faber.

Taylor, P. (1999) *Loyalists*, London: Bloomsbury.

Teitel, R. (2000) *Transitional Justice*, Oxford: Oxford University Press.

The Economist (2010) 'The new civil war: An investigation into Franco-era atrocities lands a judge in trouble', *The Economist*, 18 February 2010.

Theissen, G. (2004) *Supporting Justice, Co-existence and Reconciliation after Armed Conflict: Strategies for Dealing with the Past*, Berghof: Berghof Research Centre for Constructive Conflict Management. Online. Available at: http://edoc.vifapol.de/opus/volltexte/2011/2598/pdf/theissen_handbook.pdf (accessed on 5 December 2007).

Tilly, C. (2008) *Credit and Blame*, Princeton, New Jersey: Princeton University Press.

Todd, J. (1987) 'Two traditions in unionist political culture', *Irish Political Studies*, (2)1: 1–26.

Tonge, J. (2002) *Northern Ireland: Conflict and Change*, Harlow: Longman.

Tonry, M. (2004) *Thinking about crime: Sense and sensibility in American penal culture*, New York: Oxford University Press.

Traditional Unionist Voice (2009) 'Allister outraged at proposed terrorist payday', Press Release, 23 January 2009.

Tran, M. (2009) 'Report authors defend plan to pay £12,000 to all families bereaved in Northern Ireland Troubles', *The Guardian*, 28 January 2009.

Tremlett, G. (2012) 'Baltasar Garzon cleared over his Franco-era crimes inquiry', *The Guardian*, 27 February 2012.

Trouillot, M.R. (1995) *Silencing the past: power and the production of history*, Boston, Massachusetts: Beacon Press.

Tutu, D. (2000) *No future without forgiveness*, London: Rider.

Ulster Unionist Party (2007a) 'SF very selective over who needs Public Inquiries', Press Release, 28 June 2007.

Ulster Unionist Party (2007b) 'Republicans have a cheek demanding Truth, says Elliott', Press Release, 14 August 2007.

Ulster Unionist Party (2008) 'Eames-Bradley forthcoming report', Press Release, 25 October 2008.

Ulster Unionist Party (2009a) 'Reject Eames-Bradley Says Elliott', Press Release, 30 January 2009.

Ulster Unionist Party (2009b) 'Eames-Bradley 2', Press Release, 2 February 2009.

Ulster Unionist Party (2009c) 'Eames-Bradley £12,000 – an immoral proposal', Press Release, 23 January 2009.

Ulster Unionist Party (2011a) *Victims' Charter*, Belfast: Ulster Unionist Party.

Ulster Unionist Party (2011b) 'Victims Deserve an Agreed Mechanism for Dealing with the Past – Nesbitt', Press Release, 13 October 2011.

Ulster Unionist Party (2011c) 'End the agony – Nesbitt', Press Release, 3 November 2011.

Ulster Unionist Party (2012a) 'Nesbitt rejects Hutchinson's notion of amnesty', Press Release, 13 February 2012.

Ulster Unionist Party (2012b) 'Elliott shocked at news of Bloody Sunday murder inquiry', Press Release, 7 May 2012.

Ulster Unionist Party (2012c) 'Leader's speech to 2012 Party Conference', Press Release, 26 September 2012.

Ulster Unionist Party (2012d) 'Copeland supports La Mon families in quest for truth and justice', Press Release, 16 February 2012.

Ulster Unionist Party (2012e) 'Nesbitt calls on IRA to come clean about Gordon Gallagher bomb death', Press Release, 22 February 2012.

Ulster Unionist Party (2012f) 'Elliott welcomes extension for Smithwick Tribunal', Press Release, 23 May 2012.

Ulster Unionist Party (2013) 'We need agreed method to ensure all victims can pursue the truth', Press Release, 11 February 2013.

UTV News (2011) 'Paterson rules out truth commission', *UTV News*, 4 October 2011. Online. Available at: www.u.tv/News/Paterson-rules-out-NI-truth-commission/1276eec3-3c13-4982-90f1-3fc369ccb624 (accessed on 4 October 2011).

UTV News (2012) 'Proposals would force RUC to testify', *UTV News*, 7 February 2012. Online. Available at: www.u.tv/news/Proposals-would-force-RUC-to-testify/9e9f4f03-3fd0-4502-81a1-50d486c0b0f4 (accessed on 7 February 2012).

Villa-Vicencio, C. (2003) 'Restorative Justice in Social Context: The South African Truth and Reconciliation Commission', in N. Biggar (ed.) *Burying the Past: Making Peace and Doing Justice after Civil Conflict*, Washington, D.C: Georgetown University Press.

Villa-Vicencio, C. and Verwoerd, W. (2000) *Looking Back, Reaching Forward. Reflections on the Truth and Reconciliation Commission of South Africa*, Cape Town: University of Cape Town Press.

von Tangen Page, M. (2006) 'A 'most difficult and unpalatable part': the release of politically motivated violent offenders', in M. Cox, A. Guelke and F. Stephen (eds) *A Farewell to Arms? Beyond the Good Friday Agreement*, 2nd ed, Manchester: Manchester University Press.

Waldorf, L. (2010) 'Ex-Combatants and Truth Commissions', in A. Cutler Patel, P. De Grieff and L. Waldorf (eds.) *Disarming the Past: Transitional Justice and Ex-Combatants*, New York: Columbia University Press.

Waldorf, L. (2012) 'Anticipating the Past: Transitional Justice and Socio-Economic Wrongs', *Social and Legal Studies*, (21)2: 171–86.

Walker, G. (2004) *A History of the Ulster Unionist Party: Protest, Pragmatism and Pessimism*, Manchester: Manchester University Press.

Waller, M. and Linklater, A. (2003) 'Introduction: loyalty and the post-national state', in M. Waller and A. Linklater (eds.) *Political Loyalty and the Nation-State*, London: Routledge.

Walsh, D. (1983) *The use and abuse of emergency legislation in Northern Ireland*, London: Cobden Trust.

Watters, D. (2003) 'Is there need for a Truth and Reconciliation Commission within the Peace Process in Northern Ireland?', in B. Mitchell (ed.) *Truth Recovery after Conflict: Conflict Transformation Papers*, Vol. 3, Belfast: Linc Resource Centre.

Weitzer, R. (1995) *Policing under fire: ethnic conflict and police-community relations in Northern Ireland*, Albany: State University of New York Press.

Wessells, M. (2006) *Child Soldiers: From Violence to Protection*, Harvard: Harvard University Press.

Widgery, J. (1972) *Report of the Tribunal appointed to inquire into the events on Sunday, 30 January 1971, which led to loss of life in connection with the procession in Londonderry on that day by The Rt. Hon. Lord Widgery, O.B.E., T.D*, London: Her Majesty's Stationery Office.

Wiebelhaus-Brahm, E. (2010) *Truth Commissions and Transitional Societies. The impact on human rights and democracy*, London: Routledge.

Williams, P. and Scharf, M. (2002) *Peace with Justice: War Crimes and Accountability in the Former Yugoslavia*, New York: Rowman and Littlefield.

Wilson, R. (2001) *The Politics of Truth and Reconciliation in South Africa: Legitimizing the Post-Apartheid State*, Cambridge: Cambridge University Press.

Wilson, R. (2011) *Writing History in International Criminal Tribunals*, Cambridge: Cambridge University Press.

Winter, J. (1995) *Sites of Memory, Sites of Mourning: The Great War in European Cultural History*, Cambridge: Cambridge University Press.

Winter, J. (2010) 'Thinking about silence' in E. Ben-Ze'ev, R. Ginio and J. Winter (eds.) *Shadows of War. A Social History of Silence in the Twentieth Century*, Cambridge: Cambridge University Press.

Wood, I. (2006) *Crimes of Loyalty. A History of the UDA*, Edinburgh: Edinburgh University Press Ltd.

Zack-Williams, A.B. (2001) 'Child soldiers in the civil war in Sierra Leone', *Review of African Political Economy*, (28)87: 73–82.

Zerubavel, E. (2010) 'The social sound of silence: Towards a sociology of denial', in E. Ben-Ze'ev, R. Ginio and J. Winter (eds.) *Shadows of War. A Social History of Silence in the Twentieth Century*, Cambridge: Cambridge University Press.

Index